Q.C.'S DIARY
1954-1960

Also by Gordon Stott:

Lord Advocate's Diary 1961-1966
Judge's Diary 1967-1973

Q.C.'S DIARY
1954-1960

GORDON STOTT

THE MERCAT PRESS
EDINBURGH

First published in 1998 by Mercat Press
at James Thin, 53 South Bridge
Edinburgh EH1 1YS

ISBN   1873644 71X

Typeset in Ehrhardt at Mercat Press
Printed in Great Britain by
Biddles Ltd., Guildford

CONTENTS

In the introduction to each year (which was actually written at the end of the year) I have changed the present tense into the past. Otherwise the extracts remain as written at the time.

1954

A year which turned out to be surprisingly tranquil for the world was equally so for me. My outstanding success was in June, in a difficult action for reduction of an agreement between two partners in a public-house business. 'There is nothing that succeeds like success' is not a motto that is necessarily applicable at Parliament House—I often think that counsel can achieve more general popularity among instructing solicitors by a series of failures—but it seemed to me that following the Finnegan case I had more general enquiries for my services. Politics continued to be dull. Conservative 'prosperity' was reflected in rising share values and rising prices, and there was no sign of any break in the inflationary process. No one now believed seriously in the imminence of a general war. This country, as well as others, continued to waste much of its substance on armaments, but there appeared to be a pretty general determination that no one must attempt to make use of them. I embarked on a 4-year extension of office as member of the Monopolies Commission.

January 1st
A very interesting talk on the wireless about grizzly bears, by a gentleman with a pronounced Canadian accent, Charles Mulvey.

January 7th
Commission meeting: the new chairman is a slight, youngish-looking man who impressed me as capable and business-like.

Bus to Hampstead Heath, where I went into the local cinema, with the idea mainly of escaping from the cold. I much enjoyed the film, *Call Me Madam*, a witty, colourful musical, with lovely dancing and the scintillating Ethel Merman as the ambassadress pursuing her middle-aged romance with all the sparkle and ten times the personality of a teenager.

January 11th
In the evening I had a Record of Alastair Johnston's to revise which

gave me inordinate trouble. He has set out the case at length, in a manner which seemed likely to give rise to a lot of difficulty, and though it would have been a simple enough case to present, starting from scratch, I found it difficult to know what to do with it in its existing state. I was working on it until 10.30 and made a lot of revisions, and even then was not at all satisfied with it.

January 12th
Got up before 7.30 and wrote an entirely new condescendence of fault in place of Johnston's two. It was short, and replaced satisfactorily several pages of Johnston's pleadings.

January 13th
In the tram I sat next to Hill Watson, who told me how much pleasanter life was after one became a judge. 'I've no difficulty in making up my mind', he said. 'I may be right or I may be wrong, but I make up my mind and make a decision. A judge who dithers is no use at all.'

January 16th
Parliament House: a commission to take evidence. Birnam has appointed his nephew as commissioner, a very young counsel who performed his duties satisfactorily.

January 17th
To church: the Presbytery's quinquennial visitation. Rev. A.W. Greig of Fountainbridge Church preached on the need for the conversion of Scotland, taking as text Timothy 1,12. He preached in a very loud voice, and his sermon was illiterate, ungrammatical and sometimes absurd: but he was interesting, and what he said had a real point. Evening service on the wireless: Dr George MacLeod. He preaches with extraordinary force and power. What he says may be right or wrong, important or unimportant, but it hits you right in the eye—a preacher it is impossible to ignore.

January 19th
Jury trial: *Craston v. Short*. The pursuer, Miss Craston, and her brother Joe make up a comedy musical duo called the Crastonians. In December 1951 they appeared at the Glasgow Pavilion as 'guest artistes' in the Logan Family Show sponsored by the defender, the

father of the Scottish comedian Jimmy Logan. After taking her bow at the end of the turn, the pursuer stepped backwards through the curtain and fell over a tiger-skin rug lying on the stage, breaking her ankle. Her case is that as soon as the curtains closed the stage hands should have removed the rug, which was one of the Crastonians' own props and had nothing to do with the following turn. The defender says that in a revue, as this is supposed to have been, artistes after taking their bow always exit at the wings, and nobody could have expected the Crastons to come back through the curtains. There is a subsidiary point that the pursuer should have looked where she was going, but this seemed absurd: the pursuer in retreating through the curtain would have had to keep facing the audience. The pursuer, in spite of her 52 years, was presentable and attractive, and gave her evidence in a frank, modest way. Wheatley, who appeared for the defender, could make nothing of her.

January 20th

The trial continued. I did not make a good speech. Wheatley made the most of his case, and I left Parliament House feeling weary and by no means as confident as I had been. However, my junior rang up in due course to say that the jury had found for the pursuer and assessed damages at £500. They had held the pursuer 40 per cent to blame, which meant that she got £300.

January 21st

Commission meeting with the Washed Sand and Gravel Association. The only question I asked was completely misconceived, so that it must at once have appeared to everyone that I did not know what I was talking about. The chairman has asked me, when copper semis and tyres are disposed of, to take over the chairmanship of the panel on footwear. We should have a good group, particularly as Gallie on some excuse or other has persuaded the chairman to remove Plant out of our group into the other one and substitute Allan, who is much more amenable.

Westminster: the Mines and Quarries Bill did not give much scope for oratory or debating skill, but I liked a thoughtful, eloquent speech by Roberts, the Labour member for Caernarvonshire—in marked contrast with a ranting speech from the Labour benches by a young ex-miner, Roy Mason. It was easy to understand the popularity of Tom Brown, another ex-miner, a gentle soft-voiced old fellow like a kindly uncle at Christmas time. The reply, by Joynson-Hicks, the Parliamentary Secretary to the Ministry, was curiously academic, going into a lot of historical detail. It was a courteous, pleasant speech, different from what I thought Joynson-Hicks would be like, from reading his speeches in *Hansard*.

January 22nd

Cameo Polytechnic cinema: a French film, *Forbidden Fruit*, in which Fernandel as a country doctor with a devoted, ambitious wife is driven to introduce into the *ménage* a girl whom he has met and fallen in love with while on a trip to Marseilles. A moving, effective film—everything that happens is in character and arises inevitably out of the personalities concerned, and the ending is just what one would desire and expect for them. Also Disney's *Beaver Valley*, a remarkable film of wild life in the Canadian Rockies—not only beavers but many other creatures: otters, birds, moose, coyotes, and an extraordinary sequence of a bear standing in mid-stream catching salmon as they jump the cascades. Bus to Tottenham Court Road: Lyons' teashop—a good three-course supper for one shilling and ninepence.

January 25th

Swannie called for me with the Hospital Board's car and took me to Roddinglaw Farm at Gogar to see the bull pen which was the scene of an encounter between a bull and the dairyman—the subject-matter of an action coming up for trial in March. The manager took us round the byres and showed us the points of interest. 'How do you come to know so much about dairy farming?', Swannie asked.

January 29th

Mackay has at last been persuaded to retire: and yesterday there was a strong rumour going through Parliament House, emanating apparently from Kissen, that Wheatley was to be appointed to fill the vacancy on the bench. This strange appointment was in fact announced in this morning's paper. Douglas Johnston spoke to me about the resulting by-election in East Edinburgh. He had had a meeting with Attlee, Morrison and the Whips, who were anxious that a lawyer should be elected, to be in readiness to take on the legal work in Parliament when the party returned to power. He had given them the names of Shaw, Leslie and myself, and had no doubt that there would be strong pressure from party headquarters to get the constituency party to adopt one of us. Leslie is unwilling to stand, and Shaw is not altogether *persona grata* at headquarters by reason of his opinionatedness and unwillingness to fall in with the party line.

February 17th
Procedure Roll. Peter Maxwell for the defenders submitted a lengthy argument, with a number of authorities, in support of the proposition that a pursuer could not have an alternative case when the facts he averred were inconsistent with it. I replied in a 10-minute speech: and Birnam, according to his custom, did not bother to send for a shorthand writer but made a few short remarks: that he had listened to a closely reasoned argument from Mr Maxwell, that very likely he was right, but that the argument was far too technical to be given effect to nowadays. He repelled the defender's plea and allowed a jury trial.

February 18th
Farquharson was speaking to me about yesterday's case, in which I was instructed by him. He has a new assistant whom he left to sit behind me during the hearing, and had apparently said something to him about the tactics likely to be adopted by his counsel. When he got back to the office he remarked to Farquharson, 'You were quite right. The man on the other side made a long speech, and then our man got up and didn't reply to what the other man had said at all but spoke about something quite different.'

February 19th
Commission meeting. The chairman is clear-minded and forceful, and his conduct of the meetings is in the greatest possible contrast to that of his predecessor.

March 1st
Nancy and I to town to get a new suit for me. The jacket of a 2-piece suit seemed satisfactory, but the trousers were tight about the waist. 'What you really want', said the assistant, 'is the same size in the portly fitting'—and he produced a suit with the label 'portly'. This fitted all right.

March 2nd
A nice letter from Biddy. Replying to a remark of mine about a day

at Loch Lomond, she says: 'I do remember the day of summer you mention—I think, the one you do is Loch Lomond side but I also remember one in the Borders past a lovely loch—was it St Mary's—and I remember a warm sunny day in very early summer, passing mainly beneath a long archway of pale green leaves and seeing the blue sky through them—you won't remember that, as you were driving and couldn't like I, go along with your head laid flat on your shoulders.' She has been in London for three weeks, and was there at the time I was writing to her. 'I am sorry', she says, 'we were wandering the streets of London unaware of each other.'

March 4th

Finished *Natural Causes* by Henry Cecil, a first-rate murder story—no trial, not even an arrest, but excitement and suspense sustained to the end, with good characterisation and many witty, entertaining passages about various aspects of the law and the press.

March 6th

Elizabeth, I was told, had a present for me: and when I went in she told me to look in her wardrobe, where I found a big cardboard box. This I opened, and found two pairs of my shoes. I expressed appreciation of the present, and asked if I could take them through to my bedroom. 'Yes', she said, 'that's where I got them when I put them in the box.'

March 8th

Nancy stopped Elizabeth as she was going out at the front door carrying two of her teddy bears—saying it was too cold for her to go out without her coat, and anyhow she should not be going out in the front alone. 'I'm not alone', she said indignantly. 'I've got these two teddies with me.'

March 9th

A jury trial, *McArdle v. Edinburgh Corporation*. The pursuer had been at the Ritz Picture House and while running along Eyre Place to catch a bus was run into by the bus coming behind her and sustained a serious injury. We had one witness, a woman from Granton, who said the pursuer was knocked down on the pavement. The pursuer remembered nothing of what happened after she left the picture house, so I was faced at the end of the case for the pursuer with a motion by Guest to have the case withdrawn. I had put a question to the pursuer, 'Had you any occasion to leave the pavement?' I felt that the only possible answer to this question was 'No', and that was the answer I got: and I argued that the pursuer's 'evidence' to this effect had been corroborated by the Granton woman. I doubt if this argument would have convinced any other judge but Migdale, but I was fairly sure that he would not withdraw the case from the jury: and he refused the motion. Migdale, I think, meant to charge in the defendant's favour, but being extempore his charge was so muddled and lacking in point that it would obviously make no impression on the jury.

March 10th

Johnston gave me the result of yesterday's trial. The jury had returned after an hour's absence and informed the judge that they were equally divided, six thinking that the pursuer had proved her case and six thinking she had not. They asked for further directions. Migdale replied that there was not much more he could say, but they would remember the onus was on the pursuer, and if they could not get a majority they would have to remain for three hours. It might be that another one of them would on consideration decide that the case had not been proved. To this, Johnston excepted, but this precaution proved unnecessary, as after a short retiral the jury came back to say that they now found for the pursuer by 7 to 5. They assessed damages at £750: a satisfactory award.

March 17th

A case in Debate Roll before Lord Patrick. The counter-issue posed a question for the jury: whether the defender was acting in execution of a public duty. This would only affect expenses, and never goes to a jury, but Morison argued blandly that as it raised a question of fact it was proper to get the jury's answer to it. Patrick, who knows nothing much about present-day jury practice, accepted this. Morison remarked to me when we had come out of court that of course it was quite out of the question to put such a question to the jury and he would have to have a word with me about it.

Kelso point-to-point in Friars Haugh. On a hill in the centre I found the very pretty Countess of Dalkeith sitting on a shooting-stick, with various horsey-looking relatives-in-law standing round her.

March 18th

Called at Douglas & Foulis' and got *The House at Pooh Corner* for Elizabeth. She has to be read to quite a lot, and has a great collection of comics and children's books, particularly the Noddy books by Enid Blyton, and I wanted to have something less tiresome to read when the job falls to me. Elizabeth was pleased with *The House at Pooh Corner*, and remarked when I was reading the first chapter to her, 'I like this book.'

March 19th

Second Division: our reclaiming motion from Lord Mackay's allowance of a preliminary proof. Brand seemed to have no idea what the point was, and soon had the court completely against him. It was lunchtime when Brand sat down, and it seemed only probable that as it was Friday afternoon they would give judgement when the court resumed, without calling on the other side. However, they called on Alastair Johnston: and it appears that they had had a look at the case and come to realise that there was more to it than appeared from Brand's opening. Though in the end they adhered to Mackay's decision they announced that they did so only in view of an explanation given by senior counsel for the defender, and recalled Mackay's award of expenses. Mackintosh went the length of saying that the defender's averments were irrelevant but it would not be safe to dispose of them at that stage: an absurd result. Even without Lord Mackay, the Second Division is a weak court. Before the First Division, I think, we should have got an honest, straightforward decision without any difficulty.

Muir Society: Renfrew, the chief constable of Lanarkshire, on police preparations for a criminal trial—a sensible, fair-minded man.

March 24th

Procedure Roll before Birnam. The pursuer, a doodlebug driver at Glasgow docks, was standing by his vehicle to receive a load of packing cases. When the heave was about three feet above the ground, the wire slipped and one of the cases fell on the pursuer's foot. The defender offered no explanation of the accident beyond saying that it was caused by the fault of the pursuer in choosing to stand beneath the heave. When I saw these defences I put on a plea to their relevancy and called on the defenders to state whether it was proper practice for a doodlebug driver to leave his vehicle when heaves were being loaded on it. Ian Robertson opened on our side, briefly and to the point. Birnam sat silent, but when a young counsel got up to reply began to needle away at him, getting him to the stage of admitting that he had no averments of fact to support his statement of duty. 'Of course', said Birnam, 'you can always amend your Record—provided you've got precognitions which justify you in saying that a doodlebug driver always stands well away from his doodlebug.' The defenders' counsel rather rashly accepted this double-edged offer, and the case was continued so that the defenders could amend—with resulting expense to them, and no prospect that I can see of making their case relevant on any sensible basis. The hearing took only half an hour.

March 25th
To Birmingham, to visit one of the ICI Metals Division's factories. In the research department we saw samples of the metal titanium, which, though difficult to extract from its ore, is evidently very plentiful and may replace existing metals for quite a number of uses.

March 30th
Went into the High Court to hear William Muir defending himself on another series of fraud charges. This time he had gone to Martin's, the big furniture shop in George Street, and bought a lot of furniture and bedding. As usual, there had been something unsuitable: mattresses they had to make to a special size to conform to measurements he gave. He had got some goods from an outfitter's in Dalry Road, but the bill for most of these was paid by an Edinburgh WS, Mr Mackenzie, whom he asked to take over his affairs and pay his accounts for him pending the arrival of his monthly 600-dollar remittance from Canada. He persuaded Mr Mackenzie to advance him another £80, in three or four instalments—on one occasion he made Mr Mackenzie bring £18 out to the farm cottage in which he was staying near Ratho. There was a slight hitch after the jury was impanelled, as Muir wanted to object to someone on the jury named Macpherson, whose name he had not heard when he had been called. It turned out however that there was no one on the jury of that name. I heard Muir cross-examine witnesses from Martins, the draper from Dalry Road, and Mr Mackenzie. He made some good points, and it seemed to me that if he had had a legal training he would have been a dangerous cross-examiner. He asked a witness from Martins why

some linoleum that had been included in the charge had not been produced, to which the witness replied, 'Because you had fastened it to the floor, Mr Muir, with the adhesive we sold you, and we couldn't get it up.' Hill Watson treated Muir amiably. On one occasion he told him he was doing very well, and on another that he had got a good answer and had better leave it at that.

March 31st

I saw in the evening paper that Muir had been convicted and sentenced to four years. Bus to town after tea. We sat in the front seat, where Richard looked out ahead, remarking 'Bus' every now and again. At the top of the Mound we changed into a tram, and again sat in the front seat, Richard remarking 'Funny bus'.

April 9th

The London builders did not have counsel, but relied on Sir Alfred Hurst to put their case. Cairns cross-examined him with devastating ferocity and skill, and floored him again and again. It was a brilliant performance, but I was not the only member of the Commission to think that Cairns' attitude was not altogether judicial and that the pendulum had swung too far from Carter's woolly-minded friendliness.

April 22nd

Cairns repeated a story he had been told by Professor Goodheart, who is editor of the *Law Quarterly*. The age of Lord Asquith had been given erroneously in *Whitaker's Almanac* as 6, and Asquith having made some public reference to this Goodheart sent him at Christmas a copy of *The Tale of Peter Rabbit*. He received this letter in return: 'Dere Porfessor, Thank you for the luvly book you sent me. Mummy reads it to me, and thinks it is very funny: but I think the Law quarterly is funnier.'

Cairns, Hughes and I had an interview with Beharrel, the chairman of the Dunlop Co., who had called to give some explanations of large outlays found by Shove in the company's accounts but not appearing in other books. These, it appears, are secret payments made by Beharrel in person on behalf of the company to large customers such as the Austin Motor Company. They amount to hundreds of thousands of pounds every year, and seem to be a complete evasion of the understanding between the tyre companies.

April 23rd

A hearing of the British Motor Trade Association, who operate a price maintenance scheme on tyres by means of a semi-judicial committee presided over by a retired colonial judge. This committee takes evidence, largely hearsay, on complaints of price-cutting, and imposes fines or stop-list sentences. The Association's case was ably presented by their secretary, who knew what he was talking about and by no means got the worst of exchanges with Cairns: but they made the mistake of bringing along one of their legal chairmen, Sir Grattan Bush, a muddle-headed old fellow who left the distinct impression that justice administered by him was likely to be a chancy business.

May 7th

Goodheart takes everything very seriously, and Barnes seems to delight in putting to him some preposterous point, which Goodheart solemnly considers. Goodheart had been giving a talk on the wireless: and Barnes remarked that he liked the way he had referred to 'Lord Cook—spelled C O K E.' 'Well', Goodheart explained, 'if I had said "Cook" and left it at that, a lot of people wouldn't have known what I meant, and if I said "Coke"'— 'If you'd said "Coke"', Barnes put in, 'all your friends at Oxford would have said, "Arthur should have known better than that".' Goodheart said his great fear was that he might hiccup during the broadcast. Barnes told us the present English law officers were the poorest team in living memory. Churchill, he said, had no interest in law and no use for lawyers. If he had a legal problem, he did not bother with the Attorney-General's department but simply asked Sir Walter Monkton, who was in the Cabinet as Minister of Labour. Goodheart said Churchill had appointed Heald on the strength of one witty remark he had heard him make in a speech on the Defamation Bill. Barnes said Shawcross had been very good. At first he had been doubtful about him, but after a year in office he had been first-rate. Wheatley he seemed to think had been quite good. Thomson he had no recollection of. Cooper had been the best Lord Advocate—Reid was not so easy to get on with.

Bus to North Woolwich. A small carnival on a bombed site, shabby-looking but very vigorous. The 'Dodgems' had none of the 'one way round' rule applied in most places. Everyone crashed into everybody else as much as possible: indeed, some youths seemed to be employed by the management just to ride round in one or two cars and crash into people. I left by bus for East Ham, with lights twinkling all along the ships and reflected in the waters of Albert Dock as we crossed a bridge.

To Mrs Nancy Stott:
3 Cornwall Terrace, Regents Park.   7th May 1954.
Well, here we are starting off on London Buildings—15/16 of the full Commission, at its 100th meeting. As there are 14 others who are all more or less prepared to intervene, I think I can occupy myself more usefully by sending you my love—even if you don't get it until Monday...

Last night...I was in bed by 10.15, after a nice hot bath. On my floor there are 3 bathrooms: and having the place to myself at 9.45 I was able to measure each of the baths with the back-brush and find the biggest one...The people next door had a wireless going full blast—some variety programme—but after I had banged 2 or 3 times this went off, & everything was peaceful for the rest of the night (except the St Pancras Church clock, which didn't worry me—in fact, I rather like it during the hours at which it operates)...

May 11th
Debate Roll before Guthrie. A young junior named Ross opened for the defenders in a capable, well-ordered speech. Daiches, my junior, replied, and talked flamboyant, quite amusing nonsense which did not advance our case but kept Guthrie in a good humour.

May 19th
Finished *Mr Twining and the God Pan* by Timothy Angus Jones. Though it does not come to much, I found it entertaining, with amusing characters and witty passages. It is rather immoral, and if less skilfully handled might have been unpleasant: but the author carries it off effectively.

May 24th
The Conquest of Everest, at the Dominion cinema. It was an interesting film, in colour photography, and gave a vivid impression of the extraordinary hardships and difficulties involved.

May 26th
O'Brien was speaking about the Bible Board, for which he is standing

junior counsel. It exists by reason of an old act of Parliament providing for licensing editions of the Bible, and is run on the basis of that Act and of regulations laid down by Cooper: one of the many matters about which he busied himself while Lord Advocate.

May 28th
The final revision of the London Buildings report. Cairns, with his usual skill and expedition, got us through the whole report by shortly after one.

May 29th
Finished reading *The Exploits of Sherlock Holmes*, by Adrian Conan Doyle and John Dickson Carr: ingenious reconstructions, quite up to the standard of the original.

May 31st
Muirfield: the Bar Foursomes.

June 1st
Jury trial: a slinger in Parkhead Forge who was attaching a big connecting rod to the fall of a crane when another similar rod fell over on his foot. The defenders put in a Minute admitting liability and a tender of £850. It was common ground that the pursuer was fit only for sedentary work on account of intermittent claudication: interference with the blood supply to the foot, which we said was caused by the accident but the defenders said was due to natural causes. Their doctors pointed to various symptoms, including the state of his toe nails and the fact that he had a florid complexion. I made some fun of this in addressing the jury, and after my day at Muirfield was able to raise a laugh by remarking that it would go hardly with some of us if everyone who was highly coloured was liable to lose his foot by gangrene. I was not surprised when we got an award of £1,500.

June 3rd
Finished reading *A Voyage to Purilia*, by Elmer Rice, which I first read twenty years ago. Its witty satire on Hollywood and film conventions escaped my mother when she read it last month. When I tried to explain what it was about, she insisted that I was wrong and that it was about a voyage to another planet—as of course in form it is. What anyone could make of it on that view is hard to say.

June 6th
To bed at 10.15, in order to hear a talk recorded by Lord Montgomery recalling the surrender of the Germans to him in 1945 on Luneborg Heath. It was extremely funny. One could understand how the Field Marshal won the devotion of so many people and caused so much exasperation in others.

June 8th
Finnegan v. Graham: a proof before Strachan. Strenuous efforts have been made to settle the case, but all my powers of persuasion were insufficient to induce the pursuer to take the £400 offered. The defender has since increased the offer to £1,000, but with a condition that the business should belong to him absolutely, with no reversion of a half share to Miss Finnegan in the event of his dying before her. Miss Finnegan was prepared to take £1,000 without this condition, and Leslie had indicated to me that he might be able to arrange a settlement on those lines. Nothing further developed, and the proof proceeded. Miss Finnegan did not make a good appearance in the witness box, and at the instigation of Hughes, my Glasgow agent, I approached Leslie again at lunch time and pointed out the danger to both parties if the evidence of income tax-evasion and contravention of the licensing laws proceeded. He seemed favourably disposed to a compromise, but his agent—Stewart, of Macpherson & Mackay—was definitely of the opposite view, and nothing came of my approach. Miss Finnegan's evidence disclosed a remarkable state of affairs in regard to the public house's finances and drinking parties in the premises after closing time. Leslie put to her that on one occasion 16 priests were present at one of these parties, but she would not admit to more than 5.

June 9th
Hughes is in a great state about the case. He had spent last night compiling a long list of heads of agreement on the basis of which we might be prepared to abandon the case. Miss Finnegan was now, it appeared, willing to accept £400 and surrender the license and her whole remaining rights. I thought that now the evidence was out any attempt at settlement was hopeless, but as requested I put the proposals before Leslie. He again received them sympathetically and went off to talk with Stewart: but he again rejected them with contumely—all he would accept was unconditional abandonment. But the

proof today went much better. We had an excellent valuator called Brash, and our other witnesses were not too bad. The proof went more quickly than anticipated, and shortly before 3 o'clock the stock of witnesses summoned for today was exhausted. Hughes was talking excitedly about continuing the case for more evidence, and I had precognitions of one or two who were supposed to come tomorrow. But I took my courage in both hands and closed the proof, with the result that the defender had to go into the witness box right away. This turned out to be good tactics, as he seemed unprepared to give evidence, and gave some very ill-advised answers to Leslie during the half hour before the case was adjourned. 'I don't say we'll win your case for you', I said to Hughes, 'but it certainly isn't as hopeless as it seemed.'

June 10th

Graham completed his evidence in chief, and I cross-examined him. I had some useful material in the valuator's report, and at the end of the cross-examination it seemed to me that he was completely discredited. This impression was confirmed by my overhearing a conversation between Hughes and John George, who came in later and was evidently asking if anything had been brought out in the cross-examination. I understood Hughes to reply that it had been 'one of the best crosses' he had heard. I did reasonably well also with other defence witnesses, but, as I told Hughes when the Court rose, it is one thing to discredit the defender and another thing to prove our case. If he still got a chance of settlement, I said, he would be well advised to take it. After supper, for what I hoped was the last time, I again had to spread out the numerous Finnegan papers on the table, and set to work to compile my speech.

June 11th

I addressed for about two hours, and got a surprisingly good reception. It seemed that we were going to win. I did not wait to hear Leslie's speech, having another case in Procedure Roll before Mackintosh: *Mulligan v. Colvilles.* The pursuer was cleaning out a smelting furnace divided into compartments by 5-feet brick walls. Soot and slag had to be cleared away regularly, and employees had to drop down on to the walls and shovel the burning soot and slag from floor level into a bucket. The heat during these operations is said to have been so intense that the cleaners had to work in pairs and change places every two or three minutes, and had to wear a wet sack over their heads and a towel over the mouth. On the day of his accident, the pursuer says, one of the bricks in the wall on which the pursuer landed was loose, so that he fell among the red-hot soot and slag and was seriously burned. The defenders say the accident was caused by the pursuer's lowering himself too quickly into the soot, in which he meant to stand when doing the work, with the result that the soot came over his clogs and burned him. Oddly enough, they say also that the furnace had been hosed down some time before and the soot was no longer red hot. In the Finnegan case, my junior told me, Leslie had met with opposition from Strachan, and there had been quite a scene when Strachan had accused him of suppressing a letter from the solicitors in whose office the disputed agreement had been signed. I enjoyed this case, and never felt tired, despite the amount of work I put in on it.

With Nancy to the Gaumont cinema: *The Rainbow Jacket*, a pleasant picture, full of sunshine and the open air. The story, about a boy jockey who wins the St Leger, was largely baloney, but it was human, entertaining and genuine, with real, likable people and attractive settings—it had been photographed, in colour, at real race-courses: Lingfield, Newmarket, Doncaster and so on.

June 13th

Berwick & Haddington Labour Party's annual rally at Yellow Craig: Willis, and Penry Jones, the prospective candidate, an eloquent young Welshman, connected with the Iona Community. Willis said this was an easier Parliament than 1945: the volume of legislation to be studied was much less, and the Government supporters would not as a rule sit on beyond midnight.

June 18th

Merstham: on the main London-Brighton road, the traffic through it rather unpleasant. But as soon as I got off the main road I found myself in a complete backwater, with leafy cottages bearing a date in the late seventeenth century, and an old gentleman walking along carrying a basket and wearing a tweed jacket and clerical collar.

Finished reading *My Late Wives*, by Carter Dickson. The ending is baloney, but this does not detract from the readability of the book or the suspense and excitement created by the magnificent build-up—one of the author's best.

June 29th

A jury trial before Migdale. His charge was favourable to the defenders, and was more orderly and clear than I had expected—though, as Jack Hunter remarked to me, there was still considerable room for improvement. He said that on his telling his wife he had a number of cases before Migdale her reply had been, 'Many a Migdale makes a muddle.'

July 1st

Another jury trial. The pursuer in the course of his work as a moulder was instructed to cast a 5-inch by 15-inch offset. He had a look around for a moulding box of the appropriate size, but no box of that size was in stock, the only box available being a good deal larger. While he and his mate were lifting off the top half of the box, after ramming it with sand round the pattern, he strained a muscle in his chest. His case on Record was that it was the defenders' duty to provide a box of proportions reasonably appropriate to the job the pursuer was doing: and if they chose to supply a heavier box they should have provided lifting tackle. We had no evidence to support the latter part of the case: and though there was no doubt that the defenders had not supplied the right box the difficulty was that the boxes of the size used by the pursuer were in regular use for other types of casting. Since the box was not of the size appropriate to the pattern, more sand had of course to be used, but there was not much in this point— there did not appear to be any appreciable difference between the weight of the pattern normally used in the box and the weight of the volume of sand required to replace it. I thought it advisable in conducting the case to avoid details of weights and sizes, and concentrate on the fact of the wrong box. We led the evidence of the pursuer and his mate, and I had Dr Muir to say that the bigger the box the heavier. That was all the evidence for the pursuer, apart from a former factories medical officer, aged 84, who told the court that he himself had had a precisely similar injury ten years ago when he was boarding a tram. I got all the defence witnesses to agree—as of course they could hardly dispute—that with a bigger box one had a heavier weight and more strain on the people who lifted it. I addressed the jury: and Guest followed with a clear, logical speech, advising them to adopt a more rational approach to the case than I had done. He sat down at 3.15, but Migdale was unprepared to charge a jury without a night's reflection and sent them away until tomorrow morning.

July 2nd

Migdale proceeded to charge the jury. He seemed to be against me all through, and I daresay his intention was to charge in the defenders' favour, but what he said was almost wholly favourable to the pursuer. As Guest said sadly to me as we came out of court, he missed the whole point of the defenders' case. Verdict for the pursuer by a majority of 10 to 2.

July 5th

Finished reading *The Tortoise and the Hare*, by Elizabeth Jenkins, one of those rare novels the quality of which is such that one feels genuine deprivation after coming to the end. The people in it are drawn with subtlety and skill, and everything that happens arises naturally and inevitably out of their characters and circumstances. I hoped anxiously for a different ending, but knew that the only possible ending was that which the author has devised—though it too leaves the reader with something still to think about, the merest hint of future possibilities.

July 6th

A divorce before Migdale: *Cocozza v. Cocozza*. I appeared for the wife, who was accused of misconduct with a man named William McLean 22 years ago. Husband and wife had separated on account of the husband's association with another woman, by whom he has had five children. Some evidence had been taken on commission, before I came into the case, from two witnesses who were supposed to have seen McLean and the defender together in the house.

...How did it come that you visited Mrs Cocozza at that time? A.—Well, a man met my husband: he said, 'You've got to get down. Willie's hurted in the pit.' Q.—So did you go? A.—'You had better go down and see Willie McLean': because I knew his mother. His mother is dead. So we went down and Bella was in the room and she was running about—'Oh, don't die the now! Don't die the now!' Q.—Did you go in, after having received that message, to Willie McLean at 13 Gloucester Street? A.—Yes, I went down after that. She wanted me down on the Friday. When I left, Willie was there, giving the wains pie. He had this wee boy on his knee. Q.—You went down to 13 Gloucester Street? A.—

Yes, and he was in and I asked him what he was doing there and he said he stayed there, he was tying up with Bella. Q.—How many rooms were there in the house? A.—Just a room and kitchen. Q.—Where was Mr McLean? Was he in the room or in the kitchen? A.—He was in the kitchen alone with her. You know, it's as true as I'm telling. The next day I met her she had a boring machine on her shoulder. She was going to the pawn that day. Q.—Whose was that? A.—She said it was Willie's. I said, they'll no take that into the pawn, a boring machine.'
CROSS-EXAMINED BY MR KISSEN: …When did somebody come and ask you if you could give evidence in this case? A.— Evidence? It's not evidence at all, it's the truth…

The pursuer and his witnesses were confused and prolix, but the confusion passed over Migdale's head and I am sure he was incapable of realising what a farrago of nonsense it was.

July 15th
A Jury trial before Patrick, *Hunter v. Hanley*. The pursuer, a sufferer from chronic bronchitis, had a course of penicillin injections from the defender, a doctor practising in the Gallowgate in Glasgow. While Dr Hanley was withdrawing the needle after giving the twelfth injection it broke off at the butt, leaving the whole needle in Mrs Hunter's hip. He marked the spot with a biro pen and sent her to the Infirmary, but despite three operations they were unable to get the needle out, and she still has it there today. The defender used a No 16 hypodermic needle, and we say that this was unsuitable—a much coarser needle should have been used. These cases against doctors are always difficult—it is practically impossible to get medical men to give evidence against a colleague. The defender had plenty of evidence that the needle he used was a proper one, and we had one expert in the afternoon saying that a needle in the hip does no harm, so that a break is much less serious than the pain of the prick when the injection is given. I was handicapped a good deal by the Record, which had been revised by Wheatley and for some reason made no reference to length of needle, so that some good questions I had prepared with the help of a text-book edited by Sir Alexander Fleming had to go unasked. Wheatley had averred that the defender had been guilty of 'gross negligence', an out-of-date concept which will no doubt cause difficulty when Patrick comes to charge the jury.

July 16th

Guest made an eloquent speech for the defender, but it was easily outdone by Patrick's. He not only directed the jury that they had to find gross negligence, but set out to demolish every point in the pursuer's case. He had his charge carefully prepared, largely in typescript, and had obviously devoted his considerable intellectual powers to making sure as far as he could that the pursuer would not succeed: the most one-sided charge I have ever heard. The jury found unanimously for the defender. I had taken an exception, selecting the most hopeful of many possible passages in the charge, but in view of our averments it may not be possible to make much of the point.

July 17th

Eyemouth Herring Queen festival: a colourful, attractive ceremony, the queen coming in from the sea with an escort of fishing boats.

July 19th

Finished reading *Lucky Jim* by Kingsley Amis: not at all a bad story, and by no means as crude as it seemed at first. It was good to find everything coming right in the end.

July 21st

Motored to Alloa, for the purpose of taking the evidence of the co-defender in *Cocozza v. Cocozza*. It was half an hour before they all arrived, during which time I sat comfortably in the car, reading a book. The house was one of a Corporation housing scheme near the docks: and an elderly woman in a dirty black dress and bedroom slippers, who had been hanging about the gate, approached me, told me she was Mrs McLean and consulted me about whether she should give the children their dinner. I advised that this would be in order, and there was some commotion while she rounded the children up with much shouting and turmoil—'I'll not have any of your bloody nonsense the day'. Peace was then restored, and continued until the arrival of the rest of the Commission. We all trooped into the kitchen, and took Mr McLean's evidence. He was a funny old boy, and gave his evidence with seeming frankness, but there were some fairly obvious indications that he was not telling the truth—particularly when he was asked about having said in a letter that he had stayed with Mrs Cocozza for five months, and admitted having written the letter but not the bit about five months. As the letter was all in the same handwriting, this was not altogether convincing. On to Stirling. We lunched at the Golden Lion, at the expense of our solicitors—though they will expect to recover it in due course from the Legal Aid fund—and then set off for Gartloch Asylum to take the evidence of a witness who is suffering from paranoia but who, it was hoped, might have a lucid interval. As I had a map, I led the way. The witness was supposed to say that he had introduced McLean to Mrs Cocozza as a prospective lodger. He said this all right, but unfortunately went on to say in cross-examination that McLean became more than a lodger and he himself had seem McLean and Mrs Cocozza in bed together. He gave his evidence clearly, and seemed to be having quite a lucid interval. I thought his evidence ended any hopes for the defence.

I had a sleeper on the 10.20 to London, and left home about 9.35, taking the car, which I meant to leave at Players to be greased. When I had got almost to Abbeyhill, I realised I had forgotten to pack my shaving things, and had to turn back. This made me a little late when I came out of Players, but a taxi coming up the hill took me to the station in time for the train.

July 22nd
Peterborough Agricultural Show: one of those enormous shows with everything symmetrically arranged. Got to Kings Cross before 10 and took a bus to the hotel. I always admire the London bus conductresses, who at all hours of the day, and practically without exception, are neat, cheerful and friendly.

From Mr Guy A. Aldred:
The Strickland Press 104 George Street Glasgow C.1 22/7/1954
Both sides. Please *read* all of this epistle
Dear Comrade Stott—I want to ask you to help me. I am *not* asking you to make to me a present of money. I am in a jam out of which it ought to be possible for someone other than myself, and someone with legal knowledge to take me...

Despite appearances & coroner's verdict, I know, from his correspondence with me, that the Duke of Bedford committed suicide. It could be argued from his letters to me, unless a very great coincidence is allowed for, that this is so. Sometime before his death (about a year) he fell out with me because he went all Communist Party: and, despite my peace attitude, I am still *not*

C.P. I want peace but I believe in Free Speech and cannot agree in nonsense like the secret trial of Beria & the wiping out of his name from the Russian *Who's Who*. I never liked Beria but this is nonsense & dictatorship. This has been my attitude all along. Bedford broke almost with me over it. Anyway he was very mean. At the time of his death, he was coming round. In money he was *not* generous. He owed me £1,000 for having produced his *Road to Real Success*. I did not print nor bind this. It was done outside. I paid for it and he was to pay me. This account was not settled to me at the time of his death, altho he had sent me a little money occasionally. He told me he would pay me & in his Will he left me this exact amount £1,000. I have letters admitting it was a debt & I have the paid bills. All this does *not* matter...

I changed from the Commercial Bank to the Clydesdale. At first the Clydesdale would advance me no money. Then they advanced me £200 against a holograph instruction. They increased this to £300 against a complete bond or whatever it is termed or assignation. I have exceeded that £300 & *am being pressed to pay* the *amount over of* £39.

At the moment I have no money, not even house money. My gas & electricity will be cut off *unless I meet them at once* (they are overdue & quite heavy) because I work day & night.

About another £60 to £100 (less than the second figure & about the first) would get me out of this jam. I have money coming from USA & from New Zealand, but I cannot say when it will come. Can nothing be done?...

July 23rd

Finished reading *Performing Flea* by P.G. Wodehouse, a series of letters to a younger writer whom apparently he assisted in his career. They are kindly and helpful, and include a lot of useful advice and information about the art of writing, with shrewd comments on other authors. The book includes also some extracts from a diary kept by the author when he was interned by the Germans after the occupation of Rome. Many of them are very funny, and one also gets a pretty good impression, reading between the lines, of the hardships of life in an internment camp. This is a good book, and deserves a better title than one taken from abuse directed at Wodehouse by some ignorant person because of his broadcasting over the German radio.

Group II: it was agreed to set up a panel for the Rubber Footwear enquiry, consisting of myself as chairman, Cullen the accountant, and Archdale, a machine-tool manufacturer from Birmingham who seldom attends. This seems a good panel, and I agreed with Cullen that we should have as few meetings as possible, and conduct the business as far as we could in writing. 'And of course there's always the telephone', Cullen added.

August 7th
A fete at Houndwood House. I took part in a novel form of lucky dip, in which small boxes, open at the end, were arranged on the ground in a circle. The boxes were numbered. Two guinea-pigs, a black one and a white one, were set down in the centre, and whichever box a guinea-pig ran into first was a winning number. My first attempt, at a basket of tomatoes, was unsuccessful, but at the second try the guinea-pig ran straight into my box, and I won a dozen eggs.

August 21st
Pleased to see in Tuesday's *Scotsman* that I had won *Finnegan v. Graham*.

August 26th
Cubert: a surprisingly attractive little church. On one of the tombstones, an epitaph for a boy of 17: 'Qualis erat indicabit ultima dies'.

September 4th
Wadebridge: the road led up to St Breock Downs, and on the other side of the moor descended steeply, so shut in with hedges that it was impossible to see the countryside. Crossing a tributary of the Camel, the road then went straight up at an alarming gradient through a deep cutting half a mile long and not much wider than the breadth of the car. It emerged at the hamlet and church of Withiel, right at the top of the hill. The descent on the other side to Rock was narrow too, but not nearly as bad as the ascent. The extraordinary thing was that over this 8-mile stretch of macadamised road, between 4 and 5 on a Saturday afternoon, I did not see a single vehicle and hardly a pedestrian.

September 5th
Fistral: a short walk on the Headland. Two French crabbers were lying in the bay, picturesque in their green paint, and we watched a third coming in to anchor.

September 7th

Finished *A Passage to India* by E M Forster: a pleasure to read a book that is so well written and full of accurate observation and careful portrayal of character, British and Indian. This was our last day at Newquay, and we went to Holywell: the weather overcast and threatening, but the sea, though roughish, seemed quite safe. The surfing is always good at Holywell, and I enjoyed particularly a long run on a double wave, with rain driving on my face.

September 8th

A lovely road up a wooded hillside to Birdlip, then through fine woods where we stopped to let the children have a run along the woodland paths. We thought of having tea in Cheltenham, but as it was so nice in the woods, with open grassy glades quite dry underfoot, we had another picnic and stayed for some time in the sun before going on down the hill to Cheltenham. Lansdown Hotel: Nancy went down to dinner first, while I stayed with the children, but while I was sitting with them a chambermaid arrived to turn down the bed, a pleasant Irish girl who volunteered to stay while I joined Nancy downstairs. There was some disturbance from above after I came down, but Nancy on going up to investigate reported that the children had been playing and when she went in Margaret had been trying to get them back into bed.

September 9th

We stopped on the edge of Wyn Forest, and walked down a path beside the brook. So far everything had gone well, but as we mounted the hill into the forest after resuming the journey the car engine gave indications of trouble. Though it was every bit as bad as yesterday, I was interested to find I did not feel half as worried about it. I had not felt well yesterday, and had wondered whether this was due to worry about the car or whether my worry about the car was due to not feeling very well. As I felt all right today, I assumed the latter was correct. Very little traffic on the road to Lymm, whither Molly Rees and her husband moved last summer. As soon as we arrived, Molly phoned Tal at the works to ask who were the Ford agents in Warrington—the Warrington Motor Company. I phoned them, told them about the trouble, and asked if they could fit a new petrol pump for me before tonight. The foreman who spoke to me was sceptical about the petrol-pump story: they had no mechanic available for a big job, but he did not suppose for a moment that there was anything wrong with the petrol pump. I told him I should bring the car in straight away, and accordingly motored to Warrington, and found the Warrington Motor Company occupying a rather congested workshop in a back lane. A lot of activity seemed to be going on in very restricted surroundings. All the foreman said was, 'You've put your car right in the middle of the shop so that nothing can get in or out': and a few minutes later another man in a white overall got into the car and backed it out. I followed, thinking he was taking the car outside to look at it, but without stopping he drove it out at the gate and disappeared. I found an empty lorry standing outside, and sat there for nearly an hour. Eventually I walked round the corner, and found the car with the bonnet up, carburettor off, and some tools lying on the radiator. A youth appeared with two big rubber rings, and proceeded to fit these. The man in the white overall then appeared again, got into the car and drove out of the gate once more. He returned after a quarter of an hour, apparently satisfied: and I was presented with a bill for ten shillings and fivepence, which seemed reasonable if the trouble had been corrected. The youth who had been working on the car had remarked to me that there had been a stone in the petrol pipe, and something of the kind was confirmed by the foreman—from whom I parted on friendly terms. I was impressed by the way the job had been handled, without any unnecessary talk or discussion—I was asked nothing about it beyond what I had said on the telephone.

A game of cricket, in which Tal joined after his return from work. Elizabeth, who had never played before, thoroughly enjoyed it, though she batted oddly, bent almost double with her head hanging down in front of the wicket. As we were playing with a rubber ball she came to no harm, and was able to protect her wicket quite successfully in this way.

September 10th
The car running perfectly—I was confirmed in my good opinion of the Warrington Motor Company.

September 16th
With Nancy to the Palace cinema to see Judy Holliday in *Born Yesterday*. Miss Holliday has to be seen and—more important—heard to be believed. She has the most extraordinary high-pitched voice, and

it required a continuous effort of concentration to follow what she and the other people were saying. But the effort was worth while, and the story is entertaining and ingenious.

September 23rd

London: a day off. Train to East Grinstead, then bus to Horsham. I bought a bus timetable, and chose a bus leaving for Arundel. This route led through green pleasant country to Pulborough, where the bus turned up to the railway station and stood for about ten minutes, until two electric trains were seen to be approaching, one from each direction—when the bus at once took off up the street and rejoined the road to the coast. There is a good gap in the South Downs, through which the Arun and the railway go to the sea, but the road instead of keeping in the valley climbed right up to the top of the Downs along the edge of a wooded punchbowl—a very attractive road. At Arundel I changed into a bus for Littlehampton: a seaside resort, but no sign of the sea. The bus from Midhurst to Haslemere turned down to Shootermill, where there was a very ordinary pond with a big notice saying that unless £2,000 was speedily subscribed it would be impossible for these ponds to be preserved.

September 24th

Gallie, who is chairman of the Sand and Gravel panel, looked in to tell me his wife has to have an operation next week, when the panel is to be holding a series of hearings in Scotland: and asked if I would mind presiding and posing the questions in his stead. This was rather a blow, as sand and gravel is the one enquiry in which I have not bothered to read up anything, and I do not know at all what the association are supposed to do or what the points in the investigation are.

September 25th

R.P. Morison appointed a Deputy Commissioner under the National Insurance Acts, a full-time appointment: the most important piece of news for years from the point of view of the Bar. It will cause much rejoicing, though it is difficult to see why Duffes should be resigning or why Morison should accept such a comparatively minor appointment.

September 27th

St Andrews House for the Sand and Gravel hearings. I did the questioning. Not knowing much about it, I confined myself largely to the brief provided by the staff. It did not seem to me that anything very illuminating emerged, but it was interesting, and we were running ahead of time all day. Lunch in a restaurant on the top floor: a nice place in pleasant surroundings, priced extraordinarily cheaply— threepence for a plate of excellent lentil soup, and other prices on a similar scale. To Players, and arranged to bring the car on Wednesday to have rear reflectors fitted, in accordance with an absurd regulation which comes into force on Friday.

September 29th

A tour of sand and gravel pits. At Doune we inspected the sandpit of the Springbank company, climbing to a dizzy height at the top of a stone crusher. We stood on a crazy little wooden platform, rattling and shaking and reminding me of nothing so much as the Amusements Park at Wembley. I was in a car with Cairns and one of the Sand and Gravel people, but they were not very interesting travel companions—unfortunately as the country was looking its very best, with bright sunshine, blue lochs and lovely colourings on Ben Venue and the other hills. From Aberfoyle to Balloch I went with Hughes, and found him much pleasanter: he took a lively interest in everything we saw. There was a washing plant at Balloch pit, and Cairns and I climbed up on it, though the man there said he would not take us up because it was not safe. There was nothing to see that we had not seen at Doune, and I soon had the party down to the loch side to let them have a view up the loch to Ben Lomond. Gifford and I went in one of the cars direct to Glasgow.

September 30th

Glasgow: the Washed Sand and Gravel Association, for whom Guest appeared and put a number of points, about statistics and the future progress of the enquiry. He put them clearly and succinctly, Cairns replied with equal succinctness, and the meeting was over by 11.45.

Lunch with the Lord Provost, Tom Kerr. He is a quaint old fellow, and having asked which of us was the musician who was fond of Beethoven—I assumed this was Cairns, but he seems to have meant Hughes—went to the piano and played a few bars. He then put us through an examination as to what pieces he had been playing. For lunch I was sat down next to the City Treasurer, Mrs Roberts, a plain, sensible little woman, easy to talk to. At the end the Lord Provost got up and went through the list of his guests, saying something about each. Cairns, he said, had told him his father was 88 and still a member of the town council, which Kerr found encouraging. Cairns, he added, had been a Liberal candidate, and took a great interest in politics—at which point Cairns, as non-political chairman of the Monopolies Commission, smilingly shook his head. Kerr next recalled that he had met me when he came through to Edinburgh in connection with a little case in which I had appeared for the defence. He would say no more about that, except that he had not been the criminal. Cullen was an accountant who had travelled much in Brazil and Argentina, and claimed to understand South American economics: a remarkable claim. Hughes was a musician who liked Beethoven: it was very fine to find someone in a position like Hughes' who did that. Cairns replied briefly.

October 7th
Duffy showed me a copy of the *Daily Express* which came out a few weeks ago when Cooper had a cerebral haemorrhage, which it is said will make it impossible for him ever to come back to work. The *Express* went a stage further, so far as its northern edition, intended to go off by the early train to Inverness, was concerned. They had a big headline, 'Death of Lord Cooper': and a common-length obituary.

October 8th
Duffes said he had listened to part of my speech to the jury yesterday, and it had reminded him of rapid fire in the first world war. He thought I must be the fastest speaker in Parliament House.

October 14th
Nield addressed us all day on behalf of the British Non-Ferrous Metals Association. He is hopelessly bad, and one result is that I lose patience and ask him some questions which he regards as an insult: an unfortunate thing, as he is quite a nice fellow.

October 15th
Nield resumed his address, simply reading from the printed book that he had put in. He was interrupted from time to time for questions, but as he could not answer any of them this was just a waste of time. I kept quiet.

October 24th
Cramond church: the service at which the memorial window to my

father was to be dedicated. Mr Small preached on Acts 27,23: a fine sermon. The window portrays Moses with the serpent rod in one hand and the book of the word in the other, and Small took the three people—Moses, Paul and my father—and showed how the same strains ran through the lives of each. He referred to the restoration of the church, and stressed what a remarkable thing it was that my father should have embarked on this as soon as he came to the parish, not waiting till he had settled down in it and knew everyone there but pushing on with the work right away. It is an attractive little window, simple but appropriate.

October 26th
Duffes, in his first jury trial since his return, had what I think must be a unique achievement, obtaining, by 7 votes to 5, an award of £10: £100, with the pursuer 90 per cent to blame.

October 29th
Muir Society social. The Shaws had brought Cecil Gordon and his wife, and I had an interesting chat with Gordon. He knows Hughes, who he says is in private life a socialist. Speaking no doubt from his own experience, he remarked that if civil servants did not like anyone whose name was included in a list of possible appointments they put 'Erratic' against his name: this was very damning. Gordon was indignant that the Labour Government had made no use of John Taylor, who he said would have been willing to serve on the Coal Board or Electricity Board if he had been asked. Gordon thought it absurd that when the cement combine was prepared to pay thousands a year for the benefit of Taylor's guidance the Labour Government had been so foolish as to ignore him and fill its Boards of nationalised industries with avowed opponents of nationalisation. I took part in an elimination dance with Margaret Leechman. Dancers were eliminated by a series of instructions, and at the last Margaret and I were left against Nancy and Sinclair Shaw, when George Ritchie, who was giving the instructions, finished up with 'All couples where the gentlemen are not carrying a cigarette case leave the floor'. He knew that neither Shaw nor I smoked: but as it happened I had slipped a packet of cigarettes into my pocket before coming out, in order to be able to offer one to anybody at the dance, and I produced this and held it up—thus winning.

November 2nd

Calton Ward municipal by-election: taking voters to the poll. I was relegated to lower Greenside, a set of dark alleys under the Calton Hill, in a kind of abyss between it and the ridge on which Leith Street runs. A horrifying place: dark lanes between tenements on the one side and the rock of the Calton Hill on the other, badly lit, and filled with yelling children who could only be dimly seen in the half light. One consignment of two men and three fat women chafed one another on their weights. 'You'll hae to diet, Nellie'. 'Me? I've only yin meal in the day. I canna diet ony mair nor that.'

November 5th

Rockets and star-shells bursting over Camden Town, and a loud bang every now and again as further evidence that this was Guy Fawkes night.

To Princes Theatre to see the Japanese Ballet. It was pretty terrible: not much movement, and sometimes there could hardly be any because of the dresses, pretty but by no means convenient. In her first dance Miss Miko Hanayagui wore trousers that went down to her toes and about a yard beyond, so that it was a miracle that she was able to move at all. The worst part was the music, which consisted of someone beating a wooden drum, or two people strumming the same note over and over again on an antediluvian kind of banjo. Occasionally someone sang, or made a rhythmical groaning noise, not in rhythm with either the banjo-strummers or whatever dancing happened to be going on. I had to come away at half time to catch my train, and was not sorry.

November 9th

Quinn v. Cameron & Robertson. The pursuer was a grinder in the defender's iron-foundry from 1942 to 1951, when he was informed that he was suffering from pneumoconiosis. He has not worked since, and our medical expert gave evidence that in about five years he will be unable to breathe, with death as the result. The case is founded on faulty ventilation, and on a regulation that no grinding shall be done without adequate appliances for the interception of the dust. There is an exemption for a portable grinding machine, but the pursuer's machine, though it ran on a little rail for the purpose of adapting it to the job, seems to have been something different from a portable machine. There was admittedly no exhaust ventilation on his machine: and from Shearer's cross-examination I gathered that the main defence might be that the pursuer did not have pneumoconiosis, or that it was not contracted in the defender's foundry.

The moon tonight, which was almost full, was surrounded with circles of rainbow colouring: a lovely effect, with the moon clear in the centre and clouds round it suffused with all the colours of the spectrum.

November 10th
Tonight I spent a lot of time preparing my speech in Quinn's case, with the help of very lucid, legible notes taken by my junior, John Wilson.

November 11th
Jack Hunter recalled an occasion when I appeared for a pursuer and the case was withdrawn by Mackintosh. Mackintosh had then asked, 'What happens next?' to which, Hunter said, I replied 'I don't know— I'm not accustomed to having my cases withdrawn from the jury.'

November 12th
Finished reading *The New Men* by C. P. Snow, an interesting story about scientists engaged in atomic research. His writing has extraordinary reality and verisimilitude.

November 19th
Commission Group II: the draft conclusions on Copper. Phoned Pike and arranged to meet. We took a bus to Hamilton House, the National Union of Teachers' premises, where an exhibition of horror comics was being held. There has been a considerable public outcry about these 'comics', which are said to be corrupting children's minds. The impression I got from the exhibition was of inanity and point-lessness rather than horror: plenty of skeletons and corpses and ghouls and monsters, but so badly drawn and silly that I doubted whether most of them would strike a child as terrifying. I did not see that many children could be interested in them at all: I should think that most of them are bought by adults.

To Oxford Circus news cinema: an American coloured film of a trip to Europe, including some lovely pictures of the Lake of Lu-cerne, which made me want to go there.

November 23rd

Finished reading *The Wife of Richard Sheldon*, by Patrick Quentin. In the course of this murder story one is apt to become impatient with the argy-bargy, and even more with the ruminations of the character who tells the story: but the impatience is mainly due to the excitement of the story and the skill with which the suspense is built up: one of those thrillers that are difficult to put down until the end is reached.

December 1st

Douglas Johnston asked if I had listened-in to the broadcast of the speeches in Westminster Hall at the presentation to Churchill on his 80th birthday. Johnston thought they had typified British political life at its best. I had listened-in to the recording and agreed with him. Attlee, who made the presentation, spoke extraordinarily well: a matter-of-fact narration, addressed to the Prime Minister, of what he had done in his variegated career, interspersed with dryly humorous comments, all exactly right for an occasion when, as he said, he had not come to bury Caesar but to praise him. Churchill was equally good in his very different style. John Mackie, now prospective Labour candidate for Lanark, represented by Patrick Maitland, told me about his only meeting with Maitland, on the aeroplane from London. Maitland said he had heard about Mackie from his neighbour Thornton-Kemsley, who had told him that he and John met from time to time over a cup of coffee. This, Maitland said, might be all right for Kincardineshire, but it would never do in Lanark. John gave me also an amusing account of how the Woodworkers' delegation to the Labour Party conference was persuaded at the last moment to change its views on German rearmament and vote for the Executive resolution, thus changing a small majority against the resolution into a small one in its favour.

On the train I finished reading *The Charm of Hours*, by Peter Skelton, a peculiar novel which contains no story. Just as one thinks it is beginning, with a vivid account of the bombing of Rotterdam, it comes to an abrupt end. The book consists mainly of descriptive passages, beautifully written in lengthy sentences, one sentence sometimes occupying as much as half a page, but all lucid and comprehensible. Seen through the eyes of the adolescent who tells the 'story', it has a certain attractiveness: and though one is tempted to skip through the irrelevancies and try to get on, to find out what it is all about, every now and again one comes across a passage, descriptive of some trivial experience or emotion, which makes a tremendous impact of vividness and insight into human nature, and left me with a feeling of regret at coming to the end.

From Mr Guy A Aldred:
The Strickland Press, 104 George Street Glasgow, C.1 1/12/1954
Dear Comrade Stott—Yours to hand. Many thanks. I enclose a cutting about the Gordon case. I can send you more cuttings if necessary. Gordon came into this shop a lot during 1954 & was a pacifist in his views. Actually his behaviour was very polite and gentle. So far as this case is concerned, he seems to me to be guilty. But he wrote me from Gerona Prison, Spain, assuring me *of his complete innocence* &, as he was friendless, asking me if I could organise his defence...Bovey raises the question of expenses. I have discussed this matter with some people and they expect lawyers to work for nothing, *in a case like this*. Just for glory & fame which is nonsense.

I was studying the Camden Town murder the other night...I remember this very well: and I knew the solicitor whose last years were so unfortunate, Arthur Newton. But for Marshall Hall & Newton (not forgetting Wellesley Orr) Wood would have been executed. Yet I am quite sure that he was innocent. Everything that folly could do to make the case blacker against him he did. Anyway, Wood's father (an ill old man) had saved up £1,000 and he gave every penny for the defence. I try to find out from Bovey how much money was needed & *how quickly*. He was a little vague...

All arrangements can be made through Bovey & I will raise what balance is needed so long as Bovey tells me. The money is certain. I really intended it for myself & my propaganda. But to save a man's life is, after all, of paramount importance. Anyway, I am *most* anxious that justice shall be done: & in my opinion you are the outstanding man to secure it. As you know, I am opposed *most definitely* to the death penalty...

Gordon is nothing to me personally. But when a man is friendless, through crime or folly, his defence becomes one's business if, in his misery, he appeals. I may wish he had not turned to me. He did: & I must respond.

Yours

From Mr John Taylor:

7 Maybury Rough, Woking, Surrey.   6th December, 1954

Dear Gordon Stott,

Many thanks for you letter of 26th ulto,...

I can well appreciate that the conversation with Cecil Gordon was a bit one-sided. I am afraid political parties will never alter and they are normally interested in names not ability. Actually in much of big business the effective executive power and brains lie behind the captains of industry many of whom when one gets to know them, are fairly poor specimens.

What with playing the Germans at football, bolstering up the Japanese economy and other matters of that nature I am just appalled that the general public never thinks to conduct a post-mortem examination as to what the last two wars were all about and what they achieved.

Yours

December 9th

McKenna addressed us on behalf of the Tyre Manufacturers Conference, and answered questions, putting his case succinctly and in reasonably interesting form. I thought Cairns was hardly up to his earlier standard. He seems to be taking less trouble with his brief than he did at first, and contented himself largely with putting the questions in the form prepared by the staff, which seldom makes a really effective point. My own questions were few, and equally ineffective.

Tooting: *The Naked Spur* at the Vogue cinema, a Western of varying quality. I was amazed to find that 50 per cent of the audience consisted of teddy boys, adolescents got up in the extraordinary style favoured by such youths in some working-class areas: drape suits, with long, close-fitting jackets down almost to their knees, narrow trousers, yellow ties and socks, and hair curled back in a lump on the front of their heads—a drab caricature of the Edwardian elegance on which the fashion is based.

December 10th

About 12.20 a.m. I finished reading *According to the Evidence*, by Henry Cecil. The hour at which I finished it is some indication of its gripping power. Once one accepts the initial situation—rather a tall order—the rest follows naturally, contrived with all the author's ingenuity, wit and knowledge of the courts.

Drury Lane: *The King and I*, founded on the story of a Welsh widow who went out to Bangkok in Victorian times to act as governess to the Siamese royal children—a curious choice as the subject of a musical, but amply justified by the result, elegant and quaint, with interesting development and many pleasing tunes and settings.

December 24th
Cooper has resigned, and Clyde has been appointed Lord President.

December 25th
Elizabeth and I set off for church: a joint service in the Congregational Church in Wellington Street. A harmonium droned on until at last a door leading into a little pulpit opened and an old woman who had been standing in the porch appeared and opened a big Bible. She retreated, and two ancient clergymen appeared, one sitting in the pulpit and the other going to a seat immediately below. The one in the pulpit was a genial old fellow, but unfortunately it was the other who preached: Rev. W. R. Wiseman, formerly minister of Gladsmuir. His sermon was not the worst I have heard, but it was certainly the most inappropriate. His text was Matthew 2,1, but he soon forgot about the wise men and grumbled in a loud monotonous shout about the Germans, atomic scientists, the South African government, and others against whom he felt some grievance. He went on for twenty-five minutes, saying nothing of the slightest importance. Elizabeth was most patient, but even she mentioned that the minister had preached for a long time.

Finished reading *And Now Goodbye*, by James Hilton. I have read it many times, but found it absorbing as ever: simple, honest and profoundly moving in its happiness as in its final tragedy.

December 26th
To church. Mr Brown preached on Luke 2,7. He was very good, and seemed all the more so after yesterday's ordeal. Mr Brown's sermon was just as long, but instead of waiting for him to come to an end one wants him to go on. He told a story of a young woman whose war marriage was breaking up. Her husband was away, and she had to live with his parents—'and what's more', she said, 'they want me to go to church with them.' When it was suggested to her that that

might not necessarily be a bad thing, she said she was not a heathen. She believed in God all right, 'but not to that extent.' Mr Brown remarked that many people had only a bowing acquaintance with the Lord God Almighty.

December 27th
A very odd quarter of an hour on the wireless in which an old gentleman described as Canon A. O. Wintle told some peculiar anecdotes in an attractively concise, pawky way, as interludes in a series of tunes he played on his barrel-organs—which he seems not only to collect but to construct and sell. He sounded like anything but a canon, and produced a novel, entertaining programme.

December 31st
Mr Blair and Kate for Bridge. Their taxi came at 10.30. After washing up the dishes we listened-in to Scottish dance music until 11, when we went to bed and listened to quite an entertaining musical quiz on the Third Programme. When this ended, there was a Scottish programme, with songs by that most attractive of Scottish tenors, Kenneth McKellar, finishing off as the year ended with a short religious address from Rev. William Rogan.

1955

My mother died on 13th April 1955, game to the end and summoning up her final reserves of energy in order to carry on to the very last the perennial warfare with doctor and nursing-home staff which was one of her few remaining pleasures. She had been confined to bed for more than five years, with no other relaxation but the novels which she got through at the rate of three or four in a week, and a visit from me every second day. It was amazing that she preserved her mental faculties completely unimpaired, and kept to the end her interest in all that was going on and contempt for everyone else's way of doing. She never had a word of praise for anyone, but in this attitude of mind there was nothing mean or niggling, for the impossibly high standard she set for others was founded on the standard she set for herself: her way was the right way and she could never stoop to the hypocrisy of conciliating anyone by approving what she regarded as second-best. In some degree I think we were all a disappointment to her—Richard because he messed up his life and wasted his talent, myself because I was self-sufficient and went my own way without seeking advice or encouragement, Ian always the favourite since he was more demonstrative and apparently affectionate, because it must have seemed plain in the end that his affection like his other attitudes was more a matter of convention than anything else and had little depth or substance. My mother's rather formidable personality did not permit her to make friends easily, and she must sometimes have felt that there was not much to show for many years of unremitting work and effort. Accustomed to be in full charge, and with my father always devoted, always ready to do her bidding, however unsatisfactory his efforts generally were in her eyes, she must have felt her helplessness all the more irksome and her loneliness the more complete. Her one delight was in the children: and oddly enough her feelings in this respect were fully reciprocated. Both children enjoyed their visits to 'Granny in bed': and though it would be going too far to say that they missed her Elizabeth at least often remembered her and spoke of her with manifest joy in the recollection. In the law courts the death of Lord Cooper involved a serious loss to the Inner House. His successor, J. A.

Clyde, made a poor showing, and the Second Division was much the pleasanter of the two in which to appear. As in previous years, however, most of my work lay in the harder though better remunerated sphere of Outer House Jury trials. In these I had a remarkable run of success, not having lost a single trial from June to the end of the year. There was a general election in May: and on a wave of prosperity propaganda the Conservatives were returned to power. The whole performance was dishonest: and by the autumn Government spokesmen had to admit that there had been no improvement as regards inflation or the balance of payments position, which politicians of all parties—erroneously, as I thought—regarded as a serious problem. Faced with a falling currency and constantly rising prices, the Government continued with the extraordinary remedy of deliberately inflating them still further, by cutting subsidies, increasing Purchase Tax, keeping up interest rates, and the like. It seemed clear that there had been a considerable drop in the Government's popularity, but it was not so clear that Labour was in a position to take advantage of their weakness—particularly now that the Party's shrewd, experienced leader, Clement Attlee, had retired to the Lords and been replaced by the colourless figure of Hugh Gaitskell.

January 2nd

A broadcast series from Cramond: Mr Small on I Corinthians 9,16. He was very good, as usual, preaching with great urgency and force, and bringing out some telling, memorable phrase whenever it was needed to drive a point home. There is nothing superficial or evasive about his preaching: he always hits the nail right on the head. To Portobello for the morning service: Mr Brown equally interesting in his own way, on Revelation 11,17.

January 3rd

To Boots to change the library books. Most of the shops and offices were shut, and the town seemed deserted until we got to Princes Street. Here there was tremendous activity, with the shops starting their New Year sales. In spite of two policemen trying to keep the crowd in order outside Smalls, the pavement was so crowded with people pushing their way in and out that we had some difficulty in getting into Boots. In the afternoon to Tranent: a Scottish junior cup-tie against Ashfield, who put an end to Tranent's interest in the competition. Ashfield were an attractive team: I liked the way in which when a foul was awarded against any of their players, he rushed up to the man he had fouled and shook hands with him. Cairns has been given a knighthood in the New Year's honours.

January 7th
The final draft of the Copper report agreed for signature.

To the Cameo-Polytechnic: *The Sheep has Five Legs*—the curious title seems to have arisen from a mistranslation of the French, *Le Mouton à Cinq Pattes*. Fernandel plays six different parts.

January 8th
Nancy and I to Musselburgh, to the Regal cinema: *The Young Lovers*. This is directed by Antony Asquith, and has been compared to *Brief Encounter*. It does not quite stand up to the comparison. In *Brief Encounter* the thought at the back of one's mind all the time was: 'Yes, it was bound to happen that way.' In *The Young Lovers*, the thought rather was: 'No it wouldn't happen quite like that.' But the comparison is worth making: this picture says something worth saying, and it says it with poignancy and skill.

January 13th
Shaw recalled that he had once met Mackay in the Juridical library and had queried the value of long opinions given by judges and recorded in the law reports. Mackay, not unnaturally, contested this. It was necessary, he said, for him to deal fully with every point, since if the case went to the Lords and there was any point on which he had not done so the Lords would at once say, 'Why has Mackay not dealt with this point?'

January 16th
Home through the King's Park: the Haggis Knowe was covered with sledgers, and the park presented an animated scene. I walked along to our own park and found sledging going on there too. Andrew Smith was most insistent that I try his sledge. There always seemed to be someone in the way, and I kept heading for a gorse bush on the left-hand side, so that I had to roll off the sledge in order not to go into the bush. I quite enjoyed myself.

January 20th
My motion for a new trial in *Hunter v. Hanley*, before the First

Division: based entirely on the exception to Patrick's ruling that 'gross' negligence was required. It was my first experience of Clyde on the bench. He made one or two attempts to get out of the difficulty, suggesting that my exception did not really raise the broad general question that I was putting: but I silenced him fairly easily, and Patrick—who in accordance with the usual custom was sitting in judgement on himself along with the judges of the Division—admitted in effect that if my argument was sound in law what he had said might have been sufficient to mislead the jury. Leslie appeared for the defender, and seemed to concede that my argument was sound—but the charge was not such as to mislead a jury unconcerned with legal subtleties. There might have been something to be said on these lines, particularly as we had the phrase 'gross negligence' twice repeated in the pursuer's pleadings, but Leslie made nothing of it. I enjoyed the argument thoroughly—tracing the development of the law of negligence over the past 150 years. 10.20 train to London.

January 21st

To the Academy: *The Great Adventure*, a Swedish nature film with a thread of a story about two little boys who befriend an otter, beautifully and delicately done but hardly enough life about it to hold my somewhat tired attention. I enjoyed the supporting picture, *The Adventures of Robinson Crusoe*, a Mexican picture photographed in beautiful colouring and giving a graphic portrayal of the manner in which the castaway develops from a lithe, active young man to a queer old chap in goatskins and a skin hat. It comes to a most exciting climax—altogether something quite out of the ordinary run.

January 22nd

Owing to fog on the way north, the train was late, and did not reach Edinburgh until 8.15—an improvement on getting up before 6. Taxi home: I called out the address to the driver as I got in, whereupon the man behind me in the queue said, 'I'm going to Mountcastle Drive South—I'll come with you.' This curious coincidence saved me three shillings and sixpence.

January 25th

I was amused at a remark of Ian Macdonald's about Guthrie—who he thought was of a sadistic nature, because the only time he had heard him laugh in court was when the question was put to a pursuer in an undefended divorce whether she was willing to adhere and she answered 'No'.

January 29th
Motored with Nancy and the children to the Pentcaitland road, where they went for a walk along the road while I went through the hedge into the strip of woodland adjoining, in search of wood. It is part of the Winton Castle estate: and I emerged through the hedge with arms full of branches, to find myself confronted with a gamekeeper who had just driven up in a car with the proprietor and rebuked me for disturbing the game. The proprietor was quite pleasant, but said they were greatly troubled with well-to-do poachers who arrived in cars and did a great deal of damage among the partridges, and any time they saw a car standing on the road it made them suspicious.

January 30th
Finished reading *Adam's Way*, by Lonnie Coleman, an exciting story of an eccentric in the southern States who takes in a negro girl and tries to educate her—told with wit and charm, and an underlying seriousness which makes it interesting throughout.

January 31st
Elizabeth had a temperature yesterday evening, and Nancy phoned the doctor. He looked at her tongue and throat, and then with a sort of flashlamp which he put into her ear: and said there was nothing wrong. He made no complaint about being sent for—indeed the visit seemed to do him good. He arrived looking weary and languid, and left smiling and cheerful, waving to the children. Elizabeth is always at her best with him, and he seems to enjoy seeing her.

February 1st
Gimson was recalling a murder trial in Dundee in which the accused and several witnesses were lascar seamen. An old Mohammedan, after taking the oath by holding the Koran to his forehead, was asked, 'What is your age?' A long diatribe in Hindustani followed—as Gimson speaks Hindustani, he recounted this part of the story very effectively. At last Guthrie, who was presiding, turned to the interpreter and said, 'Well, tell us what he has been saying': to which the interpreter replied, 'He says he was eight when the horse trams were running in London.'

February 5th

A report in this morning's paper of the decision of the First Division in *Hunter v. Hanley*—allowing a new trial on the grounds of Patrick's misdirection.

February 14th

Met Charles Johnston at the station, and travelled north with him in the company of Edward Keith, the Commissioner conducting the Public Enquiry on which we are to be engaged. There was no dining car, and I had brought a pint of milk and half a pound of tongue which I shared with my junior. At Elgin we were met by our client, Mr Alastair Adam, farmer of Wester Covesea. Charles and I are staying at the farmhouse, a house equipped with all the comforts one finds in these modern farmhouses—everything laid on in the usual luxurious style.

February 15th

The Enquiry arises out of an order for the closure of two highways, necessitated by the extension of the main runway of Lossiemouth naval air station, and the construction of an alternative highway, much shorter than the old road, and maintaining a link between 10,000 acres farmed by Adam north-west of the airfield with 500 acres which he farms in three farms south-east of it—a link which would otherwise be cut. The order was supported by the local branches of the Inshore White Fishermen's Association, who wanted a direct route between Burghead and the harbour and market at Lossiemouth, but was opposed by Moray Golf Club, who objected to the invasion of their course by the proposed road, and by some farmers and landowners south of the airfield, who thought there should be a road there to replace their connection with Lossiemouth. A Public Enquiry was held in February 1953, with Grant as commissioner. We do not know what Grant recommended, but in the event the Minister withdrew his proposal, and after some delay produced the draft order with which we are concerned, closing the portions of road as before but providing as substitutes a road south of the closed portion and a length of unclassified road leading to the lighthouse which is one and a half miles west of Lossiemouth and under this proposal will be cut off from it altogether. Objections have been lodged by Adams and the fishermen, whom I represent, and by the burghs of Burghead and Lossiemouth. Until 1954 the County Council continued to support the north road, but before objections could be lodged it appears that golfing interests got to work and secured a bare majority in the council for a much weaker position—merely objecting to the alignment of a proposed Class II road to the south. This morning Charles and I made a complete tour of the area in Adam's landrover, and finally motored to Elgin. The enquiry is being held in the County Buildings.

February 16th

Adam proved an excellent witness. He stood under the map with a little pointer in his hand, and answered questions as if he were giving an impartial talk to a Young Farmers Club. On getting back to the farm we were taken to see the dairy herd: 100 attested Ayrshires. Adam had been fishing the day before we arrived and caught a big salmon, which we had hot for supper: a lovely fish. Thereafter he showed us films he had taken on his 3-months trip to Africa.

February 17th

A gale in the night cut our communications with the outer world, bringing down telephone wires and cutting also the electricity, so that there was no light. By the time we got downstairs Mrs Adam had a big fire blazing in the dining-room, and an emergency water-heater in operation. On the way into Elgin we paused at Drainie School, in a biting gale from the north, and watched aircraft circling in to land on the runway not many yards from where we were. It has emerged that the roadway at that point is 10 feet higher than the end of the runway, so that the effect of the Admiralty's safety margin of 1,000 feet completely disappears: neither the Admiralty nor the Ministry of Transport, in considering the line of the new road, had thought of levels at all. Mrs Adam, who had been with us at lunch, phoned to say she had got through to Covesea only with the greatest difficulty, through a raging blizzard, and it was said that the road was now blocked. We proceeded through Gordonstoun grounds, where a track had been cleared by a snow plough. One of Adam's men went ahead of us in a landrover, in case we should get into difficulties. I confirmed from Adam that his wife was a sister of Sandy Wishart, of Hill of Fiddes. At breakfast this morning, when the carpet had been surging up and down in the wind, I had happened to remark that the only place I had seen that happen was Hill of Fiddes.

February 18th

Woke at 5: and switching on the light sat up in bed and worked at my speech for the next two hours. After breakfast I borrowed a walking-stick and wellington boots and went for a walk to the sea. Today's proceedings began with brief speeches from the town clerks, and I then spoke for exactly an hour: solid argument, with an occasional bit of humour, as when I spoke of the fishermen's desire to get home to their loons and queanies. The two official shorthand writers, who know me from Monopolies hearings in London, were amused at this, and approached me afterwards to find out how the words should be spelled—on which I was by no means clear. The Commissioner will now consider the evidence and report to the Minister of Transport, but what may be the really important thing is that the Ministry officials will have a verbatim report of all that has been said. Last time no shorthand note was taken: and I had an advantage over the others in possessing a private report taken by Mr Adam's secretary. I enjoyed myself thoroughly.

Adam motored us to the station for the 2.15 train to Aberdeen. We were joined by Keith and Scotland, but when the train going by Forres, due to leave at 2.30, came in about that time without there having been any sign of the 2.15 they got on board and went off westwards, leaving us at Elgin. Opinion on the station seemed to be evenly divided as to whether this was a wise move, or whether they would get stuck somewhere between Forres and Perth. Anyhow, as I wanted to travel on the coast route to Aberdeen, part of which I had never been on, I had made up my mind to wait for the 2.15, however long the wait. It turned out to be nearly two hours: but I took my shoes off and put on slippers, wrapped a travelling rug round my legs, and stretched out on a seat in the station—much to the amusement, Johnston said, of the London shorthand writers before they went off on the Forres train. The train was warm and comfortable, and Charles had bought half a pound of tongue in Elgin: this we had on the way to Aberdeen, with a pint of milk from Covesea. We caught the last train of the day with five minutes to spare, and reached Edinburgh at 10.43. Charles Johnston told me that Adam had said to him he had thought at first it was a peculiar chap they had given him as counsel, but then had found to his surprise that I knew all about the places before I had even been there, and had concluded that his counsel must be a very high-powered fellow indeed. I think all our people seemed pleased, and though I am completely new to this kind of work it is the kind of work that suits me.

February 25th
Migdale gave judgement in *Cocozza v. Cocozza*, finding for the pursuer and granting divorce.

February 28th
Brayshaw told me he had had a letter from Sheriff Miller in which he recounted an incident in his court when an old shepherd was charged with not keeping his dog under control. The accused was deaf and unable to understand the question about pleading guilty or not guilty. When everybody had shouted at him for some time, Boris tried the alternative: 'Do you want a trial?' 'Oh, no', said the man, 'the dog's no fit for a trial.'

March 1st
To the nursing-home to see my mother. Dr O'Neill arrived while I was there, and told me she was in a bad way, with both lungs pretty well choked up—'and yet', he said, 'there she is, still reading away at her book, never giving in, as full of life as ever—it's astonishing.' She seemed much as usual, complaining of pain but making no other concession, and treating him and the nursing-home staff with her usual mixture of grim humour, truculence and contempt. As always, she had an answer for everything, and got the better of all the exchanges.

March 3rd
Westminster: the Navy estimates, with an amendment moved by George Thomas, a Labour member for Cardiff, about living conditions on the lower deck. He seemed a pleasant-spoken, kindly man, but as the subject-matter of his amendment was of no interest to me I took the chance to go down to the cafeteria. When starting on my apple tart, I saw on the tape that Willis was speaking, so I went back to hear him—talking quite sensibly about engine-room artificers. The best speech in the debate came from Admiral Hughes-Hallett, a dapper, attractive Unionist and a racy speaker, full of interesting ideas which he expounded with wit and originality. I liked him immensely. Edwards, an ex-stoker from the Navy who was Civil Lord of the Admiralty in the Labour Government, summed up for the Opposition with devastating dullness: and the present Civil Lord, Mr Wingfield

Digby, was so absurd that it was difficult to believe that he was intending to be serious. Intentionally or not, he made a funny speech.

March 4th
On the train north I had the company of Mrs Notman, breeder of the Normanby herd of attested Jerseys and apparently in demand as a judge at shows. I did not think much at first of this middle-aged, horsey-looking woman who strolled into a non-smoking compartment with a cigarette dangling from her lips and proceeded to powder her face with absurd deliberation. But later we got into conversation and had an amusing discussion on the merits of different breeds of cattle, and the good and bad points of Sir Winston Churchill and Graham Sutherland's portrait of him. At Dundas Street a bundle of Elgin papers had been handed in containing a full report of our enquiry, and a poem that some local humorist had written.

> 'Oh give me a road
> To my humble abode,
> Where the jets and the councillors play;
> While the years roll along
> To that hoary old song,
> "North or south—yes, it's coming—some day!"...'

March 6th
My mother seems to have given up reading for the present and was not taking much interest in anything, but she brightened up when Richard appeared, and chatted and played with him in a lively way. He and I motored to the King's Park and climbed right up the crag above St Anthony's Chapel. Richard went up at a good speed, without any sign of alarm, and was eager to go higher still: a good feat, I thought, for a 2-year old. After the children were in bed I motored to Portobello, but found to my dismay that it was a 'cinema' service: a film called *Which will ye have?* supposed to be the story of Barabbas. There was some attempt at characterisation, and Pilate gave some idea of the dilemma confronting him, but it was dull and lifeless, and the archaic dialogue, full of 'thee' and 'thou' and 'art' and 'hast', added to the general air of unreality. It was difficult to see what possible good its showing could do. I was glad to get back to my own fireside and the *Observer*—in which there was an amusing article about the playing of the instrument vertically in a recent production

of *The Magic Flute*, perhaps because it was thought that no wind instrument was blown transversely at the remote legendary time in which the action takes place. The objection that no straight-blown early instrument could possibly have delivered Tamino's flute solos may be easily enough dismissed by simply stressing the word 'magic'.' The author of the article recalls that the flute actually was played by the original Tamino, who was a flautist as well as a tenor. Mozart apparently played the bells one night for Papageno's chimes, and put in an extra arpeggio, to the dismay of the librettist, who was singing the part. Francois Brimand, a French-born player of the nineteenth century who appeared in light operatic tenor parts of Auber and other composers used to have a horn hung on a wall or a tree in any opera he was in, and if he had the stage to himself would suddenly catch sight of it and, exclaiming with immense surprise: 'Tiens, un cor! Mais j'en joue', would take it down and give a brilliant solo performance.

March 11th
With Nancy to see *Sabrina Fair* at the Kings: an excellent play, well worked out, written with charm and wit.

March 16th
With Nancy to the Regent Cinema: *The Divided Heart*, Ealing Studios' film of a displaced Jugoslav child adopted by German parents and later claimed by his mother. After a shaky start, it set out its impossible problem fairly and effectively—a memorable piece of work, which leaves one thinking.

March 22nd
Debate Roll before Blades: *Young v. Macleod*, a slander action in which the pursuer claimed £1,000 damages from the pastor and deacons' court of Harper Memorial Baptist Church in Glasgow, of which she had been a leading member for many years, prominent in every aspect of church work. At the age of 59 she married a widower of 74, with the object, she says, of looking after him since he was infirm and unable to look after himself. She says that before consenting to marriage she consulted Mr Macleod, the pastor, who told her that if she married she would be doing a good Christian work. Married life was not what she expected it to be, and after a month of two she left her husband. Macleod, who apparently sympathised with her, used his

good offices to bring the two together again, and the pursuer went back to her husband. Shortly afterwards, on medical advice, Young was admitted to Forresthill Hospital, which had formerly been a poorshouse. This was at the end of November 1953. A month later Macleod called on the pursuer and said, 'I think you should prayerfully consider the advisability of transferring your membership to another congregation.' He added that she was hindering the blessing of the church: and gave no other explanation. The pursuer, at a loss to know what he meant, wrote to the deacons' court and asked what they had against her, to which they replied that the pastor's action had their full support, that her conduct in this whole sad affair was inconsistent with the testimony of this church, and that they thought she should resign. Mr Young died in February 1954, and in March the church secretary again wrote to the pursuer, saying that as she had not resigned they had deleted her name from the roll. The pursuer said there had been a lot of gossip that she had married her husband for his money and then put him in a poorshouse, and says the statements and actings of the deacons' court were slanderous, as conveying that they had accepted this as true and that on that account she was unfit to be a member of a Christian church and her membership was detrimental to the interests of the other members. The defenders contended that the words used would not reasonably bear the innuendo put on them—a formidable point. We could however argue that the defenders have never yet given any explanation of what they meant or why they put the pursuer out, so the the pursuer's explanation was the only one so far suggested. There was a further point, that the letters were written on a privileged occasion: and the defenders finally say that by the constitution of the church, which the pursuer accepted, matters of discipline had to be kept private, and the pursuer is therefore barred from bringing the case to court. Blades was unusually silent during Macvicar's opening, and had not committed himself when I had to leave for the Licensing Confirmation Court, to oppose confirmation of a grocer's license to J. & R. Allen. I appeared on behalf of the Scottish Temperance Alliance, and expounded their objection briefly, concentrating on the already over-licensed condition of St Giles Ward and passing more lightly over the other ground of objection: that the shop is close to the University and a grocer's license would lead to the downfall of students by encouraging off-drinking. The vote was by roll-call. The Lord Provost, followed by two other members, voted 'Refuse', but

Bailie Dunbar stopped the rot for J. & R. Allan by voting 'Confirm', and in the end confirmation was carried by 9 votes to 6. The Labour representatives were evenly divided.

Returning to Parliament House, I found my junior, Forsyth, having a rough passage with Blades. He handled him with tact and skill, and I think there is a good prospect that we shall get the proof for which we asked. Meanwhile I had been asked to take a consultation at 5.30 which had originally been fixed with Leslie. It had been discovered only today that he was on the other side, and the agents had approached Sinclair Shaw—on the face of it a hopeless approach, as he would not be likely to take on anything at such short notice. I motored home for tea as I had promised, and had half an hour to read the papers in the case before going to the consultation.

March 24th

Guthrie gave judgement in *Quinn v. Cameron & Robertson*: he found for the defenders, apparently on the view that what the pursuer was doing did not fall within the statutory regulations.

March 25th

Blades gave judgment in *Young v. Macleod*: he allowed a proof before answer, with expenses to the pursuer.

March 27th

No Sunday papers today, owing to a strike of engineers which has stopped production of all Sunday newspapers. A service from the BBC's Glasgow studio, with an address by Billy Graham, who has come from America to conduct a revivalist campaign, with mass services every night in the Kelvin Hall to which bus parties are going from all parts of Scotland. I felt some prejudice against this mass-production emotionalised Christianity, but Graham preached quite a sensible sermon, not outstanding in any way, but agreeable, well expressed and containing nothing to which objection could be taken. The musical part of the service had a vitality sadly lacking in many churches including Portobello.

March 31st

London: still without newspapers, and the local porter remarking that even *Daily Mirror* readers were now reading the *Manchester Guardian*. 'Even the fish and chips is wrapped in the *Guardian* now', he said.

April 2nd

To Dundas Street—a great pile of letters and papers. 'You don't seem to have let anyone know you're on holiday', Norah said, adding that there were 24 separate things waiting for me.

April 6th

Ampherlaw: I had arranged with Brandon to go with him to Law Hospital, so that he could remove a small cyst from the back of my neck. We processed around the wards—Barney, his registrar, his assistant and I, accompanied by the sister in charge of each ward. One girl with bright red hair had been admitted yesterday with suspected appendicitis, but he did not think she had it, and decided that nothing should be done meantime. 'She won't die of peritonitis anyhow', he said: and they explained to me that red-headed people never died of peritonitis. Sir David Wilkie, he said, had told his class this: and he himself had kept a note of the cases ever since and had never known a red-headed person to die from that cause, though in the old days, before penicillin treatment, they had often had it quite badly. As soon as the operation was over, we set off for Hartwood. I drove, with Barney and the registrar as passengers. Several patients insisted on greeting us, including one old fellow who shouted cheerfully that that was the best place in the world. He was 83, and told us he had had 9 grandchildren and 4 great-grandchildren, and 2 more on the way. 'Now that Winston Churchill's retired', he said, 'I'll be ready to take his place.' I asked what was supposed to be his complaint, and was told that it was that he was elated. Unlike some others, he had no depressed periods but suffered from continuous elation. It seemed an agreeable form of complaint.

April 8th

Barney had told me to go to the doctor and have the dressing removed, and I went round to Dr O'Neill in the afternoon. It was obvious, he said, that a surgeon had done the job, and whoever had done it had done it extremely well—you would not know an incision had been made.

April 11th

My mother seemed to me to be failing. Her voice was weak and her manner abstracted. But she rallied when the children were playing round the bed, and joined in 'Sing a Song of Sixpence'.

April 12th

Nancy and I were going to the Kings Theatre to see *The Lark*: and as a phone message had come from Mardale Nursing Home to say my mother was not at all well we called in on our way to the theatre. She was obviously in a bad way, her head forward on her chest and her voice poor and indistinct: but when I remarked that the doctor had said that she was not at all well she replied—as always—'the doctor's a humbug', and went on to speak of a controversy she had had with him this evening about whether the nursing-home gave her enough jam. Her newspaper and letters however were unopened, and it looked to me as if she would not last very long: a matter of days, perhaps.

April 13th

Dr O'Neill phoned at breakfast time to say my mother had died in the night. I arranged to meet him at the nursing-home at 9.45: and he then wrote out the death certificate. He said she had great character—yesterday evening, on his last visit, she had told him as usual that he was no use at all and had never done her the slightest good. Elizabeth, she said, was the only one who had any faith in him, she did not know why. He said he had told her there was not much he could do for her, and had asked if he could get her a crucifix—he is a Roman Catholic. She had replied scornfully, 'I don't need that.' It struck me as an odd offer: I should think, if there is anything in their theology at all, that so far from requiring reassurance in the next world the truer picture of my mother is of her complaining that the place prepared for her is quite unsuitable and that things there are not being properly managed.

May 1st

To church, where Rev. Herbert McKeel, of the First Presbyterian Church, Schenectady, preached. He spoke at some length: not much substance or method, but a pleasant American voice and considerable charm. I rather liked him.

May 12th

To the Westway Hotel for breakfast. A poor north-country man was complaining at the reception desk that he had not been able to sleep, and when they told him that they had changed him to a room at the back asked plaintively whether it was a bigger room so that he could shut the window. He thought that might do, but he could not go on as he had done last night. They assured him that it would be quiet at the back, but he was not much comforted. 'I'll try', he said sadly. 'I'll do my best. But if it's not any better I'll just have to go home.' He did not seem to see the funny side of it: and the complaint seemed absurd at the Westway, where there is no traffic outside worth talking about.

Bus to Baker Street: a lovely sight to come through the passageway into Cornwall Terrace and see the mass of pink blossoms in Regent's Park. The tulips also in full bloom. Lunch with John Taylor. He took me to the Windsor Castle restaurant, where he had his own soup plate. When the restaurant introduced smaller plates, he had obtained from them a large white plate, and had taken it away and had it painted to his own design. This plate was kept to be put before him on any occasion when he had soup there. When it came to biscuits and cheese, they brought various kinds of cheese to show him, including a new camembert, which they cut through the middle to show him. As soon as it was open, without even consulting him, the waitress said, 'Not runny enough', and removed it, putting another one in front of him instead. Finally a cigarette was brought to him—only one. He explained that they had instructions not to bring him any more, so that he would not smoke too much. He was looking bigger and more prosperous than ever, and seemed to get the same simple enjoyment out of life he always has.

Train to Cheshunt. There was quite a rural appearance about Cheshunt station, and I walked for some distance without seeing anyone except a man who wanted me to direct him to the Haunch of Venison.

May 13th

Hughes was leaving us today to return to the Board of Trade. Hughes has been an excellent secretary, capable, careful and thorough, never allowing his own views to obtrude themselves. A panel hearing, with the Canadian Rubber Footwear Importers. Cullen was away, Cairns was occupied with Group III, and Archdale, the only other member of the panel, could not be persuaded that he was a member, so I had the hearing all to myself. It was interesting, and disclosed rather a tragic situation in which a valuable and useful trade had been destroyed by devaluation and similar absurdities of economic policy.

Electric train to Bushey. I emerged from the station into attractive surroundings: pleasant suburban roads green with foliage and bright with blossoms, and a grassy slope down to the valley of the Colne.

May 14th

I had gone to sleep within five minutes of settling down for the night, and when I awoke it was broad daylight and we were already in Scotland. I was called at 5.50 and took a taxi home from the Waverley. Did not go back to bed, but worked on a case in which I had a consultation, and motored to Parliament House at 10.30. I was rather dismayed to find I had mislaid the papers, including all the notes I had made on the case: but having worked on it so recently I had it all fairly clearly in mind. When the papers turned up later, I discovered that I had covered all the points I had jotted down.

May 17th

I had to make some notes for a speech at St Cuthbert's School in support of Connell's candidature in the Pentlands division: but I need not have worried, for one or two Tory youths had come for the purpose of making trouble and I got involved in backchat with them which occupied the meeting until Connell arrived. I am out of practice in dealing with this kind of thing, and though the interruptions were unusually foolish I did not make much of the openings provided: but it filled in the time. Ross presided, and made some attempts to keep me and the hecklers in order, without making much impression on either side.

May 19th

A jury trial before Lord Hill Watson: *Webster v. Lane & Girvan*. The pursuer was casting 10-gallon boilers in five moulding boxes. The fifth box was shallower than the rest, so that the sand at the gate through which the molten metal was poured was at a higher level than the rim of the box. On account of this, some of the metal which overflowed the box as the pursuer poured it in ran down the slope and came into contact with the metal edge of the box. An explosion occurred, and particles of molten metal struck the pursuer in the face and destroyed the sight of his right eye. The defenders deny that the box was shallower than the other boxes, and say the accident was caused by the pursuer's failure to control the flow of the metal. The defenders had brought in a big moulding box of the type involved in the accident: and the pursuer, with the help of the macer, a policeman

53

and the clerk of court gave a lively and effective demonstration of how the process was carried out, with Hill Watson and me urging them on and shouting a description to the shorthand writer of what was being done. Shortly after, the shorthand writer took ill and there had to be a short adjournment, during which the jury could be heard engaging in vigorous discussion about how moulding was done and what was wrong with this box. Then, when Leslie was cross-examining the pursuer, he quite innocently put a question the wrong way round, saying to him that he had claimed that the sand should slope towards the rim—whereupon the jury to a man shouted, 'No, no—the other way round'. This was all very encouraging: but in the afternoon, faced with some dour defence witnesses, I did not make much headway: and Hill Watson, who had given the impression of being in the pursuer's favour, seemed to be deserting us.

May 20th

Hill Watson charged the jury in favour of the defenders quite astutely, but we won by 7 votes to 5: and award of £1,500. I was told afterwards that the seven were all women. A consultation in the afternoon was soon disposed of: and when I came into the robing room I found McIlwraith, my junior, telling O'Brien how much he had enjoyed a consultation in which no time was wasted and we got straight down to the questions that had to be cleared up.

My back had been sore all day, and it was with some unwillingness that I dragged myself out after supper to speak at Pennywell School for Cuthbert Thomson, the Labour candidate for West Edinburgh. I found him chattering away to an audience of about a dozen. Thomson's speech was unorthodox, and he made some outrageous statements, but it was entertaining and more interesting than a stock party speech. I intimated that I should speak for only five minutes, and did so—rapidly and effectively. Much to my surprise, it was an excellent speech, and went down well with the audience such as it was. The meeting ended with everyone in good humour, and I was home well before nine.

May 22nd

Finished reading *The Figure in the Mist*, by Elizabeth Coxhead, a story about a Cockney student who goes as holiday help to a family in Arran. Everyone is alive and genuine, and though the author never fails to enlist the reader's sympathy in the right direction she is fair and understanding, putting all points of view with commendable impartiality. There is any amount of wisdom and good sense in this delightful little story, and it never gets away from reality.

May 23rd

To Stockbridge School to speak for George Scott, Labour candidate for North Edinburgh. The schoolroom was packed, and speech was rendered difficult owing to the noise of forms being brought in to accommodate late-comers. I was able to come away as soon as I had finished—indeed, I had to, for my seat had been carried off while I was speaking, to be used by someone in the audience.

May 25th

Keir Hardie Hall: Connell's eve-of-the-poll meeting. Connell was at another meeting, and I had to speak until he arrived. This meant speaking for one and a quarter hours without any note—for me, quite an achievement. I covered a variety of topics, and for the first 45 minutes got on remarkably well. After that I lost grip on my audience, but I had their sympathy, and was warmly applauded when I came away. It was a good thing this happened at the end of the election when I had got into the swing of political speaking: I should have found it more of an ordeal if I had encountered a similar situation earlier. As it was, I thought I discharged my task commendably. Though I attempted to provoke some interruption, I did not succeed. 10.40 train to London.

May 26th

In London I had seen no sign that this was polling day—no posters, no loudspeakers, no cars—but in Chertsey, though there was not much activity, every second house seemed to have a blue window card indicating support for Sir Lionel Heald. Supper in a cinema cafe. I had left myself with little enough time to get back to the station. However, as I was hurrying along the street, a car drew up alongside and the driver asked if I was going to vote. I admitted I was not, but got him to give me a lift to the polling station—giving me ample time to reach the railway station. At Kings Cross I had a sleeper on the 10.15, and soon got settled in, with my wireless. As the train left, and the announcer was explaining how the results were to be announced, the wireless went dead. I had just got the back of the set off to investigate when the transmission came on again. It turned out that the interruption had been caused by the train's entering a tunnel: the same thing happened every time there was a tunnel on the line. I had forecast a Unionist majority of 23, but after the first few results it seemed obvious that this was too optimistic. There appeared to be quite a strong swing to the Unionists.

May 27th

A case in the General Assembly, with Paterson. The Assembly's timetable was running late, but we spent an interesting half hour listening to a debate on ministers' stipends. Though pressed for time and eager to get on, the Assembly gave a good hearing to anyone who had anything to say, but anything in the way of sermonising brought protests and shuffling of feet, and even when a speaker announced that he had never addressed the Assembly he got no indulgence as soon as the members began to get impatient with him. Dr Hutchison Cockburn in the chair controlled the debate with marked skill and a degree of fairness, but it was obvious that the officials were completely unscrupulous in utilising their debating powers and command of procedure in order to silence opposition. I had recollections from my previous visit to the Assembly of finding them a good audience, and as soon as I got under way I experienced the same thing: the enjoyment of having a big meeting follow one's argument with attention and apparent interest.

May 29th

Elizabeth and Richard came into our bedroom before we were up, and Elizabeth proceeded to tell Richard a long story about a lady who met God, and God said 'What is the trouble?' and the lady said she wanted to be weighed. So they weighed the lady, and then they weighed God.

May 30th

Went with Elizabeth round to the flowering currant, and collected hordes of green caterpillars in a jam jar. They have been coming down from the gutter in the last few days, descending outside the windows on long pieces of thread and swaying in the wind as they came down.

June 2nd

A jury trial: *Smith v. Glasgow Corporation*. The pursuer boarded a tram to go home to Parkhead. The tram started with a jerk throwing her against the controls. Her injuries included a wound of the right shoulder which was still giving her trouble. At the consultation she had not been candid with us about two previous accidents: but her evidence seemed frank, and she kept her end up well in cross-examination by the Dean of Faculty. Asked by him about her reason for a change of solicitors, she spoke highly of Thornton and said he was a very nice man to speak to—'just like what I believe you'd be yourself'. Arnott had been instructed to visit the depot and have a look at the tram. Much of the evidence today was concerned with this visit, in the course of which, it was alleged, Thornton had lost his temper and called one of the Corporation officials a 'bloody liar'. Arnott having admitted that this expression had been used, I thought it best to call Thornton as a witness: and he was summoned to the witness box, protesting that he had no intention of giving evidence. He was most amusing, admitting at once that he had lost his temper and used the expression complained of, but insisting that he had merely been 'apostrophising' and had not directed his remark to anyone in particular. In the course of a good-humoured, entertaining cross-examination, he said, in answer to a question about whether the door at the end of a Glasgow tram was usually kept open or shut, that he hoped he might be excused from answering that question—he was a swell, and never travelled in a tramcar.

June 3rd

The Dean made a good speech, on the basis that this was a bogus claim corroborated by a bogus witness. Verdict for the defenders.

To the Shaws' at 8.15: the other guests Dr Meikle and Neil Beaton. Beaton proved to be an interesting old fellow, with an attractive Highland accent. His father had been a crofter near Cape Wrath, and as there had been only two families in the district, five miles from one another, the schoolmaster stayed alternate weeks with one and then the other. So the boys had five miles to walk to school daily, every other week—barefooted in the summer. There had been no homework.

June 17th

On the bus from Wimbledon to Putney some Irish labourers beguiled the journey by singing Irish songs in a pleasant brogue: 'I always come in with my swagger, As if the whole place was my own'.

June 26th

A pimple on the back of my neck seemed to be a boil, so I phoned Dr O'Neill. Motored with Elizabeth to his house. Interested in medical matters as she has always been, she declined to go into the garden and join the doctor's children, preferring to see me get the injection of penicillin in my arm. I told the doctor I was going to London, and he said he would give me a million. He said he was taking care, since my case of *Hunter v. Hanley*, to use a really coarse needle: and the injection was quite painful.

July 5th

Parliament House: the Mulligan case. Migdale's charge seemed to suggest that the point of the case was not dangerous system of work but whether a brick in the wall was loose—an incidental matter on which the pursuer did not found at all. But of course he failed equally to put the defenders' case. The jury found for the pursuer by 8 to 4. Penman, the Labour railwayman who was with me on the Trades Council executive, was one of the jury, and I rang him up at night to see how the decision had been arrived at. I asked him whether they had thought there had been a loose brick, to which he replied that they had not attached much importance to that: what they had proceeded on was the bad working conditions. It appears that a jury can be capable of finding the point of a case in spite of the presiding judge. 'It's a good thing there were some women on the jury', Penman said. 'I thought we were going to have difficulty with some of the men—I think they were employers'.

July 14th

A jury trial. The pursuer was engaged in putting a chain round a steel plate when another heavy plate fell on him. There was a tender of £600, which the pursuer refused a year ago. He was subsequently persuaded to reconsider this, but as the defenders refused to increase the tender or allow it to be accepted clear of the expenses incurred since its date it had not been possible to settle. The defenders maintained that the pursuer had struck the plate and caused it to fall: and what I had been afraid of was a 50-50 verdict that would bring the amount recovered down below the level of the tender. But after an absurd attempt to get the case withdrawn at the end of the evidence for the pursuer, on the ground that he had not proved an averment that he himself had touched the plate, Shearer—who was conducting the defence—intimated that he was leading no evidence, and the jury was left with the uncontradicted evidence that the position in which the plate had been put was generally regarded as dangerous. The evidence was all the one way, but that did not stop James Walker from directing the jury to the opposite effect: an ingenious and rather wicked exercise in the art of persuading a jury to disregard the evidence. But in spite of this the jury found for the pursuer by 9 to 3, and awarded £2,000.

July 15th

Faculty reception at Parliament House for members of the Commonwealth and Empire Law Conference. I was soon overwhelmed by people—mainly, it seemed, on the staff of University College, London —who had been in court during the case and wanted to ask me questions. The men from University College were all remarkably alike: short, middle-aged, thickset, clean-shaven, in grey business suits with white shirts. One of them introduced me to Charlesworth, the author of the standard work on negligence—a simple, kindly old gentleman, a County Court judge.

July 18th

Changed into a morning coat and motored to the Grange cemetery for Cooper's funeral. Oddly enough, there does not seem to be going to be any memorial service, and 'friends' were invited in the *Scotsman* notice to attend the service at the cemetery. Everybody—judges, advocates, officials, public representatives—stood along the pavement of Grange Road waiting for the cortège to arrive. We then all trooped into the cemetery behind it, in varying garb, for this unusual ceremony had apparently given rise to differing points of view as to what was proper. Rev. Roderick Bethune prayed. What he said was quite appropriate, but could not remove the impression that the whole ceremony was slightly absurd and nothing to do with Cooper.

July 19th

The defenders' reclaiming motion in *Young v. Macleod*, before the First Division. For most of the afternoon it looked as if Blades' judgement was to be upheld: but in the last half hour, when I came on to speak, I succeeded in turning the whole court completely against me. Motored home somewhat depressed, and spent the next hour in preparing a careful argument designed to bring things back on a proper footing tomorrow.

July 20th

Continued my speech: and slowly and laboriously set about the task of bringing a recalcitrant court back on the right lines. I think in the end I succeeded, but it was impossible not to realise the tragic loss to the court by Cooper's replacement by Clyde. Instead of bringing Sorn and the others back to the main issue when they wandered off at a tangent, Clyde would go wildly after them. I had always thought that Clyde's appointment would be a serious change for the worse, but I had not realised just how bad it was going to be. Instead of stimulating mental exercise, as it was under Cooper, pleading in the First Division has become as much of a shambles as it was in the Second Division with Mackay at his worst. My opponent, W.I.R. Fraser, found the same—it is practically impossible to present any logical or balanced argument.

A meeting of the Faculty to elect a new Dean, Cameron having been at last induced to take a seat on the bench, vacant by Birnam's death. Up to now he has declined a judgeship hoping perhaps up to the time of Keith's appointment that he might be a Lord of Appeal. His delay in accepting elevation results in the curious situation that he is junior on the bench to Wheatley, who devilled for him. For election as Dean there was only one nominee: Guest.

July 21st

Public Interest hearing on hard fibre cordage. This is an enquiry in which I have not been on the Panel: and as I had not been able to attend the clarification hearing and had not read any of the papers I did not know enough about the subject to take any interest in today's proceedings. Though McKenna, who appeared for the manufacturers, was as usual good and business-like, I had great difficulty in keeping awake.

In the tube I made the same mistake as a fortnight ago, getting out at a station too soon. As I got out, I dropped my pencil, which rolled under a door marked 'Strictly Private', and by the time I had opened the door, groped about in the dark for my pencil, and found it, the next train had come in.

July 22nd

Hearing on Rubber Footwear. The manufacturers in their written evidence had given some very disingenuous explanations of entries in their minutes, and a good deal of pressure was required to get the truth out of them. Cairns has never repeated the devastating cross-examination he conducted in the London Builders case, and latterly has been content pretty much to put the questions drafted for him by the staff. He may have decided to do this as a matter of policy, feeling he overdid things with the London Builders: but I felt today that he had not prepared the case with the thoroughness he gave to the work when he first came to the Commission. Though he did most of the questioning, I had to come in several times to make a point. Then at the Sand & Gravel meeting it appeared that he had no ideas for the conclusions chapter, and it was left to me to make definite proposals. This was quite like old times, in contrast to the usual situation since Cairns took charge, which has usually been that I have had no work to do.

In the course of this visit to London I have read *The Oracles*, by Margaret Kennedy. The characters are sympathetic, and there is an interesting thread of story, sufficient to hold my attention, but somehow I did not like it much. Perhaps there is a lack of magnanimity in it.

July 23rd

The First Division had allowed a proof in *Young v. Macleod*, but had deleted the part of the innuendo relating to the pursuer's unfitness for membership of a Christian church. This is the real point of the case, but I do not think its deletion from the Record will make any material difference.

July 24th

Morning service on the wireless from Iona Cathedral, with an address by Dr George MacLeod. As usual, he was most stimulating, not so much by anything he said as by the startling way he said it. He makes religion most exciting—nothing conventional about him, or anything that can be taken for granted. Even his prayers: 'We confess our many faults, and if at the moment we cannot think of any then we confess our awful blindness'.

With Nancy and the children to West Linton: a motor-cycle scramble at Targhaugh Farm. A big crowd was disporting itself over the grassy hillsides, giving the place a summery, Epsom-Downs kind of look.

July 26th

Drafted some conclusions on the Sand and Gravel common-price system, as a follow-up to Friday's meeting—although it is really not my business. An easy job—the first draft completed in an hour.

In the afternoon we all motored to Longniddry beach. The children fell in with a middle-aged schoolmistress who took them in hand and went out to the sea with them, conversing with them in a didactic manner which evidently pleased them.

July 27th

Train to Kirkcaldy, to attend sheepdog trials advertised for today at Wellsgreen Farm, East Wemyss. From the bus stop beyond East Wemyss I followed a road through some prefabs, then a lane between fields. The road seemed to come to an end in a farm steading, but I found my way through, under a gate, to the Cameron Bridge road. Here there was a signpost which indicated that the farm I had come through was Wellsgreen, and there was obviously no sheepdog trial there. I sat down by the roadside to see if a bus would come, and after I had sat for half an hour, quite restfully, and no bus had appeared, I turned down a mineral railway line. The track was grass-grown and overshadowed by bushes, but seemed in quite good order: and in fact a train appeared when I had gone some way along it. I had to cross into a field to avoid it: but this was a short cut to the coast road, where I got a bus.

August 12th

Called in at Greenmount to see the Campbells. I remarked to Mrs Campbell on the peculiarity of Elie: that no entertainment was provided for the visitors—no cinema, no dance halls, no amusements of any kind. 'Just the very place for you', said Mrs Campbell. 'You won't need to spend any money'.

August 18th

Dundee. We lunched at Draffens. The menu put before us was described as '3/- Table d'Hote', but there was a selection of items in each course that would have done full justice to an à la carte menu. The whole meal for the four of us cost only eight shillings and fourpence, and a very good meal it was.

August 30th

We set off home—sorry to go, having become attached to Elie. It was a boon to have a dairy farm just behind, to which I went up every evening and got 2 or 3 pints of milk, fresh from the milking—in addition to the 7 pints delivered each morning.

September 2nd

Usher Hall: Netherlands Chamber Orchestra. I had expected the seats to be fairly expensive, but even so was a little taken aback when the prices in the Grand Tier were fifteen shillings and seventeen and sixpence. The fifteen shilling ones actually were very good seats. They played efficiently but without any outstanding brilliance.

September 3rd

Borthwick Water farmers' show. About Newtongrange I picked up two youths going home to Carlisle after a hiking tour that had taken them as far as Balloch—oddly enough, no further up Loch Lomond. They were a dull pair, and I let them off at the junction of the Clovenfords road and went that way to Selkirk. On the way out of the town I got a wave from a man and a woman, Germans from Frankfurt who were making for London. I took them to the point where I turned up the glen of the Borthwick Water. Paid two shillings to go into the show: a pastoral show, and a very small one—nothing but a few pens of sheep. There were to be sports, supposed to begin at two, but nothing could be done until the sheep had been judged. This took ages. The two judges stood and stared at the sheep from every angle, pondering them with dull, expressionless faces. At last the male and female champions were selected, and I thought the judging was at an end. But no—they had to choose between the two for overall champion: and to do this they examined both animals again at great length. Finally they disagreed, and an umpire had to be sent for: a man who looked more business-like and was not long in disposing of the matter, though four or five sheep were presented for his inspection, not just the two champions.

September 6th

Nancy and I to the County: *Carrington V.C.* This is just a play put on the screen: a court martial, excellently and wittily done, with interesting characterisation.

September 7th

Collected some straw from the field for the cat's bed. They have just cut the oats with a combine harvester, and in the evenings the field is alive with children, turning somersaults in the straw or building little nests or castles for themselves.

The Sanderson (Symington) Trustees—a full meeting of the trustees in my room. Half an hour of the time of six reasonably busy people wasted in deciding to continue fifteen-shilling pensions to two old soldiers. 10.40 train to London.

September 8th

At Baker Street I allowed myself to be relieved of half a crown by a man with a hard-luck story, carrying a copy of the *Times*.

Finished *Assignment to Catastrophe: the Fall of France*, by Sir Edward Spears, Churchill's personal representative on the Supreme War Council in Paris in June 1940. It is extremely detailed, covering a period of only 14 days, and despite some verbosity and superficial moralising gives an interesting picture of the French statesmen in charge of affairs.

September 10th

Aunt Elsie was arriving today from Newquay by bus, and Nancy was to go in and meet her at the arrival time, 9.43. But about an hour before that the phone rang to say she had arrived, the bus having come in much before its scheduled time. I suppose the timetable has to conform to 30 mph running, which presumably the bus itself does not.

September 21st

Finished reading *Magnificent Journey: the Rise of the Trade Unions*, by Francis Williams. This is a book which no doubt ought to be read, but it is neither well written nor interesting, and most of the author's comments are sententious and jejune in the extreme. 10.40 train to London.

September 22nd

The train was an hour late, but the attendant very sensibly did not call me until 25 minutes before we got in. I had rather a rush to get shaved, particularly as there was no water in the taps and I had to be content with a bottle of drinking water.

Group II: Sand and Gravel. A question arose as to whether we should give reasons for rejecting one of the Association's suggestions, which led Cairns to recall the remark of a judge that he never gave reasons for his judgements, since there was one chance in two that the judgement might be right but not one in a hundred that the reasons would.

Train to Rye House, and bus to Hertford: supper at the cinema cafe. It seemed even tastier than on my previous visit. I do not believe there is better bacon and egg to be got in the country than at the County Cinema at Hertford.

September 23rd
Train to Bishop Stortford, a typical English market town, with a handsome church above it on the hillside. The interior was shut by the time I got there. I had some difficulty in finding a cafe, but eventually came on one and got a good meal. A notice on a slate intimated that customers could be served with a 'good hot meal in 3 minutes': and it was no more than that before my plate of bacon and egg was set in front of me. Got back to the station as a train from London came in—pleasant to see all the cars drawn up in the darkness outside with the wives sitting in the driving seats awaiting their husbands and greeting them as they emerged from the station.

September 24th
Ellemford Show. Rain came on shortly before three—the auction had to be held in the marquee. I got half a dozen eggs for four shillings and half a pound of butter for three shillings: the butter a good buy as prices went today.

September 25th
Finished reading *Academic Year*, by D.J. Enright. Beyond the fact that this story is set in Alexandria in Egypt, it is difficult to say what it is about: but it is well written, and amusing in a melancholy way.

September 29th
A long letter from the Ministry of Transport, indicating that my contentions in the Lossiemouth inquiry had been substantially accepted: the Minister was to make a new order for a direct main road from Burghead to Lossiemouth, on the north, and an unclassified road to serve the southern farms.

October 1st

Called at St Ann's Mount and collected three forms for the children to sit on at Elizabeth's tea-party, paying for their hire the modest sum of two shillings and sixpence.

October 3rd

Finished reading *Journey into a Fog*, by Margareta Berger-Hamerschley. This account of the author's experiences while attempting to teach an art class in a youth club is written in rather an emotional style, but it gives a graphic picture of the problem involved in dealing with the bored, mindless hooligans who apparently formed the greater part of her class. She writes with sympathy and understanding, while in no way minimising the desperate state which these classes seem to get into. The book is illustrated by drawings of the young people: slouching youths in long jackets, and made-up girls in slit skirts and elaborate hair styles.

October 6th

Kings Cross: bus to Baker Street. The conductor was a big negro, from Jamaica, I should think, who grinned at his passengers and sang and did a little step dance on the platform.

Group II discussed Cordage placidly and without much disagreement: the report seems to be well drafted. But in the last half-hour of the morning we came to a very different problem: a proposal to alter the Tyres report to meet criticisms of small factual inaccuracies brought to light by some diligent person at the Board of Trade. It was proposed that we should get our report back from the Board and amend it as suggested. I took strong exception to this, thinking that it might lead to serious trouble if ever it got about that our reports were vetted by the Board of Trade, and in any event that when a report had been signed we had finished it and had no right to correct it on the suggestion of anyone, least of all a Government department. Gifford gave me some support, but indicated that he would not persist in his view if the general opinion was to the contrary. I persisted in mine, and said that if the report was amended I hoped I should be allowed to add a note to the effect that alterations had been made. This, as I fully realised, made it impossible for them to carry out their intention: the chairman said that unless there was unanimity nothing could be done. A general appeal was made to me to give way, and allow the report to go out to the world as an accurate document, but as I would not consent it was agreed that the report must stay as it is.

October 7th

I had been rather worried about yesterday, feeling that, although I had no doubt I was right, I had perhaps been foolish to carry my obstinacy so far. Today however it appeared that it had at all events pleased the staff. Even Mrs Binney, who has nothing to do with Tyres, had heard the story and expressed delight at the stand that had been taken, and the other members of the staff seemed to be of the same opinion.

Trolley-bus through Stoke Newington—a busy shopping centre with Jewish names above most of the shops—to Stamford Hill, where there were some fine examples of modern working-class tenements, some of them apparently provided by the Guinness Trust.

October 10th

With Nancy to the New Tivoli: *The Night My Number Came Up*, an exciting, well-constructed picture from Ealing Studios about an aeroplane crash. It had a neat, restrained ending as relief from the preceding tension.

October 15th

As I pulled out the blower to put the car heater on, the wire came away in my hand, and there was a flash as it came against some piece of metal. The heater, petrol gauge, horn and traffic indicators all went out of action, and the red light which shows when the engine is in neutral went on and stayed on although of course the engine was in gear.

October 17th

Took the car to Players, where an electrician had everything in order in a very few minutes, at the cost of fourpence.

October 20th

Second Division: a case on the meaning of 'non valens agere'. The argument involved consideration of a number of old authorities, and I found the Court as interested in it as I had been when preparing my speech. It is a pleasure to get a good point of law to argue as a change from the incessant industrial-accident cases. I got an excellent hearing.

C.H. Johnston told me before I went back into court in the afternoon that Wylie had told him at lunch time that he had sat all morning listening to my argument and feeling more and more that it was becoming unanswerable. He had said that I must have put in a lot of work on the case—as indeed I had. When Keith got up to make the fourth speech he argued valiantly in a difficult situation. I shall be surprised if he succeeds in persuading the court that I am wrong.

October 21st
Finished reading *The Trials of Oscar Wilde*, edited by W. Montgomery Hyde. I was interested in Carson's cross-examination, but could not help feeling that Wilde was pretty easy prey for a skilled cross-examiner.

October 22nd
The car engine was making a lot of noise and I could not get the speed up beyond 50 mph. I could not imagine what was the matter, until I realised about a mile farther on that I had omitted to change up and was still running in second gear. Once this had been remedied, I had no trouble.

October 25th
A jury trial before Guthrie: *Miller v Sutherland County Council*. The pursuer was driving a big articulated furniture van from Wick to Blairgowrie in February 1953. Some snow had fallen in the night, and while rounding a corner near Dornoch the van skidded on the slippery surface, slithered across the road, and came into violent collision with a lorry travelling in the opposite direction. The pursuer was trapped in his cabin, and his right leg so severley injured that it had to be amputated. The pursuer blames the defenders for failing to sand the road. Ironically enough, the lorry with which the pursuer was in collision was a County Council lorry carrying a load of sand to replenish dumps along the road side from which the road could be sanded when it was thought necessary. The defenders say that the condition of the road on the day of the accident was not such as to require sanding. It had not been regarded as a hopeful case for the pursuer: but both Guthrie and the jury seemed interested, and I think we might get a favourable verdict. Douglas Johnston was against me, so a pleasant day was spent, without any displays of acrimony.

October 26th

Guthrie's charge to the jury was against us, but the jury found unanimously for the pursuer and apportioned 40 per cent of fault to him and 60 per cent to the defenders. They assessed total damages at £4,000, so that the pursuer got £2,400—this latter part of the verdict, I was told, the foreman had announced to be by a majority of '6-4-2'. I had not gone in to hear the verdict, but was told that Guthrie on hearing this had asked the foreman whether the jury had borne in mind his direction that in assessing damages they should have no regard to any apportionment they might make, and as the foreman was doubtful had sent the jury away again to reconsider it. On being told this in the lobby outside the court, I expressed the view that Guthrie had been quite wrong in questioning the jury about how they had arrived at their verdict, and the verdict should have been as announced. The jury had by now returned: the same verdict as before, but this time unanimous. Guthrie asked if I had any objection to the recording of the verdict as now given. I had none. The pursuer—a decent, sensible man—was naturally very pleased, particularly as his brother had remarked to him after Guthrie's charge that he had not a hope of getting anything. No one had been very confident about the case: indeed when I was first consulted in it ten days ago the suggestion was that it might be abandoned. My own view was that the verdict was right. Guthrie came up to me in the Law Room later, and remarked with a smile that if I wanted to criticise a judge's conduct of a case I should not do so in a voice that could be heard all over the court.

On the wireless at 9.30 there was a talk by Mr Butler on a supplementary Budget he had introduced: a stupid, pharisaical talk about a silly Budget which is intended to meet the problem of inflation by the crazy method of putting prices up still higher.

October 27th

Mr Gaitskell spoke about the Budget on the wireless. It seemed to me that although his criticisms of the Budget as unfair and dishonest were right enough he was himself to a lesser degree the victim of the same crazy idea that Butler has: that you can cure inflation by putting prices up.

October 31st

At the request of my junior, a young advocate named Cay, I had undertaken to conduct the defence in a murder trial in Glasgow. The accused, William McLeod, was a road haulage agent who in 1952 married a boarding-house keeper of 66. She had led him to believe that she was nearly 20 years younger, and he at her instance added a few years to his age of 44, so that on the marriage certificate their ages appeared as approximately the same. They set up in business on their own, and in April 1955 were joined by one John Hannah, who McLeod was led to believe was Mrs McLeod's brother but who was in fact her illegitimate son. He speedily set about supplanting McLeod, getting authority from his mother to sign cheques and generally to take part in administration. There is no doubt that McLeod resented this. On 15th July 1955 Hannah went off on a week's holiday: and at 7.30 that night McLeod drove up to a Glasgow police station and announced to the Inspector, 'I have done something desperate: I have killed the wife'. Mrs McLeod's body was found in the house, with her skull battered in, obviously by a heavy ashtray stand which was found beside the body.

November 1st

Hill Watson, who had kept very quiet yesterday, began to show his hand more today, and appeared to be anxious to demolish the defence, at any rate so far as diminished responsibility was concerned.

November 2nd

Hill Watson tried to get me to abandon the plea of self-defence, and on my refusing sent the jury away so that we could have a legal discussion. This I thought was tactically useful—it would allow the jury a period to reflect upon what they had just heard from me, before hearing Hill Watson's charge. When he came to charge the jury, after an interval for tea, he nominally left the whole case to them, including self-defence, but in fact demolished not only that but the other defence pleas as well, in a powerful, sustained argument of nearly two hours duration, directed to the conclusion that this must be murder and nothing else. It was a savage, one-sided charge, quite inappropriate, as it seemed to me, in a case of this kind: and not only did he fail to present the case for the accused but even, as I thought, overstated the case for the prosecution. This was unfortunate, as in the event of conviction on the charge of murder it would mean an appeal on the ground of misdirection: and Hill Watson being the wily judge that he is I did not think he had gone far enough to enable an appeal to succeed. I had to go to London tonight, and arranged with Cay that he would attend to the conclusion of the case. I had wondered beforehand whether I should feel any special anxiety when defending in a case in which a man's life was at stake: but I have felt no more anxious about it than about any reparation case, and just as in any other cases enjoyed my own speech and other parts of the case in which I felt I was doing well and disliked the parts of the case in which I felt I was doing badly. Nancy had my clothes for London spread out ready in the living-room, with a nice supper: and I had just started to change when the phone rang: Cay to report a verdict of culpable homicide, by a majority alleged to be 8 to 7. Hill Watson had imposed a sentence of 15 years, which seemed to me far in excess of what the circumstances required: but at all events we had done what we had set out to do and saved the man's neck.

An announcement in tonight's paper of the death of Lord Mackay—which I learned of with regret, for in spite of the trouble he caused he was a personality, and had the great merit of never bearing a grudge against anyone for standing up against him, however tiresome he might be at the time.

November 3rd
An obituary notice of Mackay in the *Times*—an extreme example of understatement: 'He was tenacious in his opinions and expressed them at a length that sometimes verged on prolixity'.

November 4th
A new enquiry, on electric batteries. We interviewed the ring representatives, who seemed an unusually candid, reasonably-minded body of men: then the representatives of an association of smaller manufacturers, unconnected with the price ring, who were completely delightful and gave us a breezy, entertaining half hour.

November 8th
A proof before Walker: *Docherty v. Walter Macfarlane & Co.* The pursuer, a labourer in Saracen foundry in Glasgow, says he was picking up a piece of scrap close to a high-speed grinding machine, and his hand came in contact with the wheel of the machine, which buffed off two knuckles. The defenders give a different account. They say that the pursuer was buffing a metal rod on the machine in order to make it red hot for lighting a cigarette. In my view the

defenders' duty to have the wheel securely fenced would apply whatever the pursuer was doing. A recent case in the House of Lords decided that these grinding machines must be fenced in such a way that the operator cannot come into contact with the wheel, even though the result is to render the machine unusable.

Finished reading *The Boy in Blue*, by Veronica Stirling, an agreeable little story about interesting, genuine people, written by an author who knows how to write.

November 9th

The C & A shop between St David Street and St Andrew Street was on fire, and I found a solid jam of traffic stretching along to the foot of the Mound, where the traffic was being diverted. The traffic was standing in two rows, head to tail, but as the tramline seemed clear I swung out to the right and drove straight along the clear space to the Mound, where I was able to turn up. No trams were being allowed along Princes Street. On getting up to the High Street I was surprised to find a traffic jam there—which seemed odd when it was so far off the route affected by the fire. I found later that this route too was blocked, by another big fire in a warehouse in Jeffrey Street. This had started in the early hours of the morning, and the fire brigade had been fully involved at it when the call came to C & A's. The fact that a full contingent of fire engines was accordingly not available to tackle the C & A fire may have accounted for the hold which the second fire was able to take: it seems to have resulted in a complete holocaust. It is remarkable that though the building seems to have been a blazing inferno for most of the morning the fire never got through to Forsyth's next door or to the shop on the other side.

November 13th

The cat had got shut in the Smiths' garage, and had spent the night in their car.

November 14th

To Churchhill to buy a tea-cosy as a present for Nancy. At the Keiths' she had been admiring a tea-cosy, which Mrs Keith said she had got quite cheaply at a shop in Churchhill. It was a nice shop, and I got a pretty tea-cosy for fourteen shillings and elevenpence.

November 15th

A jury trial before Wheatley: the pursuer a passenger in a bus which was in collision with a lorry belonging to the defenders. The defenders admitted liability and tendered £1,500. The pursuer was over 60 at the date of the accident, and the defenders say that because of pneumoconiosis and high blood pressure he would never have been fit for heavy work again, quite apart from the effects of the accident injury. In view of the difficulty of finding any loss of earnings arising out of the accident, the pursuer had been strongly advised by me and others to take the tender, but being an obstinate, self-assured man he insisted on fighting. 'You see, I'll be a good witness', he said: and in fact he was not bad at all, making a much better impression in the witness-box than he had made on his advisers. It was obvious that anything might happen, though I thought that the most likely result was that we should beat the tender.

November 16th

The jury awarded £1,800.

November 18th

A hearing with Mullards, the principal manufacturers of radio valves and cathode ray tubes. They had brought along various exhibits to illustrate what they said, and gave us a most interesting morning. I was much impressed by the managing director, Mr S.S. Erics— Swedish by birth and Dutch by nationality—who by sheer force of personality has evidently put Mullards in a commanding position vis-à-vis its parent company Philips of Eindhoven. He was an extremely candid, knowledgeable witness, who never evaded a question or hesitated to give a full answer.

Going in the dark along Regents Park Road, I had quite a long walk before coming on a bus route: and not realising that Regents Park Road had curved right round I got on a bus going in exactly the opposite direction to that in which I wanted to go. Supper at Lyons Corner House included grilled herring, which as it happened had a roe in it, and I had it to the accompaniment of Ivy Benson and her ladies' orchestra. Apart perhaps from Ivy herself, they were a present-able-looking set of girls, in scanty yellow blouses and full blue skirts. After a lively opening number, with all the girls fiddling and blowing away, Ivy announced 'a very special request', 'Blue Star', whereupon the second violin laid down her instrument, grasped a microphone, and bawled into it, while Ivy tootled away on a silver saxophone. Both this vocalist and another who succeeded her had, I think, pleasant voices, if it had not been for the microphone. For the second vocal number Ivy exchanged her silver saxophone for a gold-coloured one. It occurred to me that the girl who played the double bass must be a sister of her opposite number who plays in the band at the Corner House at Charing Cross. Like him, she was tall and thin: and she had the same features and the same vacant expression.

To the Studio Two news cinema: as usual here, an interesting programme, including a coloured film of the Austrian Tyrol. Even the cartoon was quiet and amusing—a cat conducting an orchestra, with a good musical accompaniment and no conversation.

November 22nd

Finished reading *Rough Winds of May*, by Nancy Halliman, a story about a girl and her uncle which never comes to any climax but goes on in an up-and-down manner not very different from what one would expect in real life—all quite readable and interesting.

November 23rd

Nancy yesterday gave me a Philips electric shaver, and I used it this morning. With a little patience, it seemed to give a fairly smooth shave, but it resulted in an odd sensation in my right hand, which was holding the razor: like a mild electric shock going on all the time. The great advantage seemed to be that there was no tendency to cut the skin.

November 26th

Muir Society excursion to the Glasgow police scientific bureau. As Nancy was unable to come, I phoned Biddy at Levernholme and asked her. Not anticipating an affirmative answer, I had omitted to find out the arrangements, so when she agreed to come all I could suggest was that she should meet us off the train at Queen Street station. She was the only woman in the party, and seemed much interested in it all: and though she made some pretty inane observations did not interrupt to an undue extent. She was nicely got up, looking radiant and lively.

From Mr Guy A. Aldred:
The Strickland Press 104 George Street Glasgow, C.1   30/11/95

Dear Gordon Stott—I am mailing you today the six-year volume. I think that, because it is rare, it should be sent to you, since you value the volumes. Although the paper may have many errors of thought & approach, they are *genuine* errors, and the purpose is not to deceive but to instruct. Anyway, it stimulates thought. Whatever my faults, & I am very conscious of them, I do recognise genuineness. And there is no one to whom I would rather send the volume than to yourself. I really have a deep regard for yourself & also for Creech Jones, only somehow, despite his love of truth, he lacks warmth towards life. The book is sent parcel post.

With best wishes

December 2nd
Cameo Polytechnic cinema: *Les Diaboliques*, a thriller of hair-raising quality, beautifully done and ending with a double twist of extraordinary ingenuity. Nothing could have been neater or more subtle than the final shot.

December 7th
Jack Hunter was recalling an occasion when Mackintosh had been taking a divorce on the ground of cruelty, and the pursuer was giving evidence of one instance of her husband's cruelty, when he came home drunk and put a ferret in his wife's bed. 'But', asked Mackintosh in his solemn, earnest way, 'wasn't that just a joke—a coarse joke, no doubt?'

December 8th
A jury trial before Migdale. The pursuer had to climb a perpendicular steel ladder. When he reached the fifth rung his feet slipped off. He fell, fracturing a heel bone. He claims that the accident was caused by grease on a rung and by the fact that the rung was loose. The pursuer, not a very intelligent witness, unfortunately committed himself in evidence to the proposition that grease had nothing to do with his accident, and that if a rung was loose it was his business to put it right. Otherwise the evidence came out reasonably well.

Walker in *Docherty v. Macfarlane* had found for the defenders, believing their witnesses as to what the pursuer had been doing, and holding that the pursuer's rash act in trying to use the grindstone to heat a bar for lighting his cigarette was not a danger which the defenders had to foresee.

December 9th

Conclusion of the jury trial. When Ian Fraser sat down after address-ing the jury, the very simple issues in the case were reasonably clear, but the same could not be said 40 minutes later when Migdale had finished his charge. He had had a night to prepare it, and read it out from several pages of foolscap, but it was just rubbish: incoherent, rambling and often meaningless. I certainly could not say it did me any harm. The jury were out for two hours, but in the end their verdict was unanimous for the pursuer: £1,513 total damages, appor-tioned 40 per cent on the defenders and 60 per cent on the pursuer. He thus gets £605.4.0. There was a tender of £250.

December 15th

Westminster: the Scottish Rating and Valuation Bill, abolishing owners' rates. Grant, who is now Solicitor-General, replied for the Government, making his maiden speech in the House. Rather to my surprise, he did it very well, with just the right mixture of diffi-dence and authority to catch the ear of the House. His opening was neat, and he dealt with the points in the debate courteously and not unreasonably.

December 16th

Rubber Footwear hearing. McKenna was concise and efficient, and did his best for his clients, but the evasiveness and dishonesty of the industry's representatives made questioning a lengthy and unsatisfac-tory affair—a very different set of people from the Radio Valves Association.

December 18th

Church: Nancy and the children came. Richard was quite good, merely remarking in a loud voice at the end of the prayer: 'He said Amen'.

December 31st

Mr Blair and Kate for Bridge. They came by taxi, which returned for them at 10.45. After washing up, Nancy and I went to bed and listened to the wireless. Names like Kenneth McKellar's suggested a good programme on the Scottish region: but it turned out to be a tiresome piece of scriptwriting recalling 1955 events of local impor-tance. After the Third Programme closed down at 11.30, and Scottish dance music came to an end shortly afterwards on the Light, we had to have recourse for music to a foreign station. Switched back to the Scottish station in time for the first strokes of Big Ben chiming midnight at the end of the year.

1956

The end of 1956 found me out of a job. The Monopolies Commission having been legislated out of existence so far as I was concerned, I was back in full-time practice at the Bar. At the beginning of the year I took over from the Dean of Faculty a case in which several employees of Beardmores were suing for damages on the ground that by the fault of their employers they had contracted pneumoconiosis. I found it interesting, and having had an opportunity of working on the case during the Christmas recess I knew quite a lot about it. By the time the case was over, I knew even more. It could not have entered my head when I was called that I should ever be a specialist in pneumoconiosis, but so it turned out, and in the course of the year I dealt with quite a number of those cases. The Government legislation setting up a Restrictive Practices Court was disappointing for the Commission's staff, who with practically no warning found themselves deprived of their work and in many cases of their livelihood: a reminder of how dangerous it is to get into a position in which one's future may depend on the whim of a Government. For myself, eight years' membership of the Commission had brought pleasure, interest, experience, and financial reward, far beyond anything I had dreamed of on the evening when John Wheatley telephoned to ask if I would let my name be considered. I was a diffident member in the early stages, but it was not long before I was taking a leading part, more perhaps by reconciling conflicting opinions than by contributing anything very original. As a panel chairman, again I was diffident at the thought of meeting and cross-questioning leading industrialists: and one of the Commission's greatest benefactions to me was the feeling of confidence it gave me in that kind of work. Equally novel was to have a staff of people under my control. I often did not give them much guidance or direction: but they knew that I expected them to find the right answers, and that if they did not I should probably know. The staff seemed to like working with me, and I never had any trouble with them. The events of the year were overshadowed by an ultimatum to Egypt followed by invasion planned in secrecy by the Prime Minister and his stooge Foreign Secretary. Luckily the Labour Party took up a definite line in opposition to the whole adventure, and after a shaky start, before the real issue had been pointed out to him, Mr Gaitskell led the opposition in a series of skilful speeches. The crazy affair destroyed the reputation of the United Kingdom for cool, commonsense diplomacy, free from such outbursts as had emanated occasionally from Washington. On this occasion the American Government—if one excepts their initial error which started the whole thing off—behaved with complete propriety.

January 2nd

Finished reading *Lonely Road*, by Nevil Shute, one of the author's earlier books. The plot, to put it mildly, is sheer bunkum: but his narrative power carries the book along and grips one's attention in spite of reservations about whether it could possibly have happened that way.

January 3rd

As we were passing the piggery below Woolmet, Richard asked if I knew where the sheep stayed all night. On my replying in the negative, he said, 'In the little house where pigs live. Do you know why?' 'No', I said. 'Cos they've no hulla home', he explained. Reading to Elizabeth after she went to bed, I finished an excellent book she had got for herself from the public library, *The Good Master*, by Kate Seredy, about a boy and a girl on a ranch in the Hungarian plain, pleasantly told and illustrated by some beautiful drawings by the author. This has been something quite out of the ordinary run of children's books, and a great success with Elizabeth.

January 5th

The Group was to meet at Mullards' premises at 9.15, and we motored out to their works at Mitcham. London however was blanketed in thick fog, and it was decided to go by tube to Tooting, where the cars would meet us. We were treated to lunch, and at 3.30 set off in two cars for Tooting. We were to stay the night at Eaves Hall Hotel, near Clitheroe, as preliminary to a visit to the Mullard mass production factory at Blackburn. The fog had got worse—traffic at walking pace, with no visibility. At crossroads I had to get out to guide the driver to the kerb on the other side. The four miles journey took considerably over an hour, and when we got to Euston the Preston train had gone. The Manchester express left on time, but was forty minutes late in getting to Manchester: the cars had been redirected from Preston, to meet us. The driver of the front car was timid and ineffective, and though the fog was nothing like as bad as at Mitcham he slowed to a walking pace and sometimes stopped altogether. At midnight we were just coming into Clitheroe.

January 6th
The hotel was a big mansion house, with lights still burning—a welcome sight. Inside it seemed warm and cosy. I was shown up to my room, a spacious apartment at the top of the big staircase. We all came down again for sandwiches and tea, and it was 1.30 when we finally went up. I turned off the central heating, opened both windows, and went to bed. We seemed to have come right into the country, and there was not a sound to be heard. I got up soon after 7.30 and had a walk round—a sharp morning, everything white with frost. The hotel is on the foothills of the Pennine moor, above the Ribble. There was an ornamental bathing pool, covered with ice. After an excellent breakfast I went out for another walk, and on coming in found some perturbation about the non-appearance of Cairns. I went up to his room and found him dressing. He had a vague recollection of being knocked by Pimlott, but had gone to sleep again. The staff who had been with Cairns on factory expeditions before said he had always been up very much betimes, but then he had always gone early to bed.

We motored to Simonstone, where Mullards have a big new factory for mass production of television tubes. We got round by midday, when we were due to leave for the Blackburn factory. A tedious delay for sherry drinking before lunch—after being on my feet all morning, it was tiresome to have to stand about for 15 minutes instead of being able to sit down at the table. But the lunch was good, and the factory interesting, particularly for the skill and precision in handling tiny components, mechanically and by the girls employed. The factory director, Mr de Wit—like many of the Mullard executives—is Dutch, but has spent most of his life in this country. He was enthusiastic about the General Assembly, which he had attended as representative of Dutch churches.

January 9th
A letter had come from Aunt Jean by the morning's post as I was leaving the house. I put it into my coat pocket, unopened, beside

three letters to be posted, and at the post office drew out all four letters and without thinking popped them into the posting box. No doubt Aunt Jean's letter will be delivered again tomorrow.

January 13th
Debate Roll: *McGinlay v. Nuttall*. The pursuer was a chainman employed by the defenders at Inveruglas, and it was part of his duties to read a rain gauge—canisters sunk in the ground to catch rain water, which had to be read regularly on the first day of each month. One of them was 1,500 feet up Ben Vorlich, the last 600 feet over a hillside where there was no road or path. The pursuer had to cross a burn, which on 1st December 1952 was frozen. At the point where he had to cross, the burn was about five feet wide, and just below was a waterfall 40 feet high. The pursuer slipped on a stone and slid over the frozen waterfall, sustaining serious injuries. The defenders, it is said, should have provided a bridge, and anyhow should have given the pursuer boots fitted with nails, or postponed the reading of the gauge to a later date when the burn was not frozen. Hill Watson ridiculed the case, asking if the pursuer should not have been provided with an ice axe, or a helicopter. Judgement right away, dismissing the action. I think this may be unsound.

With Nancy to the George cinema: *A Star is Born*, a new version of the old tear-jerker, this time with Judy Garland and James Mason. Though never in the least convincing, it was well done and so far as I was concerned provided two hours of agreeable, restful entertainment.

January 15th
We all motored to Waverley to see Robert Bros' circus elephants which were advertised to walk up to the Empire Theatre at 3.00. Sharp at that hour, two little elephants appeared, one holding the other's tail in its trunk, both hurrying up the roadway followed by a crowd of shouting children. Two policemen were leading the way: there seemed to be no one else in charge. The policemen after some hesitation turned the elephants along Waverley Bridge into Cockburn Street, out of our sight.

January 17th
The pneumoconiosis cases started today: *Balfour and others v. William Beardmore and Co*. The case is expected to last for at least a fortnight.

January 24th

We are still making our way through the pursuers, a remarkable diversity of types, including today one delightful old gentleman of pleasing speech and scholarly appearance, who answered questions in a cheerful, philosophic way as if he were enjoying every minute of his hour in the witness box. On Friday we had a soft-spoken Irishman from Portadown, equally quiet in manner but with a story ready for every emergency—as when Kissen asked him about a wall which was supposed to be in the foundry in 1940, between the moulding shop and the dressing shop. 'In 1940', he said, 'there was no wall at all. It came there about the beginning of 1941. Would you like now to hear how that wall came to be built?' And without more ado he launched into the tale, of how the moulders used to open a door and let out the steam of the castings, and he said there was no ventilation suitable, and how the dressers thought it was kind of cold, and the stour was blowing over from the moulding shop: and the dressers said if something wasn't done about shutting the door they would stop work and go home. But the moulders said if the door was shut they would stop work and go home: and so the management decided to build the wall.

February 9th

A defended divorce proof: quite a pleasant change from pneumoconiosis. Meanwhile *Balfour v. Beardmore* had at last come to an end, Kissen having concluded his speech. This is the longest case I have ever been in, and has involved a great deal of work. I found it less wearing than I had anticipated. One simply gets a routine of being in court all day and working all evening, and comes to take the absence of leisure as very much for granted.

February 14th

The re-trial of *Hunter v. Hanley*, before Strachan. I was pleased to see there was no sign of Guest: Shearer was appearing for the defender. Another stroke of luck last week removed one of the more serious difficulties we had to contend with last time: the absence of any averment about length of needle. We could not amend, as to do so would have meant losing all the expenses of the first trial and the case in the Division: but ten days ago the defender's agents put in a Minute of Amendment changing 'procaine penicillin' to 'estopan'— a change of no material importance. This we were entitled to answer, and I did so by averring that in injecting estopan it is usual and proper practice to use a needle not less than one and one quarter inches long. This enabled us to put the whole question of length before the jury: and this point, as I expected, became the main point in the case.

February 16th
Shearer made a good speech: and Strachan, though scrupulously fair, inevitably charged on the defender's side, repeating the criteria that Clyde had laid down. The jury took a bit longer than last time, but the decision was the same: unanimous for the defender.

February 17th
The Government's new Bill proposes that all restrictive agreements should be registered and brought before a Restrictive Practices Court. All members of the existing Monopolies Commission will cease to hold office, but a small Commission will be reappointed to inquire into real monopolies, as opposed to restrictive practices. References to the Commission on which a final report is not made before the Bill comes into operation will lapse. In view of this, it has been decided to suspend work altogether on Street Lighting. Radio Valves will probably continue on a factual basis: the Rubber Footwear report will be completed. Cairns seemed worried about the position of Gifford as a panel chairman, since neither of his panels would now be operating. I told him I thought the best course was simply to leave things as they are for the meantime until we see what happens.

Two o' clock train home—lunching with an amusing old fellow who had come from South Africa. He thought the great weakness of South Africa was the lack of fat cattle.

February 18th
Tea at J. and R. Allans: a slight *contretemps* with an elderly woman. As I was paying our bill, she came up and said something like 'Who do you think you're laughing at?' All that occurred to me at the time was that she must be a woman from our neighbourhood and had recognised me, and only later on I realised that she was a stranger making a complaint. So all I did was to greet her in a friendly way, and there was no awkwardness: she just went off without saying anything else.

February 21st
The pursuer's reclaiming motion in *Quinn v. Cameron and Roberton*.

John Wilson opened the case to a somewhat unsympathetic audience. I think we shall make nothing of the common law case on ventilation or respirators, but I do not see how Guthrie can have been right in holding that a swing grinder did not come under the Grinding Regulations.

February 22nd

Emslie, for the respondents, threw Guthrie's judgement overboard, rejecting Clyde's attempt to support it, and produced an entirely new argument on the definition of grinding as abrasion of metal by a grindstone or a wheel manufactured of bonded emery or similar abrasive. The evidence showed that the wheel was made of carborundum, but there was no evidence as to what carborundum was. This was a new point, which had never been argued in the Outer House or in earlier cases, everyone having taken it for granted that the grinding was of the type which the Regulations were intended to cover. The defenders had given no notice on Record or in evidence that they made any point on definition: Emslie however argued that it was for the pursuer to bring himself under the Regulation before he could claim a breach of statutory duty. Clyde of course jumped at this argument: and it is a formidable point. Spent most of the evening on work for my speech, including a search through the encyclopedia to find out what I could about carborundum, emery, corundum, silicum carbide and other abrasive substances—with three phone calls from John Shaw, who was engaged in similar research and had some ideas to offer from time to time.

February 23rd

Clyde was obviously impossible, and I made no attempt to conciliate him. He is a hopeless chairman, making no attempt to argue his point in the way Cooper would have done. One argument countered, he jumps to another, with no regard for logical sequence or the matter under consideration. His superficial thinking made it easy to answer him, and I contented myself with brief retorts to his interventions—concentrating on the other two. Carmont was asleep most of the afternoon, but he took a keen interest in what I said about the composition of carborundum. I asked the court, if they thought it proper to entertain the defenders' point, to give me an opportunity to lead further evidence upon it.

February 24th

The debate on the Quinn case was concluded. Shearer maintained the argument Emslie had submitted, but rather half-heartedly, preferring another argument, about the construction of the Regulation, that I think is manifestly absurd—though Clyde of course lapped it up.

March 1st

Westminster: the Army Estimates. Chuter Ede, who has retired to the back benches, started off with a violent attack on the speech with which Head, the Secretary for War, had opened the debate, following it up oddly with a speech confined to one small point: a complaint that NCOs got a bigger allowance than higher officers for attending Territorial Army camps. Shinwell spoke vigorously and eloquently, without a note, but had nothing to say. Meanwhile an Ulster Unionist named McKibbin had read from a typescript about the condition of barracks in Northern Ireland, with some unsuccessful attempts to pronounce 'Woolwich', a place of which he did not seem to have heard before. A new Labour member, Frank Allaun, made a plea for the abolition of conscription which was able and effective if perhaps a trifle overdone. To my surprise, and against my first reaction, I was favourably impressed by Brigadier Prior-Palmer from Worthing. His rapid staccato style and far from satisfactory enunciation made him difficult to follow, but he obviously believed in what he was saying and I thought his idea of a guerilla force, to operate in places like Cyprus or Kenya instead of soldiers, was not bad. Faced with a disaffected population, he said, the soldier in uniform did not stand a chance: he did not know who his enemy was, and was simply there to be shot at. Something in the nature of a Commonwealth police force would be in a different position, and—as he and another Tory speaker, Legge-Bourke, pointed out—would attract men who would not willingly join the Army because of dislike of rigid Army discipline. I found this an interesting debate: a great advance on the kind of defence debate one would hear five or six years ago. It seems to be common ground now that in a real war an army would be no use at all. Coming out, I spoke to Mrs Willis, who was in the gallery with a very pretty dark girl, the daughter of a member of the Australian Parliament: I wished I had noticed them before.

March 4th

Finished reading *The Moon in the Yellow River*, by Denis Johnston, a play about Ireland. The volume contains another play about Ireland, *The Old Lady Says 'No!'*, a surrealist play which in print is all but unintelligible. I daresay it would be effective on the stage, though difficult to produce. The author, realising the reader's difficulties and that the play 'requires in a sense to be translated', has appended notes to 'some of the thematic passages', and these certainly help to make things a little clearer.

March 9th
A divorce proof for next Tuesday has been in my diary for a long time, but Fairbairn, forgetting this, had instructed Kissen: and today I learned that owing to this mistake I was out of it and left with nothing to do.

March 10th
Lauderdale Hunt point-to-point at Mosshouses. Just before Pathhead I picked up a pedestrian, whom I took as far as Lauder. There he got off and went to have a refreshment prior to going up to the races. He gave me a tip which he had from a butcher in Dalkeith, for a horse called Red Tab. A horse of that name was running in the first race, and in fact came in first. I was sorry I had not taken the tip, and so recovered part at least of the exorbitant car-parking fee: thirty shillings. This however I felt I could afford, since this morning I was told that I was to be instructed in Tuesday's proof after all, but for the other side.

March 15th
Cairns had been to the Board of Trade and ascertained from Sir Frank Lee that they wanted me to continue in my present position until the Bill goes through—though, as Cairns said he pointed out, I could not possibly undertake to give 'half my time' to the work, as there would not be that amount of work to do. Gifford apparently is to be restored to the status of ordinary £500 per annum member, though one of the two references in which he has been appointed panel chairman is to go on.

March 16th
Finished *Girl in May*, by Bruce Marshall. No one could call it a good novel, and it is odd that Marshall, after one outstandingly good book, has never been able to do anything like it again. But in spite of the

absurdities of its plot, and its puerile jokes, repeated not once but a number of times, this is a likeable book, and the people in it, though silly, are kindly. It left a little glow of pleasure when I got to the end, mingled with a slight sense of shame at having got pleasure from such nonsense.

March 17th
Judgement in *Quinn v. Cameron and Roberton*, for the defenders. According to what John Wilson told me, they have not decided the case on the carborundum point but on the ground that an exhaust appliance fitted to a swing grinder would not have removed the dangerous dust but only bigger, unharmful particles thrown out at the back of the wheel. If this was the ground of judgement, it seems to be a complete misconstruction of the Regulation—which prohibits grinding unless an efficient exhaust appliance can be fitted. I hope to take this case to the House of Lords.

March 18th
Children's television included an instalment of the life of Jesus of Nazareth, which is being done as a serial. It was excellently done: Moving, arresting and real, with dignity but without any hint of artificiality.

March 20th
On television a party political broadcast for the Conservatives: Major Lloyd George answered questions sent in by Junior Unionist Associations—at least he purported to answer them. It was deadly dull: I cannot imagine what purpose it was supposed to serve.

March 23rd
The Labour Party had half an hour on television: Callaghan, George Brown and Anthony Greenwood, with Dalton intervening now and again as light relief, in an elderly, paternal kind of way. They all seemed to be in earnest, and got to grips with the questions: Callaghan particularly good, and even Brown, whom I do not like much, did well.

March 25th
Jesus of Nazareth: Gethsemane and the trial before Pilate. Elizabeth was much worried at the thought that 'he might not escape', and I

was glad that today's episode ended before it could appear that this apprehension was well founded. The producers got through these supremely difficult episodes with complete naturalness and without the slightest suggestion of a false note. The tragedy was inevitable and complete, and everyone's point of view fairly presented.

March 26th

Jack Payne's television programme of recording stars, *Off the Record*, included—among a lot of rubbish—Shirley Abicair, whose freshness and innocent charm had struck us very forcibly in a children's programme we had seen soon after we had television installed. She was no less attractive tonight.

April 1st

Kings Park: the usual Easter crowd of children who had come to roll their eggs.

To the Braggins house to see the final instalment of *Jesus of Nazareth*—to avoid harrowing the children with it at home.

April 2nd

In the early hours of the morning I was wakened by loud cries of 'Daddy' from Richard. I let him go on for some time, but as there was no diminution of the noise eventually got up and went through to him. All he wanted was to tell me that Elizabeth was crying: and when I went in to Elizabeth what she was complaining of was the noise of Richard's shouting.

April 3rd

With Nancy and Mrs Braggins to the Lyceum: Noel Coward's new comedy, *South Sea Bubble*. I thought at first it was going to be just a succession of witty observations, with nothing more, but it developed attractively, with a neat last act. Vivien Leigh, who had the principal part, is a fascinating personality, and very pretty.

April 5th

London. The first occasion I had gone through the City for a long time, and I was struck by the extraordinary congestion caused by parked vehicles, usually on both sides of a narrow street—in some places only a single lane for traffic between them. Electric train to Carshalton: a picturesque scene, the road crossing a pond and a park with daffodils on the other. *The Man Who Never Was*, at the Granada cinema. With every willingness to believe in the stupidity of the British security services, I found it difficult to accept that they were as stupid as they were made out to be here.

April 6th

Walked along Leadenhall Street to Pike's office. There is always something rather fascinating about the City—variously garbed men hurrying about on mysterious errands. I saw one distinguished looking gentleman walking along the pavement in a lounge suit and top hat. Green Line bus to Epping. Beyond Chingford, Epping Forest seemed to be fighting a losing battle against housing development, but soon we were right in the forest, with no houses at all—completely unspoiled country.

April 11th

We went to the Lyceum to see *Romanoff and Juliet*, by Peter Ustinov. Many of the jokes in this fantastic comedy had been made before, but they were here repeated with such subtlety and charm that they provided an entertaining evening. Mr Ustinov himself was particularly attractive in one of the principal parts, and there was a kindliness and urbanity about the whole production which made it impossible not to like it: an odd entertainment, but a civilised one.

April 12th

Nancy and I to the Empire: a new musical show, *Wild Grows the Heather*. The first twenty minutes were incredibly bad, the equivalent of an exceedingly amateur pantomime in a poor season: and the general impression was more like a homemade imitation than a genuine theatrical production—greatly handicapped by its leading lady. But it was not as bad as I thought it was going to be.

April 15th

We all set off for Stonehouse, where a motor-cycle scramble was being held on Kittymuir Farm—where the river ran through a gorge with steep wooded sides, widening out into a pleasant grassy dell. On Richard's insistence a stop was made in the hamlet of Waterloo, so that he and Elizabeth could go on the roundabout in the children's playground. There were swings too, but they were tied up—this being Sunday.

Q.C.'S DIARY

April 17th

In the evening, after the children were in bed, I happened to sneeze loudly when passing Richard's door, whereupon a voice from within called 'Don't wake me'.

April 19th

Finished reading *No Flies in China*, by George Stafford Gale, one of the journalists who accompanied a Labour Party delegation. He brings home effectively the tedium of a regime under which no one wants to think for himself, but the book is confused and contradictory and does not help much towards understanding communist China.

Harold Wilson appeared on television to criticise the Budget. It seems that he made a brilliant speech against it in the House of Commons yesterday, and it was all the more disappointing that his television appearance was a failure. He obviously did not feel at home, and what he said was prosy and unconvincing. He missed all the points, and allowed himself to be steamrollered by two supercilious Tory editors—from the *Investors Chronicle* and the *Sunday Times*—whom he had been rash enough to bring along to question him.

April 21st

The car running well on Regent commercial petrol, two shillings a gallon cheaper than the better quality.

April 23rd

With Elizabeth to the National Portrait Gallery. The ground floor galleries were full of enormous ornate portraits of Scottish kings and noblemen, and though interest increased a little as we mounted higher there seemed nothing outstanding in rows and rows of generals, admirals and sombre-coated lawyers who covered the walls. Elizabeth however seemed to be taking quite an interest in it.

Television tonight ended with *Top Town*, a contest in amateur entertainment between Soho and Dumfries. As might be expected, this was not like against like: and as I saw only part of the show I could not really condemn the judges for preferring the orthodox variety of Soho to the fine Highland dancing and pipe playing of Dumfries: but for my part I should gladly exchange all the variety in the world for 'Annie Laurie' sung with such enchanting simplicity, charm and purity of tone as it was tonight by a Dumfries boilermaker.

April 25th
Forsyths: nothing in the nature of a grey flannel suit, all the two-piece suits being in the curious drab cement-like colour, like teddy boys' clothes, which apparently is fashionable just now.

With Elizabeth to the Dominion cinema: *The Glass Slipper*, a rationalised version of Cinderella—lovely soft colours and some pleasant ballet dancing, but not I think altogether for children. It was followed by *The Wizard of Oz*. Elizabeth's first visit to the cinema—'That was lovely', she said as we came out.

April 30th
John Shaw phoned to say we had been successful in all the Beardmore cases except one.

May 7th
Steele Nicoll's death was in this morning's paper. He was a curious character, for though he must have been well to do, and lived very comfortably in that he kept two cars and enjoyed good living and fishing and shooting holidays on the rare occasions when he took any time off, he deliberately dressed in an almost shabby style, and lived in very inadequate quarters in Great King Street, mostly in the basement. He seldom had any assistance, and papers and letters accumulated on the big table in the office, in little piles which soon became dust-covered. But he could usually unearth anything if really required, and despite the volume of work never got into irretrievable difficulty, though always prepared to spend any amount of time gossiping and chatting in Parliament House. He overtook the work by working to all hours of the night, with the help of a part-time typist who sometimes came in the late evenings. He had a genius for obtaining good settlements from insurance companies and defenders' agents, and this was fortunate, for difficulties sometimes arose through failure to gather adequate evidence in cases which he failed to settle—these were few and far between. I had no experience and no practice when Ingram first mentioned my name to him and he handed me the first bundle of papers: but from that day on he gave me unfailing support, and showed the most extraordinary confidence in me. I have no doubt that my present position at the Bar is due entirely to him, for not only did he provide a substantial part of my income but he laid the foundation on which most of it could come—for at the Bar to him that hath shall be given, and without Nicoll, and with no legal

connection or relation, I doubt if I should ever have had anything. His working methods were peculiar and often trying. His instructions, and a note of the facts he had taken from a client or witness, were as often as not written in pencil on the back of old circulars or sheets from a calendar, and his favourite time for discussing cases was often about 11 o'clock at night, when he would ring up and talk for half an hour or more before coming to the point. But being no stickler myself for formality I did not mind these irregularities, and they were amply compensated for by his loyalty, fairness and willingness to go to any expense in order to get the proper result for our clients. A great deal of his work he did for nothing, and if there was money available he saw to it his Counsel had a fair share—and he was never backward in getting all he could out of the insurance companies who were our normal opponents. When I came back to work after the war, he again gave me his complete support, and enabled me to build up a good practice before his own began to fail on account of his ill-health and the death of his principal correspondent, William Philp of Kirkcaldy. Here again I have been lucky, since the falling-off began at a time when my other practice was expanding and I was beginning to get a wide range of solicitors instructing me, so that Nicoll's work was no longer of such importance as far as I was concerned. But without him to start the ball rolling, and keep it rolling for so many years, I do not see how I could have got anywhere at all.

Muirfield: the Bench and Bar foursomes. The other players made some fun of me because of the speed at which I played. 'He doesn't realise that golf's a difficult game' they said: and when, at the hole at which the match ended, I pitched over a yawning bunker to the green they remarked, 'He didn't see there was a bunker there'.

May 8th
A defended divorce. The pursuer had put his wife out after being told by one of his daughters that his wife had for some years been associating with the beadle of Martyr Church in Dundee. He learnt from another daughter that his wife and that daughter had spent a night in the vestry of the church with the beadle: and he avers that his wife and the beadle went for walks together, kissing and embracing in Soapworks Lane.

May 11th
I was handed today a copy of Strachan's judgement in the Beardmore

cases. It appeared the first report was correct—the defenders have been assoilzied in one case, on the ground that the pursuer was a welder and the defenders were not under the same obligation to provide a respirator for him as arose in the case of dressers and moulders.

June 3rd

Almondell gardens open in aid of the District Nursing. The avenue and riverside paths a mass of colour, not only with rhododendrons but with other flowering shrubs as well, and a wealth of wild flowers at the side of the path. We went into the stables for tea—tea tickets only sixpence each, and although we were told each to select one from a number of plates, having on them a piece of cake and a biscuit, more homemade cakes were handed round later, with an unlimited amount of tea. So if they had to pay the usual prices for provisions they could not have made much of a profit off the tea. I took two more tickets for our second cups of tea, but even so it was all ridiculously cheap.

Still no rain: the drought continues unchecked with all its disadvantages, and without any of the compensations one expects in the way of fine summer weather. But the countryside is looking remarkably well, with trees very green and a great display of blossom.

June 5th
Proof in *Young v. McLeod*

HARPER MEMORIAL BAPTIST CHURCH
EXCERPT from minute date 16th December, 1953.
Bro' S. Milliken reported having visited Bro' Young in company with Bros Warren & Murray. Throughout interview privacy was impossible as Mrs Young and her sister were present all the time. He had noticed in prominent position a Bible and on top letter received from Secretary accepting his resignation, and he was particularly incensed against the latter no mention or thanks having been made for past services. He told Bro' Milliken he had no intention of resigning and that he wouldn't go out he'd die out. Seeing the way the land lay the Brethren felt they could do no more...Bro' McKay Sen. then reminded Brethren of Verses mentioned in our Constitution in light of this situation and urged that the situation as pertaining to Mr & Mrs Young be dealt with

according to God's Word. If the Lord wasn't blessing under the Ministry and teaching and tears of our Pastor there must be some reason and as in Achans time and Annanias and Sapphira's he felt there was sin in the camp and until it was dealt with there would be no real blessing. Pastor thanked our Bro' for faithful and wise but costly words, and it was agreed we leave matter for special discussion...

Lord Walker seemed not unsympathetic to the pursuer.

June 6th
Mr McLeod in the witness box: a skilful witness, and under cross-examination got rather the better of me.

June 7th
The proof went much better today; I had a successful and enjoyable cross-examination of the minister and three of his deacons.

Finished reading *Roderick Hudson*, by Henry James. This is the first I have read of his books, and I found him a curiously cool-blooded writer—interesting, and the people credible so I wanted to know what happened to them, but in the end I had a feeling of being let down in some way, without quite knowing how.

June 8th
I appeared before Lord Strachan to proffer a Minute of Amendment in *Wilson v. National Coal Board*—out for proof on Tuesday next week. We had averred that the accident had taken place on 2nd August 1952; but when the Coal Board denied this in their defences some enquiry had been made and it was found that the pursuer maintained that the accident had happened on the first Tuesday of the month. In accordance with this, the date was altered on adjustment to 5th August. The Coal Board continued to deny that there had been an accident on the date averred, though they admitted the pursuer had reported an accident on another date which they did not specify. So matters remained until yesterday, when the defenders lodged the hospital records and I discovered that the accident had happened on the first Tuesday of September—2nd September. The Coal Board had intimated that if an amendment were made they would ask for a postponement of the proof. I contented myself with profering the Minute formally: but after Gimson, for the defenders,

had moved for the expenses of preparing for Tuesday's proof Strachan remarked that the Court had frequently refused an amendment proposed at the last moment and asked if there was any explanation. I accordingly narrated the whole circumstances, and pointing out that the defenders had known all along what the date of the accident was suggested that the question of expenses should be reserved for argument when their Answers had been lodged. Strachan allowed the amendment and reserved all questions of expenses.

June 9th

Markinch Games. Being uncertain about parking facilities there, I left the car in Kirkcaldy and proceeded by bus. The games, in today's brilliant sunshine, provided a pleasant afternoon's entertainment. I stayed until 6.45. Relying upon the SMT to provide a frequent service, I had not troubled to find out the bus times: and a bus to Kirkcaldy was leaving the Cross just as I came along.

June 10th

Stobo Castle: the grounds open today in aid of the District Nursing. The Water Garden a complete surprise, and very delightful. A burn had been dammed to form quite an extensive loch, from which the outflow came over a waterfall into a glen laid out with trees and flowering shrubs through which the burn ran in a number of different courses, crossed here and there by stepping stones and bridges which linked up a little maze of paths. The children found all this very enjoyable. The castle is in a lovely situation on the apex of a ridge, with wooded policies falling on each side and a lovely view of the Border hills beyond, but it is just a big bare barn. One could have spent many delightful hours roaming through the woods, and as we were coming through the wood at the back of the castle we heard a cuckoo quite near at hand. We picnicked on the grass overlooking the loch, an attractive picture with a solitary swan on the water and lovely shades of green in the woods on the other side.

June 11th

Longniddry beach for a picnic: the dunes a mass of wild roses, growing so thickly that they formed practically a solid carpet of flowers.

Finished reading *The Devil in Velvet*, by John Dickson Carr, a fantastic story about a man who made a pact with the devil whereby he was carried back into Restoration times. Despite the author's erudite knowledge of the characters and customs of the period, it is really just trash.

June 12th

Television show from North Pier, Blackpool. Television variety is usually beneath contempt, but this was an exception: a lively, intelligent show which included as its star turn a popular singer of the day named Frankie Vaughan. He had no voice, and was far from handsome, and the songs he sang were hot numbers notable more for tunelessness than anything else. But there was a remarkable fascination about his personality: we were attracted to him, whether we wanted or not, and should have liked to see more of him. The show was followed by a half-hour programme in which Sir Gavin de Beer, with films and diagrams and models, got off his chest a pet theory which he had been cultivating for the past twenty years about the route by which Hannibal crossed the Alps. Like most enthusiasts, even on a subject of no importance to anyone, he made it all quite interesting.

June 14th

Othello on television: certainly a fine piece of work, with Gordon Heath and Rosemary Harris extremely effective, but though the climax was impressive I found long portions of it rather dull—television is not a succesful medium for even the best of plays. It is more suited for the type of programme which followed, *Animal Vegetable and Mineral*, in which three experts identified various buildings, ancient and modern, from some little bit of detail shown them in black and white photography. They did it with complete naturalness and miraculous efficiency.

June 17th

Richard took us to see the footbridge which was built some weeks ago across the Figgate Burn to carry a path which has been made along the edge of the park, linking the prefabs with Baileyfield Road. This path was just alongside the existing path inside the park railings, which people used to get to work at Portobello in the early morning. As this meant that they were in the park when the park was officially closed, some were actually prosecuted and fined: and when protests were made about this the Corporation went to the expense of making this new path outside the railings, thus keeping the park sacrosanct during closing hours to some extent—though gaps in the railings allow youths and rowdies to come in at night if they so desire. After we got home I motored the children to the King's Park, where we climbed up the face of Arthur's Seat and descended by a gully on the north side leading on to a steep bit of scree which the children slid down with apparent enjoyment. I had never come down this way, and was not sure if it would be practicable for children.

June 21st
The children watching television: racing from Ascot, which to judge from the sounds coming from next door while I was having tea in the dining room seemed to be giving pleasure. When I went through, Richard turned to me and remarked 'Things with four legs go much faster than other things.'

July 9th
A note for Roy, the potato merchant, who had asked for advice as to the effect of the Restrictive Trade Practices Act on the operation of the Potato Trade Association. In his letter to me he said:

> I would like to take this opportunity of thanking you for the valuable assistance you gave me with regard to the Potato Marketing Scheme, and by using and quoting your arguments against, I have been able to get the Potato Marketing Board to completely cancel their Garnishee Order, together with their Compulsory Arbitration Order, and now I feel pretty certain that they will also have to alter their conditions on merchants' licences.

July 20th
I was told that James Walker had awarded Mrs Young £100 in her action against Rev Murray McLeod. The members of the Deacons Court had been assoilzied on the ground that they were entitled to proceed on the pastor's report. Walker held that McLeod had resented the way the pursuer had received his suggestion that she should move to another church, and in his resentment had made reckless statements to the Deacons Court which had led to the sending of a slanderous letter.

July 31st
We started packing, preparatory to going on holiday tomorrow.

August 1st

Cults: a roomy bungalow, but only two bedrooms, and the attic reached by a slingsby ladder.

August 2nd

We decided to go into Aberdeen and try to get a camp bed to put up for Elizabeth in the drawing room. At Campbell's furniture shop we were directed across the street to Millett's stores. There, somewhat to my surprise, we were supplied with a camp bed at the modest price of £2.2.6.

August 6th

Finished reading *King Solomon's Ring* by Konrad Z. Lorenz. I began this book in a gloomy frame of mind, wondering how a book about animal behaviour had got on my library list. But I found it fascinating: sensible, entertainingly written, and full of interesting things —dragonfly larva which proceeds by jet propulsion, squirting out a powerful little column of water from the tip of its abdomen which drives the animal speedily forward in rapid jerks. Then there is the cichlid fish, male and female remaining in connubial partnership and caring for their young in a nesting hole at bed time. The female jewel fish 'jerks her fin rapidly up and down, making the jewels flash like a heliograph. The father, in the meantime, searches the whole tank for stragglers. He does not coax them along but simply inhales them into his roomy mouth, swims to the nest, and blows them into the hollow'. The author tells a story about a father cichlid who when searching for truants allowed himself to be diverted by a nice hind end of earthworm—which apparently is preferred by all worm eaters to the front end. As the fish was chewing this mouthful, he saw a baby fish swimming across the tank. He raced after the baby and took it into his already filled mouth, thus having in his mouth two different things of which one must go into the stomach and the other into the nest. 'The fish stood stock still with full cheeks, but did not chew. If ever I have seen a fish think, it was in that moment!' Eventually he spat out the whole contents, ate up the worm, keeping an eye on the baby fish, then inhaled the baby and carried it home.

August 8th

Put on Mr Haggart's television for a talk by the Prime Minister about the Suez Canal 'crisis'. Colonel Nasser has suddenly national-ised the canal, ending the ownership of a company in which the British Government is an extensive shareholder: and the British and French Governments have reacted with an extraordinary display of sabre-rattling: movement of troops, aircraft carriers and the rest of it, with much talk of Egypt's perfidy and broken promises, though no-body seems able to point out any obligation so long as the canal is kept open for traffic. This the Egyptian government is apparently doing, and must be anxious to do if its object is profit, as it seems to be—the only result of the change being to transfer the canal profits from the Company to the Government. They have undertaken to pay for the company's assets at the current market price. Eden spoke well tonight, and was quite successful in concealing the poverty of his case.

August 9th
To Aberdeen with Nancy: a variety show at the Capitol. Semprini, the main attraction, was good, but among a lot of good turns I thought the best was Johnny Brandon, a singer of immense vitality and en-thusiasm and quite a bit of genius, though no doubt in a very minor sphere. It was Peter Cavanagh, the impersonator, who topped the bill along with Semprini and whose act brought the programme to a close. After so many pleasing things, he was an anti-climax: his per-formance a cheapjack affair. The aim in modern variety seems to be to make as much noise as possible, but in spite of the microphones we found this show very enjoyable.

August 12th
A service from Iona on the wireless, with a sermon by Dr MacLeod: 'Forgive us our debts as we forgive our debtors'—eloquent, forceful, moving, personal. He had something to say that one felt one could not possibly ignore.

August 14th
We motored to Park bridge: flood water made a fine stream of river. Beyond the bridge we came to an iron gate across the road, and a young man in railway uniform emerged from a cottage and said we would have to pay to go through, but it was only fourpence. He gave us two tickets marked 'British Railways. Park Pontage'—threepence for the car, and a penny for the passenger.

August 16th
Dinnet Moor. We stopped at the bridge across the Pot Burn and walked up the glen—very wet going—to the Vat, a narrow gorge in the rocks. We scrambled down to the foot of the chasm: a remarkable place, with the burn coming down in a waterfall and then passing through a very narrow gap in the rock. The glen below the bridge was different from the heathery glen above but no less attractive: a series of grassy dells concealed in woods, with the stream hurrying down the middle.

August 17th
Finished *Waiting for the Mahatma*, by R.K. Narayan, a likeable, moving little story, attractively written, with some delightful glimpses of Mr Gandhi.

The Lonach Gathering: the games included a march of the clansmen, in kilts and carrying pikes. It would be an attractive spectacle on a fine day, but in today's damp, rainy weather it was nothing much. 'It's jist the name', said an old lady. 'It's just naething. We'd be better at wir ain fireside.'

August 18th
Nairn Games. My train back went by the coast, a pleasant trip in the evening sunshine. We were 20 minutes late leaving Elgin, but made up most of it on the way to Aberdeen. I heard a railwayman at Elgin assuring a honeymoon couple in the next compartment, whom he provided with a 'Reserved' notice to paste on their door, that they were behind 'the best driver and fireman out of Forres'.

August 19th
Motored with Nancy to the coast. From Portlethen station the road followed a tortuous course and came to an end at the top of a rough, stony lane leading down to a group of houses. A man working on top of a motor van was most courteous and helpful in response to our request to be directed to the sea, asking if there was any particular kind of sea we liked—rocks, or cliffs, or seabirds. Nancy asked him where we were, to which he replied: 'Portlethen—it's Portlethen harbour I've directed you to.' It was as well he told us—we should certainly not have recognised it for ourselves. The path ran between the cottages and what seemed to be their gardens, and emerged on a rocky cliff above a narrow inlet, on which nets were drying—no artificial harbour, just this little natural opening in the rocks. In the

sea at the edge of the rocks, rising and dipping with the waves, were two cormorants with four of their young. They took no notice of us.

August 22nd

Aberdeen with Nancy: the Grand Central Cinema, *His Majesty O'Keefe*. Some fine colourful locations in the Pacific islands were thrown away on this silly film—the dialogue a miracle of ineptitude.

August 24th

Aberdeen, with the children: The Grand Central cinema, *Geordie*. This film about a Highlander gamekeeper's son, who became an Olympic champion, has plenty of absurdities, but it is a friendly, likeable picture, with some lovely colour photography of lochs and mountains. It was ideal for Elizabeth, who followed it with intense interest and delight: and apparently knowing all the conventions of the novelette realised at once what was happening and what was bound to happen next. Children in the stalls kept up a fair amount of noise, so Elizabeth's commentary passed unnoticed.

September 7th

We spent the morning on the Radio Valves report, and signed it, thus concluding the Commission work so far as Group II is concerned. Group I expects to finish its last report in about a fortnight's time. Conversation on London buses is more general than in Edinburgh: the conductor carried on a learned conversation with a passenger who looked like a brewer's drayman, on the worship of Mithras and the origins of Christianity in England.

September 8th

Breakfasted on the train with a young farmer from Dunbar, who said that in view of what the weather had done for the harvest he might as well go off to the Continent for a month—there was nothing he could do about it. Even the potatoes were rotting in the fields.

September 23rd

A mobile X-ray unit is operating in the Town Hall, and everyone is being urged to go and be X-rayed. We joined the queue in the corridor, and were entertained during a short wait by an officious little steward who got into an altercation with a woman in the queue and said we did not seem to realise that he was a voluntary worker. I reminded him laughingly that the great thing for voluntary workers was to be pleasant to everyone, to which he replied that he would be pleasant to those who were pleasant to him. 'But the important thing surely', I said, 'is to be pleasant to people who are unpleasant to you.' The actual X-ray did not take a minute.

September 24th

A curious feature of these misty mornings has been a great row of spiders' webs all along the side of the hedge, glistening with moisture, with a big brown spider at the middle of each web. The webs are beautifully made, with strands stretching away back into the hedge and fastened round different leaves.

In *Panorama* tonight on television we had Selwyn Lloyd, the Foreign Secretary, questioned on his Suez policy. He dealt with the questions skilfully: though his questioner was almost certainly right, Mr Lloyd was able to turn things round so as to indicate that he was wrong, and courteously and quietly make him seem rather a fool. Mr Lloyd is an exceptionally plausible person, and his cool, easy manner matched his skill as an advocate.

October 1st

Perturbed to find in this morning's paper a lengthy report of my talk to the Fabian Society, mainly concerned with my view that the prosecution in London of one of the Soviet athletic team for alleged petty theft, an incident which had caused a minor international crisis, would not have happened in Scotland. This view though crudely expressed in the report which one of the Fabian members had sent in, seems sound enough, but I was more worried about some slightly discourteous references to Lord Cooper when, after paying tribute to him as a 'very great man' I am supposed to have accused him of being old-fashioned and apt to make things difficult for Advocates Depute who were trying to enforce rationing regulations. I was assailed by everyone I met, on some point or other of this report.

I heard however a cheering piece of news: that Mr Murray McLeod had decided not to proceed with a reclaiming motion: I had not thought much of the prospect of defending Walker's judgement in the First Division as at present constituted.

October 3rd

A letter from James Cooper complaining about the newspaper report of my talk to the Fabians, and contrasting what I was reported to have said about his brother with what I had written to him on his elevation to the peerage. In the afternoon I wrote a friendly letter to Cooper, expressing my regard for his brother and regret that anything I said had been interpreted as disrespectful to him. It is ironical that I, who seldom spend a day in Parliament House—certainly not in the First Division—without lamenting the loss of Cooper, should be getting into trouble for appearing not to appreciate him. As I said in my letter, 'It is the simple fact that I feel Parliament House is not the same without him—nothing like the same.'

October 4th

A case in Debate Roll before Wheatley. Robert Reid, for the defenders, made a lengthy criticism of the pursuer's averments, maintaining that the case was unsuitable for jury trial. Ian Macdonald was with me, and was to have replied: but as Reid's involved, detailed argument proceeded he whispered to me, 'I can't make anything of this. You'd better take the reply yourself.' Nothing loth, I moved into the centre of the bench, and when Reid sat down made a brief reply. As I had anticipated, there was no difficulty. Wheatley allowed a jury trial, with expenses. 'I see the technique now', Macdonald said to me afterwards. 'You don't reply to the other fellow at all. You just ignore what he's said, and state your own case.'

October 5th

Another letter from James Cooper, repeating his complaint and saying that 'no one in his senses could say' that Lord Cooper was 'old fashioned in any way whatever', but in quite friendly terms. He ends up 'I greatly regret that it is your name which has been coupled with this report, since I can well recall my brother speaking to me of you on more than one occasion with high regard and indeed affection'.

Ross McLean, who spends his summer holidays going up and down the west coast on his little yacht *Kelana*, told me that he had gone into Iona this summer and met the Smalls. Being short of a member of his crew through his son's going off, he had asked whether any of the Small family would care to join him, expecting that one of the three boys would come. But before any of them had a chance to offer to come Leonard Small himself volunteered. He joined *Kelana* at Tobermory and proved an excellent member of the crew during the week he was on board. On the Sunday they had been anchored near Loch Sunart, and Small had conducted a service on board. People came from other yachts anchored there, Ross McLean's daughter accompanied the hymns on a recorder while someone else had an accordion, and Small preached an excellent sermon, taking as his text a discussion on the previous night about different kinds of anchors.

October 6th
Went into a shop at Abbeyhill to leave shoes to be repaired, and on coming out found I must have omitted to put the brake on. The car moved off, and came to rest farther along the street, bang up against the front of another empty car. As my car seemed to be headed out towards the middle of the street, it was lucky the other car had been there to stop it.

October 9th
Three pneumoconiosis cases. The defenders take every possible defence: that the pursuers have not got pneumoconiosis, that their moulding material was not sand but compo with a low silica content, that anyhow they had no knowledge of the danger, that the bakelite wheel used in the grinder was not emery or a similar abrasive, that the swing frame grinders were portable. So the proof will take a long time. Today we had one expert witness and one pursuer. When Shearer put to the witness that even in a clear atmosphere such as in that court he would get a certain dust count on his instrument—to which the witness assented—Wheatley remarked, 'Perhaps you had better not ask him what kind of count he would get in some of the other courts'.

October 10th
The proof continued. Today's evidence neither advanced the pursuer's case nor contributed to anybody's entertainment: the kind of day for which one consoles oneself with the reflection that one is being well paid for it.

October 13th
Telefilm report of the Conservative Party conference. Yates, the MP for the Wrekin, roused the delegates' wrath by standing up for Egypt and denouncing the Government's foreign policy root and branch: a friendly, likeable fellow who took interruptions placidly and left the rostrum with an engaging smile as the delegates shouted him down.

The reply to the discussion was given by Nutting, the Minister of State for Foreign Affairs, who read a lot of platitudes from a typescript, to the effect that if the Security Council did not arrive at a solution the Government would then have to consider what they would do—a point that one would suppose ought to have been engaging their attention already.

October 14th
Motored with Nancy to Cramond to attend a service in the church in celebration of the tercentenary of the existing building; we had had an invitation from the Kirk Session to attend, and I was intending to leave the car at the back of the manse. But at Cramond we found parked cars stretching right down the road, and a posse of policemen, one of whom guarding the manse gate resolutely refused to let me in unless I was an elder or a minister. I argued good-humouredly with him, disputing whether he had any right to keep me out: but he took up a dogmatic attitude, standing in the entrance and barring my way with his hand. We were holding up other cars behind, and two other young policemen arrived and said, 'Oh, well, obstruction!'—producing a notebook in a threatening manner. When I had searched in my pockets and found the letter from the Kirk Session they put the notebook away and became more civil. But they said I should have to convince the first policeman—now further back up the road. So I gave in and motored on down the line of cars until a space was reached, in Cramond village. We were in plenty of time, and enjoyed the walk up in lovely morning sunshine—I had argued the matter more for the fun of the thing than anything else. The church is vacant through Mr Small's election to St Cuthbert's, but he came back today to preach the sermon: on Revelation 3,8, and probably the finest sermon I have ever heard. He brought in everything, all the litle episodes in the history of the church from the pre-1656 ministry of Rev. William Dalgleish to my father's 'inspired' restoration of it in 1911, working everything into his theme, and on to an eloquent, inspiring climax. Not a word or sentence was out of place, and there was not a word or sentence that I should have desired to be altered—all with the appearance of effortless ease which must, I think, be something of an illusion. I could have listened to him for very much longer. They have a good organist just now, and the whole service was impressive. The Lord Provost read the first lesson, without making any serious mistake, and Lord Rosebery read the second in a

pleasant, gentlemanly way. The service was conducted by the Moderator of the Presbytery, Rev. Alexander Reid of South Morningside, who seemed a nice old gentleman. It was still lovely sunshine when we came out. We took a stroll round by the ferry until the crowd of cars abated. Cramond was looking its best, and we enjoyed our morning there.

October 16th

The pneumoconiosis proof: we started on the evidence for the defenders. I always feel apprehensive at this point, wondering whether I know enough about the case to be able to cross-examine, but when I got started on my cross-examination of the first witness I thoroughly enjoyed it.

October 31st

Final meeting of the Commission. Cairns had suggested we might meet first for lunch: and we lunched at the Chiltern—nine of us including Cairns. I had assumed that we were there as his guests, but when the meal was over Plant asked, 'Are you our host on this occasion?'—to which Cairns rather grudgingly replied, 'Well, I'm quite willing to be if you like.' Several people of course said 'Oh, no', and Cairns at once remarked, 'Very well then, you owe me thirteen shillings and fourpence each.' Before I left, I said I was glad to hear he was going back to the Bar, as it seemed obvious there was nothing worthwhile to be done here. 'Yes', he said, 'I thought it was to be a first-class job, but it's turned out to be a second-class one.' In a talk earlier with Miss Stewart, the chairman's secretary, a kindly, efficient lady who has also looked after my needs when I have been in the building, I had been astonished that she did now know even yet whether she was to be kept on. No one, she said, was told anything. Ben confirmed this when I had a talk with him, and said that though things would probably be better now he did not expect the staff would ever really settle down. After what had happened, they would never trust the Government again. He agreed that there had been no reason for the secrecy. That was always a Government department's way: the reason for it was simply cowardice. Of the old Commission members, Allen, Davidson, Hill, Birch and Barnes are being kept on, and there are to be new members. I think Gallie is probably the only one who is seriously distressed by having to go: he had made the Commission office very much his second home, and apparently expected to be allowed to stay until his contract, like mine, expired at the end of 1957. I shall certainly miss the trips to London, but I have had a pretty good innings—extremely profitable since I became a panel chairman—and I have no cause to complain.

November 1st
The morning papers were all about the extraordinary war with Egypt into which the Government has plunged amid the condemnation of practically the whole world.

November 3rd
On television tonight the Prime Minister spoke for a quarter of an hour, defending his invasion of Egypt. He spoke well: and it was terrifying to see how some judicious selection, with barely perceptible distortion of the facts, could turn an act of lunacy into the semblance of something completely reasonable. The tired, pathetic way in which he spoke made it all the more impressive: and I went to bed rather worried about the tremendous power which control of radio and television can give if perverted to the wrong purpose.

November 4th
Gaitskell on television in reply to the Prime Minister. He treated the subject seriously, and made an excellent speech, effectively answering the Prime Minister's points and concluding with an appeal to the Conservatives to get a new Government—to which he pledged support provided that it would end hostilities and carry out the recommendations of the United Nations. There had been no word last night of any reply to Eden, and even when it was announced today that Gaitskell was to speak I was not sure that he was the man for the job. But I felt much happier after hearing him tonight: I think he redressed the balance in just the way it needed.

November 5th
Panorama had interesting reports on the Suez and Hungarian crises, and the US presidential election. President Eisenhower has spoken out strongly about the war in Egypt, and if I were an American I think I should have been tempted to switch my vote to him from Adlai Stevenson, whose vague temporisings have not, I think, either added to his stature or improved his prospects of election. Eisenhower's speeches on the wireless have been forthright, vigorous

pronouncements, temperately but very positively phrased.

November 6th
At 6 o' clock an announcement that at long last Eden had consented to order a cease-fire in Egypt.

November 7th
Selwyn Lloyd gave a party political broadcast on Suez: a piece of special pleading which would not, I think, influence anyone who was not already converted to his way of thinking.

November 11th
Motored with Nancy and the children to Cranston for wood. In the 'avenue' there always seem to be some branches to be got, and we were able to collect a good load. The Government's escapade in Egypt has led to the blocking of the Suez Canal and the cutting of an oil pipe line in Syria, with the consequent threat of petrol rationing: so we were anxious to get in a supply of wood while it was still possible.

November 13th
A divorce proof before Migdale, *Morrison v. Morrison*. The pursuer is seeking divorce on the ground of cruelty, and the husband, though denying any cruelty, is very anxious to be divorced, but does not want to prejudice his claim to the custody of the 8-year-old child. So I am in the delicate position of desiring to lose on the merits but toning down the allegations of cruelty sufficiently to enable custody to be awarded to the defender. Before any other judge I think we might be in danger of winning the whole case, for the pursuer's story seemed to me to be a mass of exaggerations and inaccuracies. But Migdale is always ready to accept any cock-and-bull story.

November 16th
I had been anxiously awaiting the result of yesterday's by-election at Chester, to see how the country had reacted to Eden's sheep in wolf's clothing. The result was reassuring: nothing spectacular, the Government held the seat comfortably, but the percentage swing to Labour was sufficient to ensure, if repeated generally throughout the country, that the Government would be decisively defeated.

Elizabeth asked me if Hungary was a country, and how it was getting on. 'It's not winning, is it?' she asked. Having studied reports of concessions that the Hungarian rebels and non–cooperators had succeeded in securing from the Russians, I replied that I was not so sure about that. 'But it's not winning the fight', Elizabeth said, ' 'Cos people are fledding, Miss Clark-Wilson said, to escape'.

Sadlers Wells Theatre Ballet at the Kings—big crowds gathering in the streets to see the ceremonial passing of Edinburgh's last tram-car. The ballet started off with *Les Patineurs*, which is always delightful. The main item, *Giselle*, is a melodramatic, old fashioned ballet, and Sara Neil had such a peculiar appearance that it was impossible to associate her with any kind of romance.

November 23rd
To the City Chambers for petrol rationing book. Calculation by cu-bic capacity meant that I got even less than the horse-power of the car warranted: only 7½ gallons per month.

December 2nd
Finished reading *Return Passage*, the autobiography of Violet R. Markham. She is what Barbara Pym would call an 'excellent woman': well-meaning, right-thinking, public-spirited, and devoid of any im-agination or originality of mind. The chapters about a Victorian childhood were interesting, but the rest was commonplace, descend-ing to a lyrical chapter about the author's dogs.

December 4th
Motored to Parliament House by London Street, with idea of getting petrol at the garage there where I sometimes deal, but found a notice outside: 'No petrol today.'

December 5th
Richard was contemptuous of a Government decision he heard over the wireless, to 'ask the House for a vote of confidence in their Suez policy.' 'It's silly to ask the house', he said, 'isn't it? Because a house can't answer back'. When I told this to Lord Guthrie later, he said there was a lot to be said for Richard's point of view—you would get a better answer from bricks and mortar than from the House of Commons as at present composed. Guthrie was despondent about the situation, and thought the most charitable thing one could say about the Government was that they were all insane. The price of petrol has gone up by one shilling and fivepence, the Chancellor

having last night announced an increase of a shilling in the petrol tax: and I had no difficulty in getting two gallons at Forrest's garage.

December 6th

Morrison v. Morrison. I finished the evidence for the husband, and Kissen addressed Migdale for most of the day. His carefully prepared argument was wasted on Migdale, and when I started my reply it seemed to me that I was making more headway than my opponent had. But Migdale is so pleasant to everybody that it is difficult to tell.

December 7th

The final day of *Morrison v. Morrison.* I kept my speech short, and it seemed to me that in the crucial matter of the custody of the child Migdale was in my favour. Provided he remembers, when he comes to give judgement, what his view of the matter was at the end of the proof, I think we should get what we have been aiming for.

December 9th

A television panel answering questions put by sixth-form school-children: Mrs Mary Stokes, Father Trevor Huddleston, and a hearty young Church of England clergyman. For all practical purposes it was simply Father Huddleston, saying exactly what he thought, and reducing the unfortunate clergyman to utter insignificance. His well-intentioned wafflings were swept aside by the forceful single-mindedness with which Father Huddleston expressed his very definite views—an extraordinary display of sheer personality. A programme lasting only 25 minutes seemed absurdly inadequate.

From the Master of University College:
University College Oxford   10th December, 1956.
Dear Stott,
Thank you so much for your card. I am delighted that you enjoyed the broadcast, especially as you are living north of the Tweed. My unfortunate remark that the English tolerate the Scots seems to have given great offence to some of the more serious Nationalists. I received eleven letters in which it was pointed out that it is the Scots that tolerate the English. I shall never again make even the mildest joke on this subject.

I greatly regret that we are no longer meeting at the Monopolies Commission.

With all best wishes for 1957.
Yours sincerely,
Arthur Goodhart.

December 11th

A proof before Cameron: *O'Donnell v. John Young and Co.* The pursuer was employed as a labourer in the construction of Glendevon reservoir, and was working in a trench. Some big circular skips were being transferred by crane from beside the trench to another point further down. One skip had been set down on uneven ground above the trench. A second one, attached to the fall of the crane, swung round into contact with the first skip, which rolled down into the trench, crushing the pursuer and breaking three transverse processes of his spine. The action had been raised, based on the crane driver's negligence, against his employers. The crane had been let out on hire by them to the contractors engaged in the construction of the reservoir, and it was maintained in the defences that the crane driver was their servant at the time when the accident happened: so the contractors were brought in as second defenders. It did not matter to the pursuer which of them was liable, and it might have been thought that all the pursuer's counsel would have to do was to sit back and let the two defenders fight it out. The first defenders had however averred that one of the contractor's employees, named Gallacher, had been assisting, and as the second skip was being guided by Gallacher it came into contact with the other skip. If this was what had happened, the obvious conclusion would be that Gallacher was at fault, in which event the second defenders would be liable. But for some unknown reason whoever had drawn the case for the pursuer had made no case of fault against Gallacher, so that instead of having an easy case, with nothing to choose so far as I was concerned between the two possibilities, I was committed to exonerating Gallacher and establishing that it was the crane-man's action that had knocked the skip into the trench. Gallacher said this, and denied he had touched the skip, and another witness agreed. But that was all the evidence we had, and as the pursuer, Gallacher and this third witness all came from a little island off the coast of County Donegal—where they spend the first half of every year, coming to Scotland to work only between June and September—their evidence was open to some possibility of suspicion. The crane driver gave evidence for the first defenders, along the lines of their averment: and it seemed to me that we might easily fail to establish fault against the crane driver and so through an unfortunate error in pleading lose the case altogether. There may be some prejudice against the pursuer owing to the fact that, through some muddle on the part of a firm of solicitors in Alloa, he took four years to raise his action: and though only 31 has not done a stroke of work since the accident, maintaining that he has been totally unfit. We had medical evidence which supported him to some extent: and Cameron seemed quite well disposed towards him—rather amused by the account of how he had been spending his prolonged leisure on a croft on Aranmore, with one cow, some poultry, and a lady whom he described as his aunt, though the local doctor thought she was his mother. The doctor had been brought all the way from Aranmore to give evidence, and gave a graphic picture of life on the island, which he described as remote and the kind of place where no one would want to stay: Aranmore had had 40 doctors, he said, in the last 60 years.

December 12th

When the last witness was in the box, Cameron enquired how long the speeches would take, and on my replying that I should be quite brief remarked, 'You always are, Mr Stott, and no less effective on that account'. Actually I did not get started until well on in the afternoon, and it was not much before 3.30 when I sat down. My part in the proof was now at an end, in good time for me to be able to start my other proof tomorrow—leaving the defenders' counsel to argue the question of *pro hac vice* employment, with copious citation of authorities.

December 13th

Proof: *McCabe v. Alder and Mackay*. The case had been that slipperi-ness of the floor had arisen out of oil from a machine, but at the last moment the pursuer discovered that the accident had happened at a place where there was no oil on the floor. A belated attempt to amend and alter the complaint to smoothness of the dry concrete floor was made on Tuesday but was unsuccessful, so we were faced with the difficult task of fighting the case on a Record which really has no basis in fact. The pursuer, though stupid, is a nice old fellow, obvi-ously honest: and when asked why he had intimated a claim against his employers five years after the accident gave the unanswerable reply, 'Public opinion'.

Nancy went out in the evening to the Geographical Society: and after doing a little work on the case I settled down to supper and to *Animal Vegetable and Mineral* on the television. A team of three experts were shown a tiny detail from some painting, and had to identify the painting. Mr Michael Ayrton and Sir Gerald Kelly were pretty good at it, but the third expert, Professor Ellis Waterhouse, was magnificent, knowing in every case not only the picture but when it was painted, its history and characteristics, and in what part of the picture the detail appeared. It was a delight to watch and listen to three sensible, intelligent people who know as much about their subject as those three.

December 14th

A Faculty meeting: a committee investigating the future of the Juridical Library asked the Faculty to say that the library should not be transferred to the Laigh Parliament Hall, the basement of Parliament House most of which has become vacant by removal of the National Library to George IV Bridge. It seemed unfortunate that this space should go to waste, and I seconded Ross McLean's motion to remit back to the committee so that they could put alternative plans before us.

Muir Society: a talk by George Thomson of Green's on 'Problems of a Law Publisher'. He knew what he was talking about, and dealt with the subject factually and concisely. With law books costing about £4 a page for printing alone, it seemed clear that there was not much future in books having such a limited market as that open to Scottish legal text books. A sale of about one thousand copies was, he said, as much as could be hoped for, and an English law publisher would not look at a book which would sell only that number.

December 15th

Nancy said Richard had been talking to her about what 'manger' meant in the carol 'Away in a manger'. He had a good idea of what it was, but thought it was something down on the floor. 'The cows don't have it high up, do they?' he asked: and having got Nancy to confirm that cows were the same as cattle added that they could not have it high up, because it said in the carol, 'The cattle are lowing'.

December 16th

I have had an invitation to the Monopolies Commission staff Christmas party, and typed out a reply:

A remarkable honour for me
That you've asked me—so kindly—to tea.
But you may not have heard
What a change has occurred
And the membership's fallen to three.

When you were no more than a boy,
In the days of Dame Alix Kilroy,
The benevolent sway
Of the worthy A.K.
Made Commissioners chortle with joy.

But other and soberer views
Came in with the advent of Hughes—
A Commission and staff
Who were not known to laugh
And could seldom be said to amuse.

Lamentation and weeping were there
When, bowed down by a burden of care,
The members with Pimlott
Were really a grim lot
And often gave way to despair.

And now the last partings are said,
And the last rose of summer has fled:
And Gilbert's soft tone
Roused hardly a groan
As it sounds through the halls of the dead—

Where, free from the ignorant sally
Of a Gifford, a Stott, or a Gallie,
You may slumber in peace
Until Thorneycrofts cease
And a   shall sound a reveille.

I added two footnotes, one attached to the word 'three': 'I believe the number is rather higher, but "three" was necessary on account of the rhyme', the other attached to the blank in the last line: 'The reader may fill in any name according to his political predilections, from

Aneurin Bevan to Selwyn Lloyd—the writer is quite impartial'.

December 18th
With the drop in traffic since the petrol rationing began yesterday, the roads seemed a good deal clearer.

December 31st
Mr Blair and Kate for Bridge. It was getting on for 11.30 when they left, and we went to bed and listened to the wireless, with a short religious service before Big Ben chimed the New Year.

1957

In 1957 a successful appearance in the House of Lords early in the year consolidated my position as the leading authority on pneumoconiosis. In politics, Sir Anthony Eden did not long survive the Suez debacle: an early opportunity was taken to announce that on grounds of ill-health he was to retire forthwith. The Queen, faced with a choice of two possible Prime Ministers, preferred Mr Macmillan to Mr Butler. Panic measures by the Chancellor of the Exchequer later in the year sent interest charges soaring, with resulting chaos in the finances of local authorities, who could not afford to borrow at the rates now prevalent. The Suez Canal, when once it had been cleared, continued to function under its Egyptian masters as it had when controlled by the canal company: an interesting illustration of the theory that there is seldom any justification for war, since when the purpose of the war is not fulfilled it does not make the slightest difference.

January 9th

A surprise announcement in the middle of the television News that the Prime Minister had just tendered his resignation to the Queen.

January 10th

Considerable speculation throughout the day as to who would be Prime Minister. I thought it would be impossible for the Queen to pass over Butler, who was Acting Prime Minister while Eden was in Jamaica, but when I bought a paper while waiting for the bus home I found she had chosen Macmillan, no doubt on the advice of Lord Salisbury and Winston Churchill, both of whom had been at Buckingham Palace. The choice is a good one, and the Conservatives have the Queen to thank for saving them from disaster, at any rate for the time being. With Butler as Eden's successor, the country would soon have been in chaos: and despite his efforts to be all things to all men I have never accepted the view of Butler as a progressive.

January 13th
After Elizabeth was in bed, I read her the whole book of Jonah. When read straight on, in normal tones of voice, it made a very good story, with plenty of humour and entertainment value.

January 17th
In *O'Donnell v. John Young*, Cameron had found for the pursuer against both defenders and awarded £850.

January 23rd
On coming out of court I could see no sign in my box of jury trial papers that had been there at mid-day. The Glasgow solicitors, Dallas and Macmillan, had apparently phoned through to say that they would not have me on any account, and Ross McLean had been taken in instead. This was surprising, as I had actually had a letter of instruction from the Edinburgh solicitors. C.H. Johnston, the junior counsel in the case, was indignant about what had happened, but evidently nothing could be done about it. 'I suppose it's some political prejudice', Scotland said. The only compensation was that I would have the evening free, instead of preparing a new case.

January 30th
Garrick Theatre: *La Plume de Ma Tante*, a French revue by a French company, in English—very entertaining. The outstanding feature was the girls, scantily but attractively clothed in a variety of colourful costumes. I have never seen so fine a collection of girls.

> From Elizabeth Stott:
> Edinburgh portebellow
> Dear daddy
> I Do hope your doing well in the house of Lords, I do mervell you.
>   Ps Iv had ear ack and so has RICHARD
>   Love from as both.

January 31st
Our case of *Quinn v. Cameron and Roberton* was to come on 'not before eleven'. It came on very shortly after, and with an interval for lunch I spoke until four. I thoroughly enjoyed myself. They were a bit sceptical when I was explaining the First Division's ground of

judgement about causation, but when I had read them some of the evidence and part of Clyde's judgement I thought they had begun to realise that I had not misrepresented him and to appreciate what a travesty of the evidence his judgement was. I made no comment, nor did they: but the atmosphere seemed favourable. A knowledgeable, scrupulously fair court: Simmonds in the chair, Cohen, Oaksey, Morton and Keith. I left my bag in the robing room with coat, vest and gown: a gown which the attendant had not allowed me to wear. Obviously horrified to find on unpacking my bag that I had brought a stuff gown, he had insisted on lending me a silk one.

February 4th
I have now got my name on a peg in the Lords' robing room: I do not know what the criterion is for this, but several Scottish counsel seem to have a peg.

February 5th
Shearer spoke most of the day. Though all of course extremely courteous, they pressed him hard on the carborundum point, on which at one stage he was practically brought to a standstill. On the main point, causation, he seemed to be making more impression than the point deserved. Only forty minutes remained when I was called on to reply: and I talked out the time, on common law and the procedural position, leaving causation for tomorrow when everyone was likely to be in a more receptive mood.

February 6th
Shearer caused an unpleasant scene in the corridor outside the committee room before the case was called, evidently considering that I had misrepresented what had happened in the First Division. I did not take this very seriously, and proceeded, with gusto and considerable success, to demolish some of the arguments he had addressed to the House yesterday. Although the Lords had been quite courteous to him, it had been obvious that his arguments were not meeting with the same reception as mine, with the result that he was in a bad temper, and sat beside me muttering under his breath, while I, with calculated politeness and every expression of respect, demonstrated step by step how wrong he had been. His part in the discussion being over, he had obtained the leave of the House to withdraw at eleven: and he stalked out at that hour, leaving the atmosphere that much the

pleasanter. The extremely courteous way in which one is treated in
the Lords was illustrated by a remark of Morton's in putting to me a
point that he thought might be in my favour—saying that the fact
that I had not myself advanced the point made him suspect that it
might be unsound. Though Simmonds seemed a little doubtful about
possible consequences of a decision in my favour, there was every
indication that the Court as a whole was favourably disposed.

We went straight on to the next case, *Nicholson v. Atlas Foundry*.
As the pursuers, for whom I appeared, were appellants here also, I
was at once on my feet again, and spoke for the rest of the day. The
pursuers are the widow and children of a steel dresser who contracted
pneumoconiosis, and died as a result. Blades found that the ventilation was faulty, and also that swing frame grinders had been operated
without exhaust appliances, rejecting the argument that swing frame
grinders were 'portable' grinding machines which fell within a certificate of exemptions granted by the Chief Inspector of Factories.
The First Division reversed him and found for the defenders. They
had found it impossible to reject his decision, on the evidence, that
the ventilation was sub-standard, but held that the pursuers had not
proved that improved ventilation would have made any significant
difference as regards removal of dangerous dust, and further held
that the grinders were portable. The evidence is confused and scanty,
but it does not seem unreasonable to infer that the bad ventilation
had something to do with the presence of dust, and the points taken
by the judges of the First Division are niggling and one-sided. I
thought it best, now that my hearers knew what kind of judges they
were dealing with, to read the Opinions right away.

I had arranged to call for John Taylor at his office, and we motored in his car to the Houses of Parliament. Willis got us tickets for
the Special Gallery. The House was debating the Third Reading of
the Bill that abolishes hanging except for a few categories of murder.
The only speaker who appeared to be all out for hanging was a
woman, Mrs McLaughlin from Northern Ireland. The outstanding
speech came from Hale, winding up for abolition: a remarkable speech,
full of wit and sparkle, and at the same time rising to a great degree
of emotional intensity. I found it extremely moving.

February 7th
Everything seemed to be going well today. There was an atmosphere
of mutual confidence between counsel and the members of the court

which is really, before a good court, the greatest joy of an advocate's work, and they were asking me all kinds of questions about foundry processes and pneumoconiosis, quite apart from what appeared in the evidence, showing that they were relying on me to give them reasonable, honest answers and not put anything unfairly. On portability they seemed to be much in my favour. Keith remarked that in a sense every wireless set was portable, but a set was not generally regarded as portable unless you could readily pick it up and take it about with you, to which I replied that that was so—every machine could be described as portable provided that you had a crane or an elephant handy. I even thought I might venture on a joke at the expense of the First Division, when Cohen put a question about Carmont's view—Carmont having said that at first he had thought that the grinder was not portable but had been persuaded that it was. Blades, in finding that the grinder was not portable, had proceeded on evidence by Stabler which he had specifically accepted: and Clyde in reversing him had made no reference to the evidence at all, saying merely that he was satisfied that the machine was portable. Accordingly, in reply to Cohen's question, I remarked that what Lord Carmont had really done was to prefer Lord Clyde to Mr Stabler. Cohen was delighted: and even Simmonds, though he raised his eyebrows a little, had a flicker of a smile on his face. I could not have got away with a joke of this kind in the House of Lords unless I had been satisfied that their respect for the First Division had been pretty definitely forfeited in the course of the week's debate.

Alastair and I lunched at the same table as our opponents, Ian Fraser and Anderson, and Fraser recalled an anecdote about Lord Mackay, who soon after his wife's death had received an invitation for himself and her to some official function. He replied that he was sorry it would be impracticable for him to bring his wife, as she was dead.

When the day's work was over, I felt rather tired, and turned into the Academy cinema, where I spent two restful hours. After a Hungarian film, *Hortobagy*, which was of no particular interest but restful to watch—nothing much happened at all—I had Réné Clair's *Les Grands Manoeuvres*, a light-hearted little story of a young officer who sets out, for a wager, to win a lady's love before his regiment goes off for summer manoeuvres, and loses his heart to the lady in the process. One watched the various misunderstandings in happy confidence that all will come right in the end. But this is a French film, not an

American one, and all that happens in the end is that the officer goes off with his regiment, leaving his lady to be forgotten and to forget.

February 8th

An Opinion to work on. Maclean told me it was for London correspondents, and when they had written London to say they had sent the Memorial to senior counsel and his Opinion might be delayed because he was appearing in the House of Lords they had a worried letter back from the correspondents to the effect that, although of course they wanted the best Opinion available, they did not know whether their client could afford to take the Opinion of counsel of the standing of the one to whom the Memorial had been sent.

February 11th

The hearing finished: and Simmonds intimated that they would take time to consider. I have found the two appeals most enjoyable. Some time before I was due to come south I felt rather apprehensive, never before having been in the position of opening a case in the Lords and not being sure what was the proper way to do it in cases involving a great deal of evidence. But as the time came nearer, and I made up my mind how I was going to treat the case, I began to look forward to it, and this was justified by the event. To appear before a court so receptive and courteous, though exhausting at times, is pleasurable and rewarding. Oaksey was the weak member of the team, often missing the point and more often losing the place, but as he was amiable, and more or less in my favour, I did not find his presence any disadvantage. Keith has a commonsense outlook which is useful, though he has not the intellectual brilliance of his three other colleagues.

On the train, I shared a table with an agreeable young lady going home to Tyneside after visiting her daughter at school in the south of England. I treated her to tea and dinner, and got some return in the form of a pound of butter, which she must have left in a paper bag under the seat when she got out at Newcastle—I did not notice it until the train was almost at Edinburgh.

Finished reading *The Brabazon Story*, by Lord Brabazon of Tara, reminiscences of a shrewd, likeable man of wide interests and with a keen appreciation of his deficiencies and capabilities. His commonsense is refreshing in a politician, but does not make a particularly interesting autobiography.

February 13th

I had a sore eye and felt out of sorts. It is curious that when I have been so busy I have enjoyed excellent health, and came to feel the effect of my exertions only this evening, when I had nothing to do.

February 19th

Migdale in *Morrison v. Morrison* granted decree of divorce in both actions, and custody of the younger child to my client: exactly what we were aiming at.

February 22nd

Television has started a good programme of news and topical items to fill the time between 6 and 6.45 which previously was 'truce' time free from television, for the purpose of letting children get off to bed.

February 24th

Finished reading *Sunset and Evening Star*, by Sean O'Casey. The author does nothing by halves, especially his likes and dislikes. Chesterton comes in for a good measure of abuse, with any literary critic who has attempted any criticism of the author or his work: but the book is at its best when praising Hugh MacDiarmid. When he goes on to deal with his terrifying experiences in having to take shelter from air raids at his house at Totnes, his exaggerated, emotional outlook just seems silly: and a good deal of the book is of this hysterical character.

February 28th

A jury trial before Migdale. The pursuer, then a girl of 16, was being brought home from the potato fields in a van belonging to her employers. She says the van stopped near where she was to get off. As she was doing so, the van moved forward and she was thrown into the road. The defenders say the accident happened when the van slowed down because of cyclists in front, and that the pursuer had been skylarking with one of the lads in the back of the van—he took hold of the strap of her handbag, and when he let go she fell backwards. The pursuer's injuries led to an epileptic condition. However, she has since the accident been able to get married and have a baby, and she looked a plump, healthy girl. The case seemed to be going satisfactorily, but then we put in a youth who had come up overnight on the train from Bristol, and in the middle of being cross-examined he suddenly shouted out that he was tired of it and wanted to go home. The next witness, the pursuer's sister, collapsed altogether under cross-examination and had to be helped out of court. The defenders produced an independent witness who had been given a lift in the van: and unfortunately it came out in the course of his evidence that the pursuer had been to see him and asked him to give evidence on her behalf. The pursuer, both at the consultation and in the witness box, had pretended that she had no idea who the man was who had been given a lift, a view that was untenable when she had been to see him. So, though there was something fishy about the defender's case as well as ours, I was not hopeful about the case when we rose.

March 1st

I made quite a good speech, but Ross McLean's was better: and it was no surprise when the jury returned a unanimous verdict for the defenders. They cannot have been out for more than ten minutes.

March 14th

The Lords were giving judgement today in *Quinn* and *Nicholson*. They reversed the First Division and allowed the appeals in both cases.

March 15th

Made a point of speaking to the Lord President, telling him that the Lords did not agree with him about carborundum. Mentioned the result to Kissen—his comment being 'Shearer will have a relapse'.

March 17th

Motored to Ruskin House for North Edinburgh selection conference. I drew up at a point in the street where I thought Ruskin House was, opposite a door with a big nameplate: but on getting out found that the nameplate read 'Old Contemptibles Association', and realised I was in the wrong street. This mistake was soon rectified. Two other nominees: Ian Hamilton, the young Scottish Nationalist advocate who stole the Stone of Destiny from Westminster Abbey, and Alex Reid, a Post Office worker. As we were taken in alphabetical order, I came last, and occupied myself in working on the notes of evidence in the Harrower divorce case. We were each given ten minutes to speak, and ten minutes for questions. The man who had come up for us patted my back as we were going down the stair, which I took as indication that I had won. Shaw told me with characteristic candour that if he had not known us both beforehand, and had been going on the way we had acquitted ourselves at question time, he would have voted for Reid.

March 21st

The hearing in the Harrower case: Migdale apparently doubtful whether he could find against me on cruelty. There seems quite a danger that I shall win on the merits, and my client not be divorced as he wants.

From Mr William Muir:
Untried Prisoner's Letter...
Register number 629   Name William Muir
The Prisoner's writing to be on *the blue lines only.*
H.M. Prison, Edinburgh   30.3.1957.
Dear Sir
Will you please appear at Edin Sherriff Court next Friday morning to apply for bail. If case is not dealt with if you are unable will you advise some other regardless to the amount of Fee required I will pay
        Yours faithfully

April 1st

After buying myself a pair of nineteen shillings and elevenpence flannel trousers at Parkers', I motored home, and finished reading *The Woman in the Case*, by Edgar Lustgarten, an account of four well-known murder trials. There is no one to match the author at this kind of thing: and this book for the first time gave me a clear picture of such familiar cases as Oscar Slater's and Madeleine Smith's. I had tended to assume that Slater, though convicted on a verdict improperly obtained, had probably been guilty: the book makes it clear that there was no evidence against him at all, and that the case was a frame-up on the part of the Glasgow police.

A letter this morning from William Muir, who is back in Saughton Prison. I took the letter up to Bowen, who phoned the Procurator Fiscal—remarking that he had happened to see Muir the other morning in George Street and had at once said to himself that some jeweller was about to be defrauded. That, it turned out, was what had happened. Muir had gone to a jeweller's in George Street and asked to see some watches for a niece that was to be married. He had been given three on approval, and shortly afterwards brought them back saying that none was suitable. Ultimately he was persuaded to buy a different watch, for which he paid three pounds and ten shillings. He then asked to see some rings, and took them away on approval. Shortly afterwards he brought them back, saying they were not suitable, and asked to see some better ones. They gave him four rings, valued at £1,050. He brought them back too, saying he could not decide on any of them, but eventually said he would buy all four as an investment, but would not be able to pay for them until 20th April. They said that would be quite all right, and gave him the rings away with him. Next day he pawned them in Stockbridge for £160. The police got on to him through the pawnbroker, and arrested him. He maintains there is no fraud, as he is not due anybody anything until 20th April.

April 4th
Finished reading *Scales of Justice*, by Ngaio Marsh, a good murder story, with excellent characterisation, which held my attention—even if on reflection one may have some doubts as to whether murder could be committed with the weapon in question.

April 6th
Oatridge point-to-point. Buses were being run, at a return fare of three shillings, an improvement on the car parking charge of thirty shillings. I knew nothing about any of the horses, not even their names, and hearing someone asking for a bet on No 6 I followed this example. As I did not know which of the horses in the race was mine, this was not much fun, so I bought a race card and in the second race followed the fortunes of Good Scout. In the last race my choice was Irresponsive—yellow, red cap—and as the horses came round for the second and last time to the final jump I observed with some excitement that only two were left, and on one of them the rider had a yellow shirt and a red cap. They crossed the fence neck and neck, but I was pretty sure that in the final spurt Irresponsive got ahead and passed the winning post first. So I hurried up to the tote and was paid out seven shillings and threepence.

April 8th
Finished reading *A Prospect of Britain*, by Andrew Young, in which

the author quite at random wanders in print about Scotland and England, discoursing in his usual erudite but friendly style of places, people and things—all written with judgement and good sense. A good *Panorama* programme with Duncan Sandys, the Minister of Defence, was followed by Victor Sylvester demonstrating Rock 'n Roll in immaculate evening dress and thereby turning it into a very attractive dance form.

April 10th
A pleasant surprise: a warrant for repayment of income tax to the amount of £236. I have no idea how these payments are calculated.

April 12th
Scottish Labour Party conference at Dunoon. I had said to Nancy that we could go if she wanted, and this week she suddenly decided she would. At Gourock we fixed on the Ashton Hotel. Its frontage on the street was not impressive, but on the other side it was directly on the sea, and we were shown into a lovely room, just above the water, with an enormous bay window giving a magnificent view of the Clyde and the mountains. We had a walk round the pier, looking at two ships moored there and a forlorn little group of foreigners sitting on a small pile of luggage and trying to shelter from the wind and threatening rain. It was impossible to imagine what they were waiting for, or why they should not wait under cover in the station just behind. Back to the hotel for high tea: a table in the window with a gorgeous view over the sea, and a school of porpoises gambolling not far out. Nancy then put Richard to bed—the manageress was willing to keep an eye on him—and we motored to Greenock to see *Ill Met by Moonlight* at one of the cinemas. It was not a success. In a much more interesting supporting film, *Once upon a Time*, all the parts of a melodramatic and rather terrifying fairy story are played by live animals. A duckling is the hero of the story, and the animals included also a delightful little fluffy Persian cat.

April 13th
We took the steamer to Dunoon, where I went to the conference. Mackintosh, the prospective candidate for Pentlands division, impressed me as a sensible and personable young man. I met Mrs Willis, who said she thought she had been responsible for suggesting to Broughton Ward that I should be asked to the selection conference.

She said her intention had not been to have me adopted for North Edinburgh, but simply to let it be known that I was in the running for some better constituency. I replied that North Edinburgh was good enough for me. On the boat back to Dunoon I encountered Ross, the MP for Kilmarnock, and his wife. He had made a good speech in giving the report of the parliamentary Labour group, and in conversation with them on the voyage I thought them a pleasant, sensible couple. The hotel was having a 'supper dance', according to its Saturday night custom. Before I went to bed, I looked into the dining room, and found four or five couples dancing a St Bernard's waltz, including the girl from the kitchen in her white apron. No sound of music penetrated upstairs: only the occasional sound of waves below the window when a passing ship made a wash against the shore.

April 14th
A pleasant sail brought us to Dunoon shortly after eleven. A debate on Shaw's pet subject of Scottish devolution had been going on for some time. The Scottish Executive had with unusual temerity submitted a report concluding baldly, and without anything substantial in the way of argument or evidence, that a separate Parliament for Scotland was impracticable. Though no enthusiast for Scottish devolution, I had no difficulty in voting for remitting back the Executive's report—which was obviously what my constituency party wanted, and in view of the unsatisfactory character of the report seemed reasonable. It was carried against the Executive by a big majority.

April 15th
Home by 4.30, after a pleasant holiday. I enjoyed being at a Labour conference again after so many years: as Shaw remarked, it was a friendly gathering, and having no responsibilities and no duties to perform I was able to come and go as I pleased, free of all worries. *Jesus of Nazareth* on children's television. This evening's instalment was excellently done, bringing out the real drama of the story and the humour of Jesus' teaching.

April 16th
On television tonight the second programme in a series entitled *Portraits of Power*. The first dealt with Hitler: a remarkable production, portraying by films and interviews the hold that Hitler had on great

masses of people—an extraordinary, fantastic, terrifying picture. To-night's programme, on Gandhi, was less dramatic but hardly less interesting. The highlight was the voice of Nehru, recorded as he broadcast in simple, unpretentious but very moving words his extempore tribute to Gandhi immediately after Gandhi's assassination.

April 17th
Finished reading *A Friend in Need*, by Elizabeth Coxhead. Though perhaps lacking the rapture of some of her other books, it is a kindly, readable story, and carried the reader contentedly along to a happy, sensible ending.

April 18th
Perth Hunt races. A profitable afternoon: my gains not only exceeded my losses but paid my admission fee of four shillings and one shilling outlay on a race card.

April 21st
Motored Mrs Braggins to church. It turned out to be a choral service, excerpts from Stainer's *Crucifixion*—by no means as bad as I had expected. While the choir sang, I occupied myself in reading St Mark's gospel. It makes fascinating reading, much more so than any commentary or most sermons.

April 29th
Tonight on television included a very odd interview with a young Cockney couple who had invited Spiritualists to come and rid them of a couple of ghosts who were troubling them in their bedroom. They appeared in a variety of forms: and although they had got the priest in and he had sprinkled holy water that had not done any good. They did not believe in Spiritualists: they had got them into the house simply to try and get rid of the ghosts. The woman was obviously terrified and at her wit's end. One of the ghosts had apparently agreed to go, but the other had not been contacted, and there was to be a second meeting. The woman said they had been told to keep the date secret.

May 6th
Glasgow High Court: *H.M. Advocate v. Graham and Sweeney*. We were appearing for Sweeney: Daiches and a young junior named

Davidson appeared for Graham. They were charged with the murder of a young man named Craney in a tenement at 430 Argyle Street. Craney was an acquaintance of a woman, Nancy Fletcher, who lived in that tenement, and he and his wife had spent the evening in the Douglas Arms with Nancy, her uncle and aunt, and another woman. About 10 they all came back to 430 Argyle Street, and as they reached the close Craney was accosted by a man who had been with him in the Forces in Korea, and who after a short conversation said to Craney, 'You've married a cow'. Craney not unnaturally took exception to this, and butted the man with his head. A short fight followed, in which the man lifted his hand and brought it down on Craney's head. It seems that he had some small weapon in his hand, for Craney was found to have a cut on his temple, which bled profusely. The other man had gone off: nobody knows who he was or what happened to him. Craney now became involved in some altercation with his wife and struck her in the face. She set off home: and he was next seen on the top flat, where he went into the house of a total stranger named Swandells and asked if he was Sergeant Black. He is said to have been quite peaceable here, but Swandells thought it prudent to say he was Sergeant Black, whereupon Craney shook hands with him and went with the Swandells family to a friend's house next door. On leaving here, Craney came downstairs and went into a room next door to the Fletchers', where he became involved with the occupant's brother, a man named Haig. There was some butting with the head, which opened up Craney's wound: but after he had it bathed he became quite friendly. Meanwhile my client, who lives on the top floor, had come home from the cinema with his co-accused William Graham and the latter's brother James. They had been to the Gaiety to see the *Gold Rush*. When the party had come in from the public house, Mrs Fletcher had had some words on the stair with Mrs James Graham, asking her what she was moving about for, always looking at people who had had a wee half. This was reported to James, and he went down to see Mrs Fletcher about it. Mr Fletcher persuaded him to leave the matter over until morning. He set off back to Sweeney's house, whence Sweeney's girl friend had been sent out for fish and chips. On the way up, he went into his own house on the middle floor to speak to his wife, so that Sweeney on going down to look for him missed him and instead encountered Craney, who he says accused him of being the soldier who had hit him with a bottle. Sweeney was in battledress, and this was no doubt a genuine mistake. Sweeney came back upstairs, told the Graham brothers that he had been 'claimed' for something he had not done, and asked them to go down and tell the man they had been with him all evening. They all trooped downstairs, and found Craney in Haig's house. An argument between him and Sweeney led to blows with the head, and William Graham and Sweeney then dragged Craney out of Haig's house and put him into the Fletchers'. There they say he picked up a chipping hammer. The Fletcher party deny that there was any chipping hammer in the house, and say that Craney was shouting that he had had enough. Anyhow William picked up a chair and crashed it over Craney's head. They then hauled Craney out to the landing—or, as they say, Craney followed them there continuing the fight. Somehow or other Craney's head seems to have struck against the stone floor. Sweeney gave him a couple of kicks, while Graham apparently told him to leave the man alone: and Mrs Graham having shouted that the police were coming they all went off, leaving Craney on the landing in a pool of blood. An old woman who lived in one of the other rooms had gone to a police box, but two policemen there gave her a ciga- rette and told her they were busy, and it was some time before any police arrived. Craney was taken to hospital but never recovered consciousness. An operation was performed, apparently with the object of relieving any pressure there might be on the brain, but he died the following night. A post mortem was carried out by Allison and Imrie, who have certified that death was due to sub-dural haemorrhage. It was obvious that Craney had been looking for trouble, and had got more than he bargained for: and in that state of affairs I did not see much likelihood of a murder verdict. The real issue seemed to be culpable homicide, and here it seemed that the Crown's difficulty would be to exclude Craney's earlier injury as the possible cause of death. It seemed possible that the sub-dural haemorrhage had been caused in the first fight, in the street, in which the accused were in no way concerned. The evidence on this point came out more favour- ably than I had expected: it turned out that on getting up to the Fletchers' Craney had collapsed in a dead faint for four or five min- utes. His wife however said that such black-outs were not uncommon with Craney. She herself fainted in the witness-box: but after a short adjournment she had revived and we were able to cross-examine her. She had been married only two days before, but—as we knew, though this did not come before the jury—had been living with him for some years and, as Mary Gough, had herself been sentenced by Lord

Carmont to four years penal servitude at the outset of the judicial drive against razor slashers some years ago. Most of today's witnesses did not implicate the accused at all, and their evidence should have gone through very quickly: but Daiches proceeded to cross-examine them at length, apparently with the object of showing that the sinister person in the Swandells' house might not have been Craney. It took me some little time to re-establish that he was—which seemed very much in the accused's favour as showing how curiously Craney was behaving before he ever met the accused.

May 7th

The evidence continued to go quite well. Haig, whom fortunately Daiches decided not to cross-examine, made it clear that Craney had struck the first blow in the fight with Sweeney. The old woman who had gone to the police box came into the witness-box shaking from head to foot, and at one point practically collapsed from sheer terror, saying Graham had threatened her that night that if she went for the police she would get the same. As she was obviously a very nervous person, I doubt if this was as bad as it might have seemed. She was able to finish her evidence with a policewoman holding her by the hand. At the end of the day there was a surprising development when Irvine, the surgeon who had carried out the operation, said sub-dural haemorrhage had exerted no pressure on the brain, and he was satisfied from the clinical symptoms that death was due to damage to the brain structure. This would have caused immediate unconsciousness, and he had no doubt that the fatal injuries had been inflicted in the final fracas, not in the earlier fight in the street.

May 8th

Irvine was cross-examined, and proved an excellent witness: courteous, knowledgeable and definite. I could not shake him on his main point, but he agreed that if sub-dural haemorrhage was the cause of death the fight in the street was of undoubted and critical relevance. This I thought was probably good enough, as whatever Allison and Imrie might say now their post-mortem report was obviously going to put them in a very awkward position. Allison started off in his usual pompous, know-all way. He seemed to assent to the view that on the information now available death had been caused by damage to the brain structure. He agreed with Skae that that meant that the fatal blow had been struck at the time the chair had been used. Daiches made nothing of him in cross-examination, treating him with great deference: but I, knowing his obstinacy and fatuousness, felt pretty sure he would deliver himself into my hands, and so he did. After a few innocuous questions about bloodstains, I asked whether when he made his post-mortem examination report he had had sufficient material to reach a conclusion as to the cause of death. I expected him to answer 'No', and I should then have got some fun out of asking him why in that event he had certified on soul and conscience that in his opinion death was due to sub-dural haemorrhage. But to my pleased surprise his answer, though in his usual longwinded and circumlocutionary style, was in effect 'Yes', and he continued to maintain that sub-dural haemorrhage was a cause of death. He tried to say 'potential cause', and when I knocked him off that tried 'contributory cause'—which would not do, since he had already said there had been no intracranial pressure, the only mechanism by which sub-dural haemorrhage could have caused death. So he floundered deeper into the mire, asserting that what he had to do was to attach a label to the death and state the facts—which of course brought the retort that according to his own evidence what he had stated was not fact but falsehood. In the end even his verbosity failed, and he was brought practically to a standstill. It was an easy cross-examination— so long as the initial mistake was unacknowledged, the cross-examiner's job was simple, and my cross-examination left the Crown medical evidence in confusion. Allison had provided Skae with a 1942 text book of brain inquiry and got Skae to put a passage to him: and at lunch time, looking through the book—which was written in almost unintelligible jargon—I found another passage which seemed to me to throw some doubt on Irvine's clinical symptoms. I finished the main part of my cross-examination by putting this passage to Allison and asking if he agreed: and he, now thoroughly demoralised, began to read aloud from another passage, at considerable length and carrying no meaning whatever. 'I don't want to interrupt', I said, 'but I didn't ask you to read the whole book'. At this Russell came in, saying it was useless to read long screeds which no one could follow and it would be much better if the witness would answer questions 'Yes' or 'No'. 'Yes', said Allison miserably, 'I understand': but before he had time to say more I said, 'Perhaps I needn't pursue the matter. I take it you would agree that you're not a brain specialist any more than Mr Irvine?' Allison fervently agreed, and we passed to one or two minor points about external injuries—which in his now chastened manner he agreed were superficial, and could have been caused in the first fight or by a fall. Imrie required different handling, and I was dismayed when Daiches proceeded to try to cross-examine him on the lines I had followed with Allison. There was a serious danger that Imrie, with his usual honesty and ability, might be able to clear the whole thing up: but luckily Daiches did not know enough about it to go very far with him, and I handled him delicately, putting a few questions of no particular significance. The case for the Crown came to an end about 5.20, and Russell asked Daiches if he had a short witness. Daiches explained apologetically that he had sent his witnesses away, whereupon I obligingly suggested that he might call one of the witnesses on the Crown list who had not been called and whom I wanted to ask one or two questions of. Daiches jumped at this offer, and the result, as I had expected, was entertaining: when he had the witness in the box he realised he had no idea who the witness was or what he was supposed to ask him. 'Ask him his age', I said, 'and his name and address'—which Daiches did, and sat down. I then rose and proceeded to ask my questions, amid some murmurings as to whether I could cross-examine Daiches' witness. When Russell intervened to ask about this, I explained that I had merely attempted to assist the Court, but if objection was taken the whole thing could just be wiped out and I should put the witness in, myself, tomorrow. Stevenson had meanwhile been in earnest conversation with Russell, and persuaded him that as the witness was on the Crown list either accused could use him and ask what questions we pleased: and Russell invited me to proceed. The witness's evidence was actually of no importance.

May 9th
Both accused went into the witness-box, and did very well. Graham was a careful, intelligent witness, but Sweeney was if anything the more attractive of the two: a dark, curly-headed Irish lad. I stood beside the jury box and shouted to him every now and then to speak up: and otherwise left him to tell his own story. Daiches in a longwinded examination of his client brought him to the verge of disaster by getting him to say he had never been in similar trouble before. This might have had deadly repercussions if the Advocate-Depute had been anyone less scrupulous and fair to the accused than Skae. I did not make a good speech, but it was factual and reasoned, and probably made quite an effective supplement to Daiches' rhetoric—in the

course of which he described the Crown productions as 'this mass of gory haberdashery'. Russell left both murder and culpable homicide to the jury, but made it clear that in view of the breakdown in the medical evidence the proper course was to acquit. I did not wait for the verdict, but set off for the 6 o'clock train. All the work I had done on this case had been done on the train, and with nothing to do in the evenings I have found work no burden, and enjoyed it. Davidson rang up later to say that both men had been acquitted.

May 23rd

A divorce proof. The husband, a somewhat unprepossing man at first sight, turned out to be quite a picturesque witness. Answering questions about why he had not defended an action of adherence, he described a visit to a lawyer in Glasgow—whom he named—to whom he said, 'I've got a defence'. 'Then he said, "Have you any money?" and when I said "No" he said, "Well, you've had it son".'

June 21st

Sorry to see that Willie Muir had been put away for another five years on being found guilty of defrauding a jeweller. I had looked into the High Court yesterday and heard him examine some witnesses called at his request: a farming family from Southfield Farm cottages who said he had always plenty of money and had been very good to them. One of them was a young girl to whom Muir remarked with sobs in his voice that he didn't like to see her in such a place. One of the things that induced them to let him have the rings was that he was able, in paying for the watch, to flourish a big bundle of bank notes: and Bowen explained to me how this had happened. Muir had been living in a caravan which he rented at Southfield Farm, and during the winter had been ill with pneumonia. The doctor attended him regularly, and with a good deal of trouble got him back to health. On one of his later visits he admired the caravan and said he was looking for one himself to take on his summer holidays. 'Don't look any further', said Muir. 'I shan't need this one after the Spring. I'll let you have it for £150'. The doctor pointed that the caravan was worth a lot more than £150, to which Muir replied that the doctor had been very good to him—he probably owed his life to him—and he would not think of charging him any more. So the doctor wrote out a cheque for £150, unaware that the caravan had never been Muir's to sell nor that, as is rumoured, Muir had already in any event sold it to someone else. The doctor has declined to make any charge, saying he is not going into the witness box to say he made a fool of himself.

July 3rd
Isabel Sinclair was speaking about a plaque that was unveiled in the Corridor yesterday to the memory of Lord Macmillan. The plaque includes a coat of arms, and Isabel in conversation with some more conservative members of Faculty had suggested that this should have had a springboard on it, Macmillan's main connection with the Faculty having been that he treated it as a springboard for his own career. 'Oh, well', was the reply, 'quite a lot of people have done that'. 'Yes', Isabel said, 'but quite a lot of people haven't got a plaque for doing it'. Actually Macmillan is the last person the Faculty should have honoured, since it appears that he more than anyone else was responsible for depriving all future members of borrowing rights in what had been their own library.

July 5th
Ian Macleod, the Minister of Labour, had to face the journalists tonight in a television 'Press Conference'. He is a capable person, with a reasonable, friendly manner: a man who would be a useful member of any Government rather than a party politician.

July 9th
First Division: *O'Donnell v. James Young and Co*. The contractors were challenging the judgement as regards negligence both of their foreman and of the craneman supplied by Youngs. I have no doubt that Cameron's judgement is sound, and I should have no anxiety about the case before any court other than the First Division. Donald Ross spent the day opening the case, in his usual competent, attractive manner.

July 10th
The O'Donnell appeal continued. Today again the pursuer's counsel had nothing to do but listen—what would have been an interesting, pleasant day in any court in which one did not have to be on the look-out all the time for some indication of how they were aiming to inflict injustice on the pursuer.

July 11th

Shortly after lunch Alasdair Johnston, who was replying for the second defenders, was persuaded to sit down: and Forsyth, who was with me, then made a very tactful intervention, more or less inviting the Court to say that he was not required to reply. Clyde fell for this, and Forsyth accordingly said very little more. After Kissen had summed up the first defender's contentions with equal cogency and speed, and McKechnie had fought for some time against lengthening odds, I adopted the same line as my junior and said next to nothing. It looked as if they would find that the crane driver was *pro hac vice* in the second defenders' employment, thus imposing 100 per cent liability on them: but in view of the way the case developed it does not look as if the pursuer can suffer any disadvantage, whatever happens.

July 13th

Eyemouth Herring Queen celebrations: an excellent speech from the retiring queen. The children of Eyemouth seemed to be favoured with a very good education, so as to be able to express themselves well.

July 14th

Reading *April Lady*, by Georgette Heyer. It is an exasperating book—one feels that the misunderstandings that form the basis of the story could easily have been cleared up or avoided, and it is difficult not to feel impatient at the slowness of their unravelling. But it is a tribute to the author's skill in creation of characters that one wants them to be unravelled and goes on reading with some anxiety until everything comes right.

July 16th

Stewart v. Stewart: the case in which the defender and her young daughter Eliza are supposed to have spent the night in a church vestry with the co-defender, the beadle. It is an odd feature of the case that the husband's essential witness Eliza is living with the wife, and wants to go on living with her. She was a slow and diffident witness, but stuck to the essentials of her story: that her mother and the beadle had been kissing in the vestry, and when she went to sleep the beadle was sitting on her mother's knee. Having given this evidence, she went off arm in arm with her mother.

July 20th

A national bus strike has brought passenger transport to a standstill on the roads everywhere except in towns served by municipal transport systems.

July 21st

We all motored to Blackness and went in to see the castle. While we were talking to the custodian, the children rushed into a little door at the foot of the castle wall, up a flight of steps and through another little gap at the top. I hurried after them, and found them running along a narrow rampart at the top of the castle wall, with a sheer drop of twenty feet to the rock below. They treated this alarming place with complete contempt, as they did with all the other stairs and gables and battlements over which they climbed, with me in as close pursuit as my age and girth allowed. The custodian had said, 'Go into every room in the castle', and they made sure that they did. It was a most exhausting tour, physically and mentally.

July 23rd

Finished reading *The Caine Mutiny*, a remarkable novel which held my attention in a manner which—considering I had already seen a film and part of a televised play on the same theme—was quite outstanding. The thing about it is its complete authenticity, both in the details of the story and in the way people speak and act. The author never lets his sense of the dramatic run away with him: there is always, he seems to say, something to be said for the other point of view.

July 25th

The African Queen, at the Regal in Musselburgh. Apart from a short but effective appearance by Robert Morley, this picture is entirely Katherine Hepburn and Humphrey Bogart. Miss Hepburn—bedraggled, unadorned, completely unglamorous—gives a fine performance, and Bogart is the perfect foil, content to sit back and let Miss Hepburn carry it through. The story is improbable but exciting, and there is some fine photography of river and jungle—not a bad film at all.

Finished reading *Autumn Term*, by Joan Whitty. Its only merit is brevity. The story, if it can be dignified by such a title, is told by the widow of a headmaster of a small preparatory school, and if she talked the same sentimental gup to the boys that she talks in telling her story the boys must have had an awful time.

July 27th
Killearn Show. On the way home I came round by Larbert to take four Denny girls to a dance, but there were surprisingly few people wanting lifts—my total did not come up to a dozen, coming and going. If motorists were prepared always to give lifts, it looks as if a bus service would hardly be necessary on the main roads: cars could cope with all the passengers.

July 30th
With the children to Marks and Spencers, a fine, airy, spacious shop just opened on the site where the New Picture House used to be, filled with a most enticing array of goods of all kinds.

August 1st
We packed up the car with our holiday luggage, and left for Kirkcudbright: even less of a place than I had remembered it, practically nothing in the way of shop, and not even a cinema. It is evident that we are going to have a quiet holiday.

August 2nd
Finished reading *Sincerely, Willis Wayde*, by John P. Marquand. The author builds up his principal character with his usual subtlety and skill, and it is only as the story nears its end that one appreciates the delicate irony of the title: a double irony, for though the reader is left to draw his own conclusion it can hardly be anything else than that Wayde is indeed sincere from his own point of view.

In the afternoon we motored down Kirkcudbright Bay. The tide was out, and big banks of thick oozy mud sloped down to the river. As we proceeded down the estuary, there was a strip of sand, where a lot of people were disporting themselves. The sea was a long way out, with what looked like mud between: but when we had taken off our shoes and socks and were making our way out we found it was hard and clean. The tide was coming in at a great rate, and there was soon a vast expanse of shallow water, delightfully warm as the sea came in over the hot sand. After supper Nancy and I went for a walk round. Hardly anybody in Kirkcudbright cultivates his garden: most of the plots, in contrast to the Deeside plots we saw last summer, are wilderness. In various parts of the town there is a curious dank smell, like hay that has been cut wet and left lying for some time. But fresh air appears to be greatly valued: almost every house has its windows wide open, even at nine o' clock at night and despite a white mist hanging over the meadow in the lower part of the town.

August 4th

St Cuthbert's church: Rev J.E. Mothersill, the minister, preached on Genesis 49,1. He spoke in a slow, melancholy voice, attractive but all very pessimistic and sad. Other people, he agreed, might think differently, but he could not see any salvation outside the church—'I grant you it may be a long way off'. There had been a baptism earlier in the service, in the course of which he gave quite a long address, telling us the sacrament of baptism seemed to him to be completely futile when parents never came to church. He might be wrong, but that was the conclusion he was coming to, after many years in the ministry. He seemed a likeable person, and his sermon was interesting, genuine and brief. During the collection the organist played the *Londonderry Air*, which consorted with the gentle melancholy that pervaded most of the service. Richard at his own request stayed throughout, and was as good as gold.

In the afternoon I went with Nancy and the children to look for a sea beach. Turning off the Borgue road we could see what looked like a broad sandy bay, with a grassy shore: Bridgehouse Bay, a fine expanse of sand stretching out to where the sea was breaking on rocks on either side. No 'development'—not even an ice-cream van. I bathed with the children, a very nice bathe in little rolling breakers coming in over the hot sand, no mud at all. This lovely beach was a great find, so near to Kirkcudbright.

Finished reading *Justine*, by Lawrence Durrell. It is set in present-day Alexandria, and I suppose is about love in various curious forms—well done, but at the end I was completely uncertain who was who and what it all meant.

August 7th

Wigtown: a higgledy-piggledy place, with odd patches of ground, and nettles growing between the houses.

August 8th

A successful excursion to New Galloway gala day. New Galloway is said to be the smallest burgh in Scotland, and it must have the smallest gala. The street was decked with flags, but there was nothing in the little park but a row of forms, sufficient to provide seating for all the members of the public who were there. There was however an excellent programme of children's races. Richard ran in the race for boys of five and six. He finished well towards the rear, but the race had to be run again owing to the finishing tape's having blown away. Each of the runners got a prize of threepence. Richard and Elizabeth went in together for the wheelbarrow race, and finally sat with other children on the edge of a big tarpaulin to hold it down while older ones competing in the obstacle race went under it. This seemed to please them more than anything else. For the third successive evening I had fried salmon steak for supper, part of a six pound salmon that was brought on Tuesday by a fisherman whom Miss Picken had asked to call on us. He charged £1 for the fish, about half the price we should have had to pay in the shops.

August 9th

A letter from Donald Shaw and Co., with fees for the Beardmore cases. The auditor has been generous in taxing the pursuer's accounts, and has allowed 460 guineas as fee for incidental procedure in the other 11 cases. This is the biggest fee I have ever had.

Finished reading *A Train to Tarragona*, by Anthony Carson. It gives a vivid, entertaining picture of people the author met and consorted with in Spain. Occasionally the humour seemed the least bit childish, but that no doubt is part of the picture.

August 10th

Port William sports, a professional games meeting, with all the equipment, but it must be about the smallest in the country. A woman who had set up a stall to sell funny hats and similar novelties was bewailing her error in coming to Port William, and on a fine day at that. I heard her remark to a companion, referring to her stock in trade, 'They can't even look at them for fear I mesmerise money out their pockets'. But in view of the prices she charged when she did at last manage to detain some customers I had not much sympathy with her.

August 11th

Found a collection of verse for children in Miss Picken's bookcase, and read Richard and Elizabeth some of the familiar poems such as *Young Lochinvar*. Elizabeth does not seem to get any of those well-known poems at school, only trivial pieces of airy-fairy rubbish by women that no one ever heard of.

August 13th

We motored to Low Boreland to see the milking. We saw 32 Ayrshires being milked, and the milk cooled and put into cartons: very good milk, of which we get 9 pints a day.

August 14th

Kirkcudbright is a great place for artists: in the fine weather when we were here at first we saw them sitting with their easels at odd corners all over the town—ladies, mostly, of uncertain age. The other feature of the place seems to be nuns, whom we see going out either in pairs or walking two by two in a kind of crocodile. They are friendly nuns and return the children's waves.

August 15th

Television performance of Rossini's opera, *Le Comte Ory*: gay and tuneful, and exquisite singing by Sara Barabas.

August 17th

Finished reading *Guilty Men 1957*, by Michael Foot and Mervyn Jones. Though not the best of the Suez books, it constitutes a damning indictment of Government policy. Infuriating that everything is glossed over and forgotten, and there does not seem to be anything one can do about it.

August 18th

St Cuthbert's church: Mr Mothersill on Psalms 139,7. He does not say anything very definite, but in his slow, ruminating, tentative way throws out ideas and leaves you to think them out for yourself: and what he says is thoroughly sensible. Pointing out that the idea of God as spirit was incompatible with limits or dividing lines, he remarked that we set up fences and barricades and notices against trespassers, and if that was not enough we had soldiers and sailors, with atom bombs and depth charges. 'I wonder what God thinks of it all'.

August 19th

Our plans for the afternoon were disrupted by continuous rain, and I motored with Nancy and the children along the street to Broughton House, where a local painter named Hornel had built a small picture gallery on to the house and left it to the town, with a collection of his own paintings. The pictures were mostly of children: all the same children, whether the scene was described as Burmese or Brighouse Bay. There was no charge. The museum, where we had to pay sixpence, was worth visiting: an excellent collection of things related to the locality, including a complete range of local birds, animals and fish.

August 22nd

A picnic to Sandyhills bay. Looking seaward, we could see nothing but bank upon bank of mud and sand, all at different levels: a dangerous place, one would imagine, with an incoming tide. But there was no incoming tide today, so far as could be seen. The sea must have been a good five miles out, and remained there throughout our stay. Nancy and I walked across the beach to cliffs, where we had a view of more and muddier banks stretching up the Solway as far as the eye could see.

August 27th

Just after midday I heard a hoot on a ship's siren: the oil tanker that comes periodically up the river to Kirkcudbright to pipe petrol into storage tanks—the only ship now coming to Kirkcudbright 'harbour'. I hurried the children into the car, and drove down to the harbour. The visit of the tanker is quite an event and a small crowd had gathered. The ship was a good sized tanker, *BP Distributor*, and made an attractive picture as she came up the channel on a full tide, with a background of green hills. Opposite the jetty she swung slowly round, her stern almost touching the bank on the other side, and moored heading downstream.

August 30th

Took the children to the museum, at Richard's request. An old gentleman in a deerstalker hat, who seems to be the curator, asked Elizabeth what she most liked doing, to which she replied, 'Writing poetry'. He asked Richard if he liked writing poetry too. 'No', said Richard, 'I like fishing'. 'So do I', said the curator in great delight, adding that both had made very good choices.

September 9th

Richard's arm was blistered as a result of his falling yesterday into a small bonfire we had on the bank at the side of the road, and we thought that the doctor should look at it. There was a consulting hour at 10 in the hut at Niddrie Mains. The number of waiting patients must have been over twenty, mostly blowsy women with babies and young children. Richard had brought a book, which Elizabeth proceeded to read aloud to the assembled company. Everyone seemed interested.

October 2nd
Guest was installed as a judge in place of Hill Watson. I thought some of the older judges looked a little melancholy, as if thinking 'Well, I may be the one to leave the next place to be filled'.

October 4th
Television *Press Conference* turned out to be with Dr George MacLeod: a melancholy occasion, as the journalists asked silly, argumentative questions which MacLeod found difficulty in answering, his thinking being on a different plane from theirs.

October 6th
Finished reading *The Long Walk*, by Slavomir Rawicz, an account of a Polish lieutenant's escape from a Siberian prison camp. To the uninformed reader very little of it rings true, though if the author made it up it is odd that he did not make it a little more interesting.

October 10th
The Faculty committee on counsel's clerks has been asked to make some recommendation about counsel's use of tape recorders. Five juniors now dictate their summonses and other writings to these machines, and the clerks have refused to type from them, so that counsel have to employ an outside typist at their own expense while the clerks get from the solicitors a shilling a sheet for writings they do not write.

October 11th
A vivid dream: that Lillie had been elected Dean of Faculty.

October 12th
A television programme about the Conservative Party conference at Brighton: Lord Hailsham ringing a bell which he waved wildly in the air, shouting 'Ring it for victory, and say to the Labour Party: "Seek not to know for whom the bell tolls, it tolls for you".' The Prime Minister's speech fell rather flat.

October 18th

A faculty meeting to elect a new Dean. All the backwoodsmen were out in force to vote down Douglas Johnston—retired Sheriffs and other ancient members whom I had never seen in Parliament House before—and C.J.D. Shaw was elected by 72 votes to 32. He would of course have been elected even on the vote of practising members. On being brought in after election, he made a nice little speech, saying particularly to younger members that they should regard the door of the Dean's room as open at any time if he could be of help. He will make an excellent Dean, better than Douglas, and though I voted for the latter I have always thought Sinclair Shaw's idea of nominating him rather foolish. I told him at the time that it was stupid to put up a left wing candidate when the right wing candidate was a particularly popular member of Faculty, but nothing would persuade him that a conservative person like his namesake could be popular among the younger members. He has an extraordinary capacity for ignoring any evidence that does not fit in with his point of view.

Motored Elizabeth to Portobello for Brownies. She was very late in getting back. As it was a wet night, Nancy got much concerned and went out to look for her. It appeared that she had chosen to walk home, instead of coming by bus, and Nancy met her strolling along Duddingston Road all by herself in the dark and rain, evidently enjoying the walk.

October 22nd

A proof before Wheatley, *Aitchison v. Aitchison*, an action of divorce by a husband on the ground of the wife's insanity. A curator had been appointed to the wife, and I appeared on behalf of the curator to defend on the ground that the pursuer's misconduct had conduced to the insanity. The pursuer told a cock-and-bull story, full of contradictions, about his wife's drinking habits and cruelty to the children. As he led no evidence from members of his family, and we had three of them who said the opposite, it seemed clear to me that no credence could be given to this: and the eldest daughter proved an excellent witness—frank, straightforward, intelligent, making no bones about her dislike of her father but freely admitting her mother's weak points as well as her own. In cross-examination she gave a lively account of an occasion when she had hit her father on the head with a jelly jar, and he had to be taken to hospital and got eight stitches. She frankly admitted that she herself had not been in the least afraid of him. Her two sisters were nothing like as good, but as they had been young children at the relevant time I thought this was not surprising. What did surprise me was Wheatley's attitude to them—he seemed to think they were being deliberately dishonest in not remembering what had happened, and was quite rude to one of them. When the evidence finished, between 3.30 and 4, Kissen indicated that he would prefer to begin his speech tomorrow: but Wheatley, who seemed in a cantankerous mood, insisted on his starting right away—though of course he had not got far when it was time to rise.

October 23rd

The Aitchison case. Wheatley seemed to show a curious lack of discernment in appearing to prefer the evidence of the pursuer to what seemed to me the transparently honest evidence of the eldest daughter. In view of his attitude yesterday, I was not altogether surprised, but I was disappointed and a little resentful of his unfairness towards a daughter who had come of her own free will and stuck up for her mother so gallantly against the slanders of the pursuer—who, as Kissen admitted to me privately, was simply a brute. It does not matter to the defender, who has no knowledge of what is going on: but for the girl's sake I felt rather sore about the way Wheatley seemed to have taken her evidence.

October 24th

King's Theatre: the Sadler's Wells Theatre Ballet, now rather absurdly called the Royal Ballet. In *Pineapple Poll*, Brenda Bolton danced the leading part with joyous abandon, an appropriately pert manner, and a captivating smile.

October 28th

Panorama included an interesting summing-up of the results of the Suez adventure, exactly a year ago. Amusing to see the feverish way in which they had to rake around in order to find anything to say on the credit side.

October 30th

A television programme about the 1930s, with a commentary by Malcolm Muggeridge: intelligent and to the point, though a little too supercilious. It is easy to be wise after the event: and though his sneers at Baldwin and Ramsay Macdonald, and even perhaps Neville

Chamberlain, were no doubt justified it occurred to me that Hitler and Mussolini, for whom he seemed to have unbounded admiration as they ranted away to vast, hysterical crowds, were the ones who came to a bad end in the long run. Fascinating to see the change in political oratory since then—far less of the posturing which in Ramsay Macdonald's case seemed ridiculous on any view of what he was saying. Possibly the advent of television has had something to do with the change.

November 1st
Wheatley found for the pursuer in *Aitchison v. Aitchison*. I was glad to notice that so far as appeared from the newspaper he had not said in terms that he disbelieved Marion but had proceeded on the ground that there was no corroboration of her evidence, which may be right.

November 2nd
Finished reading *Beyond the Black Stump*, by Nevil Shute. Written with the author's meticulously detailed realism, this story takes a little while to get under way. But the problem that it poses is real and interesting, and it is deployed in a manner that leaves one in no doubt as to the rightness of the solution. Whatever the ultimate fate of the girl from the Australian wilderness—and that is still in the future when the book ends—it is easy to realise that she could not do other than reject the comfortable negation of life offered by marriage with the small-town American engineer, where everyone knew everyone and the family settled down happily every evening to watch television.

November 4th
We all went to the George cinema to see *The Happy Road*: two children who run away from school in Switzerland and are pursued across Europe by the American boy's father and the French girl's mother, somewhat unwilling collaborators in the chase. The great thing about it is that it is a happy road: everyone with whom children or parents come into contact is friendly, and though efforts at help may be misguided or unavailing they are always well-intentioned. Many of the incidents are very funny: nothing is overdone, and even the ending is sensible. I think everyone enjoyed it.

November 5th
Motored to town to take voters to the poll in the municipal by-election,

and for the next two hours I climbed tenement stairs, rang bells and knocked at doors. I must have been at well over 100 houses, and in all that time got seven passengers to take to the polling at Broughton School. My assistants produced no passengers at all. I found it quite entertaining. Everyone had some excuse, or else merely said, 'Not tonight, thank you', or explained that he or she had already been to vote or was going later—an explanation that if true would have meant an excellent poll instead of the poor percentage that votes in municipal elections. In one house when I knocked at the door footsteps approached inside and stopped: and when I knocked again a woman's voice said 'Who's there?' I said my piece, and the voice replied, 'I'm not voting for any of them—not any of them': and I came away without the door's having been opened. At another house, from the sounds, barricades had to be taken down and locks and bolts undone before the door opened and two nice old ladies appeared, one peering over the other's shoulder. 'We've been', they said, interrupting me happily, 'we've both been'. One impoverished looking man was 'just scraping the ceiling'—though he and wife were eventually persuaded to come out. I was struck by the comfortable, cosy look which many of the houses had from the glimpses I got into them, even in poor tenements. A less attractive feature was the constant noise of wireless and television: practically every tenement had at least one house where it was going full blast, so that you could hear it all up the stair.

November 7th
A case in Procedure Roll before Wheatley. The pursuers are the widow and son of a man employed by a Dundee dentist as a jobbing gardener. The garden was on two levels, and part of the upper level formed the roof of a coal house. There was a hole in the roof: and one day while the defender was on holiday the gardener fell through the hole. He died in hospital not long after. The pursuers say that before going on holiday the defender told the deceased to come and work in the garden as usual. The defender denies this. He says he told the deceased not to come during the holiday period. I had adjusted the case for the defender and had put on a plea to relevancy: and when I saw the papers again yesterday I could not at all remember why— there did not seem to be any point of relevancy but a plain issue of fact as to whether the deceased had been in the course of his employment. On consulting my junior, Charles Johnston, he reminded me that the case had been sent to Procedure Roll to let us argue that it

was unsuitable for jury trial because it raised the question of the capacity in which the deceased was present: employee or trespasser. Thus reassured, I had a look at the authorities, and found it had indeed been laid down that when a case raised a question as to the category into which an injured party fell it was the usual practice to send it to proof rather than jury trial. Charles was occupied elsewhere, and I opened the case. I made no headway, since while recognising that in some cases a question of categories might present a difficulty Wheatley obviously thought—and said so several times—that no such difficulty arose in this case, when all the jury had to decide was whether the man had been told to work during the holidays. I had no answer to this, and after 20 minutes or so was considering whether it was worth while to argue the matter further when the clerk of court got up and reminded Wheatley that no Issue had been lodged. Anyone wanting a jury trial has to lodge an Issue, so the debate came to an abrupt end, and a proof was allowed.

November 8th

Got up before seven to see if I could see the satellite which the Russians have launched into outer space and which circles the earth two or three times a day. It has a dog inside, whose reactions are remitted by wireless to Moscow. The sky was overcast, and I went back to bed.

To Dundas Street for a consultation with an old smallholder who by obstinacy and intransigence had landed himself with liability for several thousand pounds of tax, and stormed up and down my room cursing the Inland Revenue, his lawyers, his relatives and everyone else concerned.

November 10th

Elizabeth, reading a comic to Richard, read out that the 'water was full of fierce men, eating sharks'—a misreading of 'man-eating'.

November 15th

Press Conference on television: Derek Walker-Smith, the Minister of Health, a suave customer who evaded all their questions with remarkable skill and aplomb—an infuriating man.

November 16th

My Income Tax demand for 1957-58, which I was horrified to find amounted to £651.19.0.

November 17th

Finished reading *Thin Ice*, by Compton Mackenzie. Surprisingly, in view of its highly unusual subject, this novel is not in the slightest degee unsavoury or unpleasant. The characters are delightfully drawn, particularly the respectable old widower who tells the story and who, while doing his best to keep his distinguished friend out of trouble and rescue him from the predicaments into which his perversion leads him, simply does not understand the force or nature of the perversion. The weakness of the book is that it leads the reader to expect some climax or denouément, and then tails away into an irrelevant ending.

November 18

Panorama included an interview with Mr Hare, the Secretary of State for War, on whether it will be possible to get sufficient volunteers to replace National Service as the means of recruitment for the army. He seems a nice, ineffective kind of fellow.

November 19th

Duffes was expressing annoyance because of an Opinion he had written for someone in England. Some question of English law arose, on which Duffes had written that he was not an expert but speaking as a lawyer he would express such-and-such an opinion. He had just had a copy of the typescript of his Opinion, and observed that in what had been sent to England he had been made to say 'Speaking as a labourer'.

November 20th

The starter jammed as the car was on a steep slope, facing down hill. Rather than put the engine into top gear, I thought it might be safer to put it into reverse and try pushing the car forward. Nothing happened, so I changed into top and sat in the driver's seat, pushing the car backwards with one foot on the street. At once there was a loud click, the starter freed itself, and I was able to start the engine and proceed.

Finished reading *Westminster Wader*, by Rufus Noel-Buxton. The author is concerned with his efforts to wade across the Thames in order to find the track of the old Roman fords, and also with his position as a second-generation peer. The two themes are ingeniously interwoven, and the author presents—or vaguely suggests—some sensible ideas, wrapped up in an attractive air of antiquity. He seems to be obsessed with the prospect of a flood which will overwhelm Westminster and restore it to its old condition of uninhabited marshland—a prospect from which he is apparently not at all averse.

November 24th

A special meeting of North Edinburgh Labour Party. Marshall had come from Glasgow, and started the proceedings off: and then all the members proceeded in turn to air their grievances. I had prepared a political speech, but as this seemed out of place contented myself with an effort to get them into a more cooperative frame of mind. It seemed quite a success: and the meeting, though it had no visible practical results, may have done some good in starting to dissipate the atmosphere of defeatism. As June Hay sensibly pointed out, it is a peculiar party and a peculiar constituency, with no community spirit and a sharp dividing line between two incompatible types of people. I think it would be difficult to weld this party into anything like a coherent whole, of the old West-Edinburgh style.

November 26th

Finished reading *Homecomings*, by C.P. Snow. This is, as one would expect, a highly civilised novel: people's conversations intelligent and so much in character that it is always interesting. I felt however that this time their actions seemed contrived rather than compelling. The author's long study of the life of Lewis Elliot and his friends is beginning to have the air of a kind of intellectual's Mrs Dale's diary.

November 30th

To the bank to pay in some money. In view of the increase in Bank Rate arising from the Government's new policy of bribing foreign investors to keep their money in the country, the interest rate on deposit receipts has gone up to $4\frac{1}{2}$ per cent. Mr Bruce said they had been doing quite a trade in deposit receipts since the rate had gone up.

Kate and Mr Blair came for bridge in the evening. When they were leaving, there was some excitement caused by Kate's car. She had just started the engine when it failed, and a violent buzzing noise came from under the bonnet. Kate leapt out, yelling for a flashlamp and for me to 'switch off the battery'. Never having had the occasion to switch off a battery, I was at a loss what to do: but on hitting one of the terminals a good bang I apparently, quite by accident, moved a switch at the bottom of the battery, and the noise ceased. Kate was profuse in her thanks, jumped into the car and drove off—the fact that the battery was 'switched off' seemingly making no difference to engine, starter or lights.

December 5th

Debate in a divorce case, *MacLennan v. MacLennan*, the question being whether artificial insemination constituted adultery. The point was completely novel, and apart from one unsatisfactory case in Chicago has apparently not been the subject of judicial decision anywhere in the world.

December 6th

Motored to Parliament House, expecting a free day. But my expectations were agreeably disappointed: Ian Macdonald appeared saying I should be wanted for an interdict hearing this afternoon—a petition by an Englishman named Kennedy to restrain his daughter Tessa and a man named Dominick Elwes, the son of a famous portrait-painter, from marrying. The young couple had come to Scotland on 26th November. Tessa's father, having learned of her intention, had applied on the previous day to the Court of Chancery to have her made a ward in Chancery—which automatically became the situation on the presentation of the summons. Being a minor—she was 19 today—she was thereby prevented from marrying without the consent of the Court of Chancery: and on 27th November Mr Justice Roxburgh pronounced an order prohibiting her from marrying or leaving the jurisdiction. The couple took up residence in the Caledonian Hotel, with the object of establishing the necessary residential qualification of 21 days in Scotland preliminary to getting married here, where no consents of parents or others are necessary. The petition is an attempt to stop them, on the ground that Tessa cannot contract a valid marriage without the consent of the Court of Chancery, and while she is prohibited from marrying by an order of that court. The petition seemed to me to be incompetent—lack of consent cannot be an impediment to marriage, since by the law both of England and Scotland, provided there is no incapacity for marriage by the law of the parties' domicile, any question of what consents are required is a matter of form, to be determined in accordance with the law of the country where the marriage is being celebrated. I made a good speech, to which Douglas Johnston had little to say in reply, but it was all wasted on Migdale. After a moment's hesitation at the end of the argument, he consulted his clerk of court and announced that he would defer his decision until tomorrow.

December 7th

I did not go in to listen to Migdale's judgement, but was not surprised to hear he had granted an interim interdict.

December 10th

An appointment at 4.30 at Ian Robertson's flat to meet Tessa and Mr Elwes. News had come through that Mr Justice Roxburgh had this morning pronounced an order committing Elwes to gaol for failing to return Tessa to the jurisdiction, and that a court official was on his way to Scotland with a warrant. So when I came out of court I went up to the Crown Office to consult Bowen. He was fully *au fait* with what was happening, and said that though he had not seen the warrant he assumed it would not be a criminal one so as to be enforceable in Scotland under the Indictable Offences Act. He was sure the police would be unwilling to do anything on the faith of such a warrant. Armed with this assurance I motored to Moray Place, in a minor snowstorm, and we had an hour's chat about the prospects. It was obvious that Tessa was the dominant personality. Throughout the evening the telephone kept ringing with enquiries from my colleagues in the case, who were engaged in preparing an interdict petition to serve on the Court of Chancery's tipstaff as soon as he put in an appearance at the Caledonian Hotel. The last news of him was that he was leaving London by the night train, and would be in Edinburgh early tomorrow morning.

December 11th

First Division. It was clear that all four judges were determined to decide against us, and it was indeed observed that Clyde had his judgement all written out before the debate began. So far as my speech was concerned, this was a type of situation which I enjoyed, and I had the stimulus of a good audience. Having complete contempt for all four, I did not allow their interruptions to put me off, and had no difficulty in meeting any point they put to me—in what was, I think, one of the best speeches I have made in court. As soon as I sat down, without even consulting his colleagues, Clyde hastily remarked to Douglas Johnston, 'We don't need to trouble you', and proceeded to read his judgement. I did not wait to hear it. As I remarked, my clients had been two years too late in coming to Scotland to marry: while Cooper was alive and head of the Scottish judiciary, he would have made short shrift of any argument that a decree of an English court could be an impediment to marriage in Scotland. I felt we had nothing to reproach ourselves about in the conduct of this case, which should certainly have succeeded before any Scots court worthy of the name.

December 20th
The schools had broken up today—or 'broken down' as Richard puts it.

December 26th
A consultation with a solicitor, who by a piece of almost incredible folly has exposed himself to a serious criminal charge. Having given a dishonest answer in the witness box when giving evidence in a 'hotel' divorce which had been arranged by the defender's solicitor, he was asked to produce his books, for the continued hearing the next day: and the two solicitors spent the night in faking their books and letter files, destroying all the letters relating to the arranged divorce and substituting others to fit in with the oral evidence. The papers have been sent to the Crown Office, and no one knows what may happen.

1958

Apart from a motor accident in the King's Park, in which my car was overturned, and Richard and I were lucky to escape without injury, 1958 was devoid of excitement. My practice continued to flourish, with briefs from an ever-widening circle of instructing solicitors, and two successful appearances before the House of Lords. In one, a dispute between two defenders, I had no interest other than to satisfy the House of my right to be present: and though they shook their heads over the expense involved in my unnecessary appearance they treated me with the good-natured tolerance and courtesy I had come to expect from them. In politics the important factor was the impression given by the Prime Minister of calm and sweet reasonableness which, despite his support of Sir Anthony Eden in the Suez adventure of 1956, was not, I thought, altogether misleading. Many of his ideas were on the right lines, and his was a more attractive personality than that presented to the public eye by the leader of the Labour Party. But fundamentally there was no doubt that the Conservatives' philosophy was false, and that their hold on the country was maintained not so much through the propagation of any particular policy, as by spreading an atmosphere of synthetic prosperity which had no foundation in fact.

January 4th
Started work on Tuesday's jury trial, but coming through to the living-room I found Nancy starting to watch Patrick Hamilton's play, *The Man Upstairs*, on television. This attracted my attention by the neatness of the dialogue and the excellence of the acting, and I got no more work done tonight.

January 7th
The jury trial by a stroke of luck had been put out before Migdale. Since Hill Watson had rejected *res ipsa loquitur*, the pursuers were left only with a case that the fall of baths which caused Mrs Lindsay's husband's death had been due to the fault of his fellow-slinger,

McFadyen, in failing to put the sling on securely at his end of the batch. Apart from the fact that it was a mystery how the baths had come to fall, this case had the serious weakness that there was no evidence but McFadyen's as to which sling had been put on by him and which by Lindsay himself, nor any satisfactory evidence as to which end of the baths had fallen: the waste end, on which McFadyen said he had put the sling, or the scoop end, which presumably had been slung by Lindsay. After a good deal of time had been taken up in enquiries which added nothing, we decided to amend by deleting the case against McFadyen and attacking the system of work. We were not hopeful about the case, even on these lines, but thought it was the only chance of getting to the jury without having the case withdrawn for lack of evidence. But when the motion was enrolled at the end of last term Guest rather high-handedly refused to allow it. It was decided, on instructions from London, that for reasons of policy we should let the case proceed and fail, rather than abandon it. I felt that by now taking up the line that the defenders' system was perfectly safe it could be argued that the accident could only have happened because someone had put a sling on insecurely, and with a bit of luck—Migdale being the judge—we might get it to the jury that it was McFadyen's sling that had been insecure. I had to put McFadyen in as a witness, and in order to be able to tell the jury that we had put in every witness who knew anything about the accident, favourable or unfavourable, I called every witness who had been anywhere in the vicinity. Several of them could say nothing about the accident, and I got through eleven witnesses, and closed the pursuers' case, all in just over two hours. I had not been able to get any witness to say he remembered which end of the baths had fallen first: but one witness, although he said he did not really know and it would be only guessing, said he could assume from the broken pieces—though he did not actually look at them—that it had been the waste end. The craneman had said at the Fatal Accident Inquiry that it had been the waste end, but no amount of pressing could bring him to repeat that evidence today—he said he did not know. Finally, on the suggestion of my junior, Alistair Johnston, I read him the sentence from his evidence at the Inquiry. Even then all he would say was that he could not remember: and only at the end of a long series of questions he gave a grudging assent to my suggestion I had to put to him three times before he at last said 'Yes', whereupon I at once sat down. Migdale refused to withdraw the case. The defenders led no evidence—there was none left for them to lead—and Migdale's charge was completely neutral. I changed and was preparing to leave the building but had hastily to resume my wig, gown, stiff collar and fall, in order to go back to court to deal with a question the jury had raised: whether it was competent for them to take into account evidence given at the Fatal Accident Inquiry and not included in the evidence today. To this the answer was obviously 'No', but Migdale agreed to add a rider that they could have regard to the evidence in so far as it had been adopted by a witness in the present case. The jury had been sent out while the point was argued, and there was an amusing interlude when Migdale got the shorthand writer to read out the relevant part of the craneman's evidence—everybody in court convulsed with laughter at my lengthy effort to wheedle or bully the requisite sentence of evidence out of him. The verdict came about twenty minutes later: they found the defenders liable, and awarded the widow £2,300, a fair award considering that Lindsay was 63 when he was killed.

In the evening's television we had a programme about the Outward Bound school for training young industrial workers in endurance, a gruelling course of hard living, rock-climbing, mountaineering, fell-walking and so on, which it surprised me to think that any young industrial worker could be induced to undergo.

January 8th
The *Tonight* programme on television has been promoted from a 6 o'clock start to 6.45, with the result that the children, who had been accustomed to watching it in preference to the children's hour, are now deprived of it. I had it this evening, and found it, as usual, excellent, including lively filmings at a schoolboys' chess congress and a schoolboys' model exhibition, with both lots of schoolboys full of enthusiasm and eager to impart chunks of weird and wonderful knowledge—particularly, at the exhibition interviews, about space travel. The highlight of the programme was an interview with Frank Muir and Denis Norden, the script-writers of a regular radio programme, *Take It from Here*. These turned out to be genuine comedians in their own right, and with deadpan countenances carried on a fantastically funny conversation with their interviewer on how two people combined to write a script. 'Do you think fashions in jokes change?' they were asked. 'Oh, yes', they said, looking solemnly at one another. 'People don't laugh at the same jokes today as they did forty years ago. A joke about the Kaiser doesn't go down so well today.

Then on the other hand about twelve years ago we tried a joke about a sputnik, but that didn't register—before its time, you know'.

January 10th

Wheatley was giving judgment in *McLennan v. McLennan*, and as I had nothing else on I went along to listen to it. In a long, discursive judgment he held that artificial insemination could not constitute adultery by the law of Scotland. I daresay he is right, but the judgment was disappointing: it seemed to concentrate on superficialities, without getting down to principles.

On television tonight there was a short American documentary about German flying bombs and V2 rockets: an alarming demonstration of what a tiny margin of time saved Britain from destruction, simply a misjudgement of Hitler's which held up production until it was too late.

January 12th

A meeting in the Free Gardeners Hall organised by the City Labour Party to protest against loading hydrogen bombs on American planes flying above Britain, and against the proposal to establish atomic rocket stations in Scotland. The hall was packed with an enthusiastic, receptive audience. John Mackintosh made a good speech. Thoughtful and well reasoned, but, as he said to me afterwards, it rather lacked humour. I supplied the humour, among other ingredients, and it was an enjoyable, impressive meeting.

January 19th

Finished reading *Outbreak of Love*, by Martin Boyd. Though it takes a little while to get going, this is a likeable book. One knows and understands the people, and feels that what happened to them would happen just in that way. The quiet, undramatic ending, inevitable from the start, is exactly right. Free Gardeners Hall: a protest meeting on old age pensions, organised by the Trades Council. I spoke first this time, and Mackintosh at the end, after an excellent speech from Ned Hoare, representing the pensioners. Mackintosh spoke well—his speech certainly the highlight of today's meeting.

January 20th

Panorama on television: the international situation—two apparently intelligent MPs, Mr Dennis Healey and Mr Fletcher-Cooke.

January 21st

I had nothing on in court, and about midday was working in a leisurely fashion on the case for tomorrow when a solicitor appeared asking if I could take a consultation this afternoon with a gentleman who had expended £62,000 on the purchase of certain shares and was in danger of losing through a difficulty that had arisen regarding the quotation of certain other shares on the Stock Exchange. No details were available, but the advice of counsel was urgently required, and he would bring the papers with him for the consultation at 2.30. This was worrying, as it seemed that the consultation was likely to be about something that I did not know the first thing about and there was nothing I could do about it—I could hardly start to read up the whole of Company Law in the hope that I might remember a bit that should turn out to be relevant. However, the consultation went off not too badly. I was able to preserve an air of wisdom reasonably well while allowing the three other people present, who of course knew the answers far better than I, to do most of the talking. Luckily they seemed all to be agreed on the best line of action. In a conversation today in the hall, Douglas Johnston happened to ask Duffes whether in his experience there had ever been such a bad appeal court as the First Division at the present time. Duffes was emphatic there there had been nothing like it: he had known bad courts, but the present First Division was in a class by itself.

January 23rd

Douglas Johnston rang up about the Kennedy case, in which he is senior counsel for the petitioner. He said Mr Kennedy was to abandon the petition and allow the couple to marry if they wished.

January 27th

Elizabeth has had an essay to write for Brownies on some nature subject, and for some unknown reason has chosen the subject of 'Bear's Garlic', the name of a flower which she found in a book about wildflowers. Using material from the book, she has composed a convincing essay:

> One day I was walking in a wood, when I saw a white flower, Bear's Garlic. I picked it and smelled it. It smelled of garlic. It was like a star in loose clusters, the flower I held was of nine flowers and had a long stalk, but I saw some with twelve flowers.

I took it home Mummy told me it was of the Lily family and Daffodil family. We found out the stalk was three sided. Bear's Garlic's leaves remind me of those of the Lily-of-the-Valley.

The consultation on the Company Law question seems to have been regarded as satisfactory—among the papers is a letter from the Glasgow solicitors to the Edinburgh ones saying 'We must thank you for the very helpful and expeditious way in which you have dealt with the matter'.

February 4th

The Kennedy petition. Unfortunately, before Mr Kennedy's decision to throw his hand in could be communicated to the respondents they had—unknown to their solicitors—left the hotel in North Berwick where they had been and taken an aeroplane to Holland, and thence to Curaçao and finally Cuba, where they have since gone through a form of marriage. Whether or not this is a valid marriage, it provided the petitioner with an excellent excuse for not proceeding with his petition, and I was not surprised that Migdale made no award of expenses.

February 9th

Finished reading *On the Beach*, by Nevil Shute. The scene is Australia, and as one reads the book one gradually comes to the realisation that all life in the northern hemisphere has been destroyed by the radiation effects of a short nuclear war. Radiation is slowly spreading southwards, and is calculated to reach Melbourne in seven or eight months. The story deals with the life of a particular group of people during that time, up to the end. Everyone is kind, friendly and peaceable, and this enhances the grotesque horror of the plot. The end of the world, one feels, might easily come just that way, unless the nations learn some sense pretty quickly. I should imagine that if every politician were to read this novel it would have a much more salutary effect than any blue-book or statistical treatise on the dangers of radiation.

February 10th

To Watson's for Richard. In the park the road surface was wet, with patches of frozen slush, and just beyond Samson's Ribs, when Richard was pointing out to me the spot where Mrs Carrie's car had stuck on the way to school this morning and had had to have a push from Mr Hannah who had been passing with the children, our car suddenly went into a skid. Instead of taking a slight bend to the left, it shot forward at an alarming speed straight towards the wall and steep slope beyond, down to the hollow beside Duddingston Loch. Luckily we crashed into a lamp-post on the edge of the footway, striking it a glancing blow which deflected the car in the opposite direction, so that it crossed the road, mounted the grassy bank below the cliff on the other side, and eventually overturned. It was all over so quickly that I was not sure what was happening, but I had a distinct sensation as we were tumbled about that at one time the car was right over on its roof. It finished up on its side on the bank, facing up hill. Even when the car was charging into the bank and toppling over, I had no expectation whatever that either of us was going to be seriously injured, and so had no feeling of fright or shock. Disentangling myself from the seat, I crawled out through an open space at the front and helped Richard out after me. He was upset and crying, but not really hurt. Contemplating the car lying on its side with the nearside wheels in the air, he said tearfully, 'We'll have to walk home'. But just at that moment a little car came up heading for Duddingston, and the driver readily agreed to give us a lift. I crawled back into my own car for my briefcase: and the car driver kindly brought us right to the top of our road. I had a plate of soup then went up to Nancy's garage for her car and motored back to the park to retrieve things I had left in the car, including my shoes and slippers—I had been wearing Wellington boots. Richard was alarmed by my intention to go by car, and urged me at all events 'not to go through the park'—a somewhat unpractical warning. I found my car as I had left it, and was amazed to find that the windscreen had come out all in one piece, and was lying propped up against the door pillar, without a scratch on it. The gap by which Richard and I had got out was the space where the windscreen had been. Some bumps on the roof confirmed my impression that the car had at one time been upside down, but the working parts did not seem to have suffered much, if any, damage. I crawled in again, gingerly, for fear that the car would topple down on the road, and get out all the belongings. The lamp standard had been broken off, and there was a sound of escaping gas, with the smell of gas added to that of petrol dripping down from the cap of my petrol tank. Having motored to the police station in Braid Place, I gave particulars of the accident to a peculiarly unintelligent constable, who wanted to put in a great many particulars about my having braked on seeing a bad patch of road ahead. I said that was all right provided it was understood that that was his account, not mine, whereupon he said wearily, 'What is your account then?' He noted Richard as the only witness. Nancy had gone up to the doctor's with Richard, as a precautionary measure, but so many patients were in attendance that they did not wait. I myself felt none the worse, apart from slight bruising in the lower part of my back, and was able to continue the work Nancy had been doing of clearing slabs of frozen snow off the pavement.

February 13th
The insurance company's engineer to see me. He asked if I would be willing to deal with the case on the basis of total loss, and said he would recommend a payment of £400. This was satisfactory: more than I had expected to get for the car in part exchange for a new one.

February 14th
Motored to Players and collected some odds and ends from the car. The engineering manager confirmed that the car must have landed on its roof in order to produce the damage that had taken place.

February 15th
Drove round by the scene of the accident to see if my tyre-pressure gauge was lying anywhere about. I looked over the little two-foot wall on the right-hand side, and was rather alarmed at what I found. Though I had realised there must be a steepish slope, I had thought of it as a grass bank, but in fact there was a sheer drop of 40 feet on to the railway line where it comes out of St Leonard's tunnel. If we had gone over, it seemed to me that we should probably both have been killed: and if the lamp standard had not been there I did not feel much confidence that the two-foot wall would have sufficed to keep us from going over.

February 19th
A present from R., the solicitor whom I advised in regard to the divorce proof where the papers had been sent to the Crown Office on a perjury question. I heard some time ago that the Crown had decided to take no action, nobody apparently having discovered that the books and correspondence had been tampered with. Since R. was a

simple, well-meaning kind of man who had obviously been led into trouble by his Edinburgh correspondent, I had been much relieved to hear that things had turned out all right, and that it had not be necessary for R. to take the advice Douglas Johnston had given and leave the country. He had sent me a magnetic inkstand.

February 20th

First Division: an action of damages by a lady who had been injured by falling on the footway of Wellington Street in Glasgow. Though Wellington Street is a public street, the footway has never been taken over by the Corporation, and the defenders disputed that they had any duty to inspect the footway or repair it. My junior, Isabel Sinclair, stood up to them well.

February 21st

I enjoyed myself in the Division. I presented a careful, logical argument treating Clyde good-humouredly and squashing him with a humorous or ironical retort whenever he intervened. Isabel was delighted, saying it had been devastating and extremely funny. When Clyde asked if I was insisting on a decision on a particular matter— one that Reith had argued at length—I replied in the negative, adding that I was however concerned to see that if they were to decide it they should not decide it wrong. There was a general laugh, and Clyde remarked, 'It sometimes happens you know'—to which I replied, 'Not, I hope, in this Court'. On another occasion when I took up one of his points and put it in an extravagant form—to which he in his usual rash way assented—I remarked that my learned friend Mr Reith had certainly not had the audacity to argue on those lines— 'though of course', I added, 'he had not then had the advantage of hearing your Lordship's observation'.

March 10th

To Armadale to take the evidence of a witness on commission, with John Shaw. We motored out through Bathgate, passing some of the foundries involved in our pneumoconiosis litigations. 'I always raise my hat when I pass a steel foundry', Shaw said.

April 4th

Motored to Portobello to have a look at the sea. A spring tide and a gale coming right in from the east was bringing up a tremendous sea:

the Promenade and the little gardens in front of the houses awash, and every now and then a 30-foot wall of water flung up against the house fronts as high as the roof.

April 9th

Finished reading *Korean Reporter*, by Réné Cutforth. He did not see much of the war, but what he saw is sufficient to demonstrate the appalling misery, destruction and death that the 'United Nations' brought upon the Koreans in preserving for them the right to live under what the author describes as the 'festering corruption' of the Government of the Republic of Korea.

April 10th

We went to the New Victoria to see *Around the World in 80 Days*. It is a long film, and I found some of the earlier stages of Phineas Fogg's travels rather wearisome, particularly a long sequence about a comic bullfight. But on the whole it was lively and entertaining, with a lot of original touches and a remarkable cast of celebrities—one of the incidental amusements is to try to spot the many distinguished people who play various bit-parts in the different episodes. It is not a film to be taken seriously, but as an extravaganza it is in a class by itself, and an appropriate climax to the adventurous life of its producer, Mike Todd, who was killed in a flying accident a few weeks ago.

April 11th

Finished reading *Personal Identity*, by C.H. Rolph, an extremely readable and interesting book about identification. In addition to such well-known cases as Adolf Beck and Oscar Slater, the author discusses some even more alarming instances of false identification, and brings out in a remarkable way how ruthless the authorities in this country can be when they want to suppress anything that would bring their mistakes or misdemeanours to light.

April 13th

We all motored to church. Mr Macmorris from Newcraighall preached on John 1,14: a short, simple sermon. Nothing he said was quite right—his analogies were faulty, his sentences did not reach a conclusion—but he had a point to make, a good point if in no way profound or original, and everything he said was directed towards the point. His trouble is that he is not really a professional preacher: he gives the impression of an earnest and well-intentioned layman suddenly called on to conduct the service.

At lunch-time in a conversation about derivation of words I remarked, 'I remember my mother buying me a French reader'. 'I remember', said Richard solemnly, 'my mother buying me a French cake.'

April 15th

Bruce Campbell on children's television, introducing a programme called *Out of Doors*. He was good, and seemed very much at ease, but not as handsome as he used to be.

Finished reading *Jutland*, by Captain Donald MacIntyre. I thought this was going to be a gossipy book, but once the author gets to the battle he gives a lucid, exciting narrative, and shows how both Jellicoe and Beatty were hampered by the extraordinary lack of intelligence among the professional long-service Navy men who constituted their senior officers—a lack of intelligence which no amount of courage could make up for.

April 16th

The Chancellor of the Exchequer's Budget is a pedestrian affair, and Mr Heathcote-Amory had nothing to say about it worth hearing, when he appeared on television last night—though he is friendly and likeable, and within the limitations of Conservative party policy has, I imagine, a lot of commonsense.

April 24th

With Nancy and Richard to Midmar Avenue to see a house: square, compact and well built. Its serious defect is the absence of a garage, and the price of £4,500, plus an incalculable amount for the construction of a garage, makes it a hardly practicable proposition. On the way home we saw a car with a pram on the roof, and Richard with his usual interest in any kind of hypothetical problem asked what they would do if they came to a low bridge that they could not get under. Nancy said they would just have to go round some other way, but Richard would not have this. 'They could take the pram off and push it through the bridge and then fasten it on again. Or else', he added, 'they could break down the bridge'.

April 25th

Finished reading *Rachel Weeping*, three stories by Shelley Smith. In each, the central figure is a child. The endings differ, but each has an element of tragic perfection which as tension builds up one knows all along is inevitable.

April 26th

Nancy wanted to see tonight's instalment of a serial she is watching on television, and we kept the television on through the *Benny Hill Show*, which I thought very good—chiefly through the wit and versatility of its hard-working principal. The guest artiste in the finale was Alma Cogan, a painful woman who could not sing at all.

April 29th

This evening on television Kenneth McKellar sang a number of old favourites with his usual felicity, and combined serious singing with an air of lightheartedness which he carried off very effectively. He was ably abetted by his pretty guest singer, Patricia Braden, particularly when he sang 'Trottin' to the Fair'.

April 30th

I had promised to go to another of Robert Irvine's meetings, in Leith Walk school: and McGowan rang up to ask if I would give the use of my car for an hour to go round advertising it. I drove the car slowly along back streets, stopping from time to time while Irvine and McGowan took turns to harangue the windows through a loud-speaker. We gathered the usual accompaniment of children, and found an audience of two, both sympathisers. Without conscious direction, we all—Irvine, the audience, McGowan, McKail the chairman, and myself—got into an interesting informal discussion about various municipal topics, which developed on philosophical lines. I came away after half an hour, which had certainly passed more interestingly than any municipal election meeting I have been at for a very long time.

Got home in time for a television reconstruction of the Tay Bridge Disaster inquiry. This was a failure. The BBC had been handed an excellent subject on a plate, but destroyed its dramatic value by fussiness and failure to appreciate the real point. There was not even a picture of the bridge: only a lot of fake 'interviews'.

May 1st

Greenhill Gardens: the house on view was dilapidated, but it was a roomy house with some character, and a lovely sunny garden. It seemed it might be worth thinking about if we could get it cheap and do it up completely. The agent who had come to show the house said the price asked was £3,050, but appeared to agree that it might be necessary to come down a bit.

May 6th

A consultation in a series of pneumoconiosis proofs out for trial next week. Lawrence of Glasgow in accordance with his usual practice had Watt instructed as senior counsel, but now, when tenders had been lodged in all thirteen cases, it was evidently thought advisable to take me in as the expert in pneumoconiosis. Though I meant to come down quickly after lunch and read the papers, I forgot about it and stayed gossiping with Leechman and O'Brien: but found, as I had anticipated, that I seemed to know as much about the cases as anyone else at the consultation.

May 7th

At Home, by William Plomer, an autobiography in which the author keeps assuring his readers what an eccentric, unusual fellow he is. From aught that appears in the book, no one could be more commonplace.

A television show put on by the Unionist party: Lord Hailsham and a Conservative MP discussed housing and education in a blatantly partisan way that could hardly have taken anyone in, particularly as it was also pretty dull. Odd that neither of the big political parties seems to be able to make any proper use of television.

May 9th

Debate Roll: *Nicolson v. Cursiter*, an action by the widow of an old man who was knocked down and killed by the defender's jeep when walking westwards along the road between Fidge and Kettletoft in the island of Sanday. In our narrative of facts it was stated that Nicolson had been walking on the north side when he was struck by the jeep, travelling in the same direction, an averment which would lead to the inference that the jeep was on its wrong side. By some inadvertence we had omitted to include this among the grounds of fault, and Strachan seemed to be having some sympathy with the view that difficulty might arise before a jury if we were to prove something that amounted to negligence but was not made one of the grounds of action. Peter Maxwell had suggested that the averment about walking on the north side of the road should be deleted, and McNeill asked me if he should agree. I shook my head: and in defending this part of the case said I did not want to be obstructive and, if Mr Maxwell wanted, was prepared to insert an averment that it was the defender's duty to drive on his own side of the road and he had failed to do so. I explained that it had hardly seemed fair to say that to drive on the wrong side of the road between Fidge and Kettletoft was itself a fault, since on roads of that kind one probably simply picked the best part of the road. But if Mr Maxwell thought the omission of this ground of fault might create difficulties I was very willing to put it in. Maxwell got up to explain that my proposal was the opposite of what he wanted, and that he would prefer me to take out the reference to the north side of the road, but in reply to Strachan he agreed that my amendment would make the pursuer's case relevant. The amendment of course does not affect the pursuer's case in the slightest.

In television press conference we had Henry Brooke, the Minister of Housing, defending the Rent Act: amiable, unperturbed, completely divorced from realities. It was difficult to believe that he was as innocent as he appeared, or so wholly unaware of the meaning and effect of his Act.

May 10th

Sinclair Shaw said he had been walking down the Mound with Matthew Fisher and had been surprised to see him buy the *Evening News*. Fisher told him that he always took the *News* now instead of the *Scotsman*. McLarty was astonished at this, and said he had not imagined there was a household in Edinburgh that did not take the *Scotsman*. This remark amused Kissen, who said it reminded him of people who said that in August London was empty.

May 12th

Alex Thomson told of an occasion when David Anderson, who had been holidaying in Norway and met a man there who shared his enthusiasm for bird-watching, arranged to put him up for the night when he had come to Edinburgh a year or two later. Anderson was to meet him at the station when he came through from Glasgow, and as it was some time since they had met it was arranged that his friend would carry a bundle of papers so that Anderson would recognise him. As it happened, there came off the Glasgow train Charles Mackintosh returning tired and irritable from a lengthy Glasgow circuit, carrying a bundle of papers. Coming up on him from behind, Anderson mistook him for his visitor and greeted him: 'Ah, Hans, how good it is to see you again after such a long time'. Mackintosh, in no mood for joking, replied, 'Don't be a fool, Anderson'. To this Anderson answered that he was so sorry—'I mistook you for a Norwegian ornithologist': a further attempt at humour, Mackintosh thought.

May 16th

Caley Picture House: *Orders to Kill*, a film worth seeing, tense, exciting, honest, and no less interesting in its development of character than in its plot. It has something to say, and says it with tremendous effect and yet without the slightest over-emphasis. Anthony Asquith's direction has made it a film to remember.

May 17th

Finished reading *The Sword of Pleasure*, by Peter Green, a fictional reconstruction of the life of Sulla in the form of a narrative by Sulla himself: a successful piece of work, bringing the contemporary people and events vividly to life—though by the end I was beginning to weary of the incessant wars and bloodshed which characterised Sulla's life.

May 18th

Bothwell Castle: a massive ruin set on a curious sandstone promontory above a bend of the river—the policies carpeted with bluebells, growing so thickly that you could not see the ground.

May 20th

A pneumoconiosis proof: *Campbell v. North British Steel Foundry*, and two other cases against the same defenders—what was left of the thirteen cases into which I was brought for the consultation a fortnight ago, the other ten having been settled. Instead of coming on last week, they came on today, enabling me to take part along with Watt. Watt took all the witnesses except Stabler, and got everything into an extraordinary muddle. He seemed not to have made any effort to understand what his case was, nor even to be able to read the precognitions, though as most of them have been got from Shaw—the ones we had in the Sheriff Court case—they are reliable. In the evening I did some work on the case. I have prepared it just as if I were taking it myself, so that I can take over from Watt at any stage if he wants.

May 21st
We managed to spend the whole morning and part of the afternoon on the evidence of two general practitioners, who on their own showing knew next to nothing about pneumoconiosis. Watt took them both, and it seemed to me that he was not so bad today—it may be just that I am getting accustomed to him. Watt then asked for an adjournment until Tuesday. Shearer opposed the motion, but it was granted with surprisingly little fuss, and the case came to a stop until Tuesday. This suits me, since it will allow me to get to the Fife farmers' show tomorrow and to take a case that I have been offered on Friday.

May 23rd
I had the television on for Mr Truman. His fascinating personality is always impressive on television, where sincerity and absence of humbug are all-important.

May 24th
On television tonight Ed Morrow and another American questioned Mr Macmillan. They treated him gently, and he gave his usual impression of a kindly, sensible, well-intentioned person, but one in marked contrast with the impression left by another kindly, sensible, well-intentioned person: Mr Truman. While Truman had a definite view and a positive answer on each question, Macmillan really said nothing.

May 27th
Watt's cross-examination was a weird and wonderful affair. He seemed to have nothing prepared, and asked long, rambling questions apparently at random and without any idea of establishing any particular point. With Kelman Robertson however this method had some success. It was obvious that he had no idea what Watt was driving at, any more than Watt himself, and in his zeal to contradict whatever Watt put to him he often gave an answer which was useful to the

pursuers. It looked as if the cross-examination was going to last a long time.

May 29th

The pneumoconiosis proof was completed, with Shearer's speech. I looked in for a short time. Nobody seemed to be in any hurry, and for long periods Shearer stood in hushed silence while he and Walker ruminated on some problem such as the measure of damages for shortening of life.

June 4th

House of Lords: *Miller v. South of Scotland Electricity Board.* I was sitting in counsel's box looking up some cases when the official who attends the Lords arrived and remarked, 'You made a great impression yesterday, sir, from the talk afterwards.' I said it was kind of him to say so, to which he replied, 'It's the fact, sir, I assure you'. This was comforting: and when the hearing was resumed it seemed to be becoming fairly clear that they would remit the case for proof. In view of Simonds' doubts about relevancy, it was obvious that I could not press for a pronouncement that the case was suitable for jury trial, and I did not argue the matter, simply explaining what the statutory provisions were and indicating that I was content to leave that matter entirely in their hands. Called on for a reply, I spoke briefly, pointing to averments which supported my case of reasonable foreseeability. Finally, when asked whether I did not agree that the case was not really suitable for a jury, I replied that in a sense it raised a question which was pre-eminently a jury question. 'No doubt', said Simonds. 'But don't you think a judge might have some difficulty in directing a jury on the law applicable to those facts?' 'Well', I said, 'I must admit that that too is perhaps within the bounds of reasonable foreseeability'. They all laughed, and I sat down, saying nothing more. The general feeling is that they will allow a proof before answer, which is good enough for me and will enable us to recover our railway fares and something to help to meet expenses— all that is allowed if one succeeds in a case *in forma pauperis*. But to appear in the Lords is always such an exhilarating experience that whether one gets paid for it is a minor consideration.

June 11th

To St Andrews House to give evidence before Lord Strachan's

committee on civil jury trials. I was questioned for a full hour and made no secret of my view—which I think most people would privately accept—that the major cause of uncertainty among legal advisers in Scotland just now is not vagaries of juries but the gamble of whether one's case on appeal comes before the First or the Second Division.

June 13th

A debate before Migdale: *Mayor, Alderman & Burgesses of Ramsgate v. McGhee*, in which the pursuers are suing the defenders for £1,150. In discussion with my junior, Charles Johnston, we agreed that there was no relevant defence, but we thought, as the case had come out before Migdale, that there were two arguable points which would at least enable the case to proceed, giving time for our clients, which apparently is regarded as some advantage. When I came into court I found Charles embarking on a third, quite ingenious argument. There were obvious answers to all three, but before Migdale anything might happen. Kissen, who was appearing for the pursuers, sat writhing throughout the day while Migdale wresttled with the puzzles we put before him. I spoke at some length, and thoroughly enjoyed myself tying Migdale into knots. He reserved judgement.

June 30th

A House of Lords appeal: *O'Donnell v. John Young*. The dispute is between the first and second defenders, and there is considerable doubt as to whether we are entitled to be here. But it is our award of damages, which in the end of the day will have to be paid to the pursuer, though he is indifferent as to which defender pays it. Anyhow it is always a pleasant experience to be in the Lords, even if it has to be at our own expense. Kissen was reading the judges' Opinions: and I am not sure that his rapid, shorthand method of pleading is suited to the House of Lords. His mind runs ahead of his words, so that instead of finishing a sentence he starts off on something else.

From the appearance of the people in the streets, I observed that the return of the short-skirt fashion of the twenties which has been sponsored lately by leading fashion designers had by no means prevailed with the London public.

July 1st

The second defenders have instructed an elderly English silk, Mr

Beney. He, when Kissen intimated at 4 o'clock that he had said all he
wanted to say, was asked about the prospects, and indicated that he
would take two hours but was not sure what Mr Stott's position was.
I merely said that I was not sure what my position was, either: and on
that, today's hearing ended.

July 2nd

Beney was as good as his word, taking just two hours, and made an
excellent speech: dull, but cogent, concise and beautifully arranged,
every point developed in the form most effective for his purpose. Up
to the time he spoke I had been in some doubt as to how the decision
would go, but Beney has given them such a clear, logical line that I
think they will find it difficult not to follow it. Kissen strongly opposed my motion for costs, and contradicted my assertion that in a
similar situation in the Court of Session I should certainly have been
found entitled to be present and get my expenses. He cited a passage
he had noted from *Maclaren on Expenses*, but as the book was not
obtainable here it was impossible to check the context. Luckily however he went on to say that in the present case it had been said in the
Inner House that there was no need for the pursuer to be represented. This was untrue: and Keith, who had the record of the
proceedings, remarked that anyhow the pursuer seemed to have got
his expenses there. 'Oh, no', said Kissen. 'Only from the second
defenders, because they were contending that their foreman was not
negligent'. Keith at once pointed out that the award of expenses in
the Inner House was joint and several, against both defenders, and
Kissen had to apologise for his mistake—an error that would, I think,
detract from any weight they might have been inclined to give to his
other assertions. Denning was clearly in my favour, and I thought
they were all reasonably sympathetic, though Simonds obviously
thought that someone should have cleared the matter up so as to
obviate any necessity for my attending. Forsyth, my junior, remarked
that after the discussion this afternoon he thought things looked
much more hopeful for us.

We got to Kings Cross in good time for the four o'clock train.
Kissen and his junior, Donald Ross, had seats booked, but we got in
all right in the next compartment, with an elderly woman, an awful
example of the abuse to which the new fashions are subject. Her
tight, knee-length costume disclosed enormous ham-shaped legs that
were the quintessence of ugliness and could have been concealed

without any loss to their owner and with considerable gain to the spectator. She was one of those insipid, unattractive females peculiar to first-class compartments, but would perhaps have been a passable sight but for her short skirt. Apart from her, it was a pleasant journey, and the engine-driver put in some exhilarating running. We were twenty minutes late leaving London, and there were signal checks farther north, but we reached Newcastle ahead of time. Rain all day—floods all over the east side of England, and on our way north a constant succession of flooded fields, rivers over their banks, and sodden grass and turnips.

July 3rd

Procedure Roll before Strachan: *Lawson v. United Cooperative Baking Society*. The pursuer is claiming damages for injuries she received when working on a machine used to grind biscuit material—which it is agreed frequently contained, in addition to waste biscuits, such things as coins, nails and hairpins. These had to be taken out to prevent damage to the machine, and when she was doing this, she says, the machine suddenly re-started, with the result that her hand was caught.

After coming out of court I was cheered with the not unexpected news that the Lords in *Miller v. South of Scotland Electricity Board* had unanimously recalled the interlocuter of the Court of Session and directed a proof. Forsyth's devil, Coutts, had put in Forsyth's box a copy of *Maclaren on Expenses*, open at the page to which Kissen had referred in yesterday's debate: and I was shocked to find on reading the passage that it was in a section headed 'Poor Law Cases', referring only to actions by Poor Law inspectors to determine which of two local authorities was responsible for the maintenance of a pauper. It was grossly misleading to cite this as a general proposition, and I at once got hold of Layden and said he should write the solicitors for the first defenders and insist that they send a letter to the clerk of the House of Lords correcting the mistake. Kissen had meanwhile come along himself, and said he would write if the position was as I had stated. He went into the Law Room with the book, and shortly after produced a letter in which he pointed out that the passage he had cited dealt with Poor Law cases. This was good enough for us, since it will send Keith and the others to the book and they will then see the position. I kept an eye on Kissen while he addressed the envelope, and went out with him to the hall, where he happened to meet John George. To him I said laughingly, 'Go out to the lobby with him, will you? and see that he posts the letter'. I took care to ascertain from him later that the letter had been posted. It seems hardly believable that a man of Kissen's ability would have made such a mistake, but as it turned out the incident may, I think, be in our favour.

July 4th

Pleasantly surprised to see in the current number of Session Cases that in reporting the argument for the appellants in the House of Lords in Nicholson's case the reporter included my remark: 'Machines which weighed as much as half a ton, although they were moveable, were not portable unless you happened to have a crane or an elephant at hand'.

July 5th

Thornton Games: the usual pony trot, in which the winner in one of the races was a pony referred to by punters round me as 'Joy de Vear'.

July 8th

Finished reading *Henry James and H.G. Wells*. This is a full documentation of the relations between these two distinguished writers, and includes an extract from one of Wells' books containing a devastatingly wicked parody of James' involved style of writing. This is extremely funny, but only occupies a page or two of a book which consists mainly of tedious correspondence. It has been edited with a pedantic pernicketiness that would no doubt have appealed to Henry James himself.

July 11th

A Bar dinner—held periodically when any members of the Bar get engaged, the bridegrooms-to-be being guests of the Faculty. I had never been to one, but as the dinner was being held in the Reading Room for the first time, instead of some hotel, I thought I might go and see what these dinners were like. The three guests were Ross, Cowie and Cay. The Dean proposed their health in an excellent speech, brilliant in its sustained wit and the effective way in which each point was made. Ross made a good reply, but Cowie—as no doubt befitted a former Rugby International—had not the slightest idea of how to make a speech. The company gradually drifted into conversation among themselves which drowned most of what the speaker was saying. This was unfortunate for Cay, whose speech, though peculiar, might have been good if it had not been for the babel of voices with which his gentle tones had to contend. Norman Sloan, for whom Ross had devilled, had come from London to propose the customary toast of Sweethearts and Wives. The reply, given in accordance with tradition by the most junior member of the Bar— Gavin Douglas—was a good, amusing little speech. We then had a terrible song written by George Walker, about an Egyptian mummy belonging to the Faculty which has for many years been reposing in the Laigh Parliament Hall and has now been disposed of to someone in Glasgow. I was sorry for Nigel Thomson who had to sing such unmitigated drivel. A song on the same subject from Cameron Miller was much better, but I did not think the subject really offered much scope for humour. Things brightened up when the Dean suggested that Ireland, recently appointed Professor of Law at Aberdeen in succession to T.B. Smith, should propose the toast of Aberdeen University, coupled with the name of the Lord Advocate. This meant that Milligan, who has no connection with the University of Aberdeen, had to reply, and he was very funny indeed. He has a reputation as an after-dinner speaker, fully justified by his skill as master of an inconsequent style of humour. Laughter and applause for this speech had not long subsided when the Dean rose and said it had been suggested to him that Mr Gordon Stott who he heard was attending a Bar dinner for the first time would now give us some reminiscences of his 25 years at the Bar. It had hardly occurred to me that I should be asked to speak: and though it was easy afterwards to think of some embellishments which would have made it a much more polished and effective speech I think it was not really bad for so completely impromptu an effort. To be called on without notice had at all events the advantage that I did not have a speech to worry about through the earlier part of the dinner: and I quite enjoyed myself when I was actually speaking. The dinner was officially concluded by Leslie, who had apparently been destined to propose the health of the Dean, and after making one good joke carried out his task with his usual propriety. A number of the diners were settling down to drinking. Ross McLean seemed to be most affected, but was in good humour, merely ejaculating 'Muckle Flugga' in a loud voice on a number of occasions while Ireland was speaking.

July 15th

A deluge of rain, with thunder and bright flashes of lightning. A torrent was flowing down our road, washing away what was left of the surface. When it subsided the road was down to its rock foundation at several points.

July 17th

Dismayed to see from this morning's paper that the Labour Party had not divided the House on the Government decision to support the Americans in the landings they have made in Lebanon. All the good which Mr Hammarskjöld's United Nations' intermediaries have done will of course be undone by this futile display of force. The Labour Party's ambivalent attitude was well illustrated by a television press conference in which Herbert Morrison answered questions about the Middle East situation, or rather refused to answer. Though amusing in a way, it was fundamentally a pitiful exhibition of unwillingness to take the responsibility of expressing any opinion whatever. No doubt if he had expressed an opinion it would have been the wrong one, but that did not make things any better.

July 24th

O'Donnell v. John Young & Co.: the House of Lords have dismissed the appeal, with costs to both respondents—very satisfactory.

July 25th

Langholm: the Common Riding Games. I sat down in the sun, with my back to the fence bounding the course for horse racing, and was joined by a very drunk man, who after an ineffective attempt at conversation—he evidently came from the north of England, and I could not understand him at all—turned over flat on his face and went to sleep. Unfortunately his head was projecting under the railing on to the track, and I had to take him by the feet and haul him to safety. Later another drunk man came up and greeted me warmly, remarking that he had not seen me for 35 years—no doubt true as far as it went.

August 6th

Elizabeth and Richard had a great game of detection while she questioned him about a crime he had committed and he gave detailed explanations. She was also going to cross-examine the members of his household, but that, said Richard, was impossible: the woman worked both by day and by night, the girl was away at a Guide camp, and the boy was drowned.

August 8th

Truro—to look for a sports jacket. After abortive attempts at Burton's and a much more expensive shop, I got a nice one in a little shop near the cathedral which advertised 'Industrial Clothing'. The old Cornishman who served us had an ingenious explanation of how he was able to stock Harris tweed jackets for sale at six pounds ten shillings. There had been a split-up, he believed, in the Harris family, and so his boss had been able to get his consignment at a low price. Whatever the real reason, they had a remarkably good selection.

August 9th

A man stopped me for a lift soon after Indian Queens. I was a little perturbed on hearing from him that he was out on parole from a mental hospital in Bodmin. According to himself, he had escaped from a criminal lunatic asylum, and the police at Camborne had been nice to him and instead of sending him back arranged for him to be sent to Bodmin. He assured me that he was now quite sane. Parole allowed him to go only three miles from Bodmin, but they did not mind how far he went provided he got back for tea. He seemed somewhat unstable emotionally, bewailing the fact that his father had not been a policeman: he would have loved his father if he had been a policeman. He asked my advice as to whether he should go back to London—he himself seemed to think it a bad idea. He got quite worked up, and I was not sorry to get to Lanivet crossroads, where I had to let him off as I was turning off the Bodmin road.

August 30th

We got home from Newquay—to an immense pile of papers.

September 1st

To Parliament House, where I spent the day working. An interval for lunch before returning to Parliament House, where on reaching my workplace in the Corridor I found I had sustained a setback: I had only so far managed to dispose of one set of papers, and during my absence several other sets had been deposited there by Scotland for my attention. It is of course pleasant to have some work to come back to, but I cannot see any immediate prospect of overtaking the amount that seems to have come in this August .

September 2nd
Parliament House. Made good progress today, and felt for the first time that I was making some inroads on the accumulation of work.

September 3rd
Television *Press Conference*—with Mr Desai, the Indian Finance Minister. I did not like him much—he seemed too good to be true—but he was certainly the perfection of cold, unruffled imperturbability, with never a trace of emotion or excitement, and complete indifference as to whether he or his questioners got the better of an exchange.

September 4th
Took a holiday today, and took Nancy and the children to Loch Lomond for a sail up the loch to Inversnaid.

September 6th
Shotts Highland Games were being held today: but as I went out along the Glasgow road it got blacker and blacker, with damp mist all round and lightning flashing all the time about the windscreen—conditions quite eerie as cars emerged from the gloom with lights on. I have never seen an afternoon like it. At first there was no thunder, and not much rain. Later there were loud cracks of thunder just overhead before heavy rain came on—useless to go on to Shotts, and I made for home.

Finished reading *Mama I Love You*, by William Saroyan. Despite its title, this is a likeable book, fairly free from the toshy sentimentality that has bedevilled recent Saroyan books. Everything is acutely observed, with just that touch of quaintness that might come from the observer being a child. The last chapter seemed to me to go wrong, but the author managed to extricate himself in a kind of way in a final paragraph.

September 7th
Not surprised to see in today's paper that the railway line near Winchburgh had been flooded yesterday afternoon. The main Glasgow road had been blocked by flood water at Newbridge shortly after I passed along it.

A television play, *The Heiress*—excellently done, and most absorbing. I thought Catherine's final revenge on the philanderer who had jilted her was a little cheap, and out of character. It would have been a better play if it had ended more enigmatically ten minutes earlier.

September 12th
Nancy and I to the Empire: *Ballets Premiers*, presented by the Edinburgh International Ballet. Six new ballets were commissioned for the Festival, and tonight we saw four of these ballets. *The Night and Silence* provided some lovely dancing by Paula Hinton and David Poole. Alone throughout, they danced this dramatic ballet with great distinction: Miss Hinton shimmered across the stage in the true poetry of motion, dancing with every fragment of her mind and body. *The Great Peacock* no doubt was intended as the *pièce de resistance*, and it certainly was a brilliant ballet, brilliantly danced: but a ballet about insects is the kind of ballet I do not like.

September 14th
Finished reading *A Family in Egypt*, by Mary Rowlatt. The author has obviously a deep affection for Egypt, which has been a second home to her family for two generations: and she surveys every aspect, old and new, with a sympathetic but discerning eye. She has an amazing gift for bringing a scene vividly to life, so that the most humdrum incident—crows fighting, or a bathe from a Mediterranean beach—becomes full of interest. Old-fashioned she may be, but she takes care she misses nothing, either in perception or in enjoyment, and her generous, far-sighted views about the country and its people put the politicians' clap-trap to shame. This book really made me feel I should like to visit Egypt and see for myself.

September 15th
North Berwick. Edinburgh Autumn Holiday had brought out tremendous crowds. The tide was high, the sea dead calm and a beautiful blue: and the beach sloped down a little towards the land, with only a litte ridge of sand between the depression and the sea, so that with the sea practically at eye level one got an impression of fulness, as if the bay was brimming over with blue water. I have never seen North Berwick looking so lovely.

September 17th

Television *Press Conference* with Sir Ronald Howe, a former commissioner of the Metropolitan police, whose frank avowal of old-fashioned 'commonsense' views was refreshing. He had no use for psychiatrists, since frankly he thought most of them as crazy as their patients. Of course murderers like Haig and Heath were completely mad, and of course it was right to hang them—no sense in keeping people like that alive. It would not be a good thing to put prostitutes off the streets: in some countries where that had been done arrangements were made by telephoning hotels, and that was unsatisfactory—much better to see what you were getting. He could not remember a case in which he was concerned where anyone had been wrongfully charged or convicted. He had no doubt Timothy Evans was guilty, though the jury would no doubt have thought it a curious coincidence if they had known that there were two murderers in the same house, one of them the principal witness against Evans.

September 19th

Nancy had been to collect a pedigree corgi puppy from Pembrokeshire which she had ordered, at the price of 12 guineas: a quiet-looking thing with a nice head and a very fat brown body, travelling along vigorously on its four short legs.

September 24th

Charles Johnston had been consulted by Grimond in regard to a letter from Attlee. In a speech at the Liberal Party conference last week, Grimond had attacked the system of political patronage by which he said politics were maintained under both Conservative and Labour governments and had spoken of how no one could be appointed to high ecclesiastic or legal posts unless he was agreeable to the ruling clique. Attlee had chosen to regard this as an attack on himself personally, in regard to his appointment of judges, bishops and so on, and had written demanding a public withdrawal and apology. Charles and I agreed that there was not much substance in Attlee's complaint, and approved the draft of a letter Grimond proposed to write explaining in friendly terms what he had had in mind and saying nothing about a public apology.

October 2nd

One of the speakers on an amateurish Scottish programme, *Compass*, on television, was Sinclair Shaw, commenting on the failure to alter the Scots law of intestate succession—this as a text for a vigorous denunciation of Westminster and M.P.s' neglect of Scottish problems. He was very much in earnest, and I thought very effective, though possibly he overdid it a little. One of the things at the back of my mind in tuning in to the programme was that it might be the kind of thing I could take part in, some day, if I knew how it was run and what it was about. But I did not grudge Gerald his appearance, and thought he was probably a good deal better at it than I should have been.

October 16th

Ian Fraser was complaining bitterly of Clyde's habit of producing a prepared judgment which he read 'extempore' as soon as the final speech had been delivered. Fraser thought this, apart from its discourtesy and departure from ordinary rules of justice, was a bad thing for the Faculty, since it might mean that solicitors would cease to incur the expense of instructing senior counsel when they knew that the Court's opinion would be prepared before senior counsel had been heard. Ross McLean suggested that the Faculty should pass a resolution and get the Dean to send it to the Lord President.

October 22nd

To Glasgow, where evidence was being taken on commission in *Chestnut v. Barclay Curle*. The job at which the pursuer had been injured consisted of sealing the ballast tank of a ship called *Queen Eleanor*. A small oval manhole leading through the engine-room bulkhead was about 18 inches in diameter and obstructed by pipes. The pursuer says that attempts by some members of the squad to get in were unsuccessful, and he as the smallest man there was sent in. He managed to get through, but gave himself a bad twist and developed a hernia. The foreman, whose evidence was being taken today, had been awkward and had refused to answer Thornton's questions when he interviewed him: but today he gave his evidence fairly enough, and though stubborn at first soon came round under cross-examination and ultimately agreed with me that the hole was obviously dangerous and just the kind of place where a man was liable to injure himself. He and I got on very friendly terms during the cross-examination, and he shook hands warmly with me as we were leaving.

October 31st

Brand was recalling a trial in which a housebreaker had defended himself, with Strachan as presiding judge. The accused did not go into the witness box, but in addressing the jury at the end not only reviewed the evidence but gave his own account of the facts—which led Strachan, when charging the jury, to tell them that the accused, 'no doubt inadvertently', had referred in his speech to some matters that had not been spoken to in evidence.

November 4th

The Pope's coronation televised this morning. Everyone concerned seemed curiously confused: and the ceremony, though an interesting spectacle, fell a long way short of the dignity and solemnity of the Queen's opening of Parliament.

November 7th

A Gorebridge farmer had dumped a great bundle of paper into Dundas Street about the injustices inflicted on him when his land was requisitioned for open-cast mining. As he had already been writing to the Prime Minister—'Dear Mr Macmillan, I know you are very busy, but...'—I thought the case had gone beyond my level.

November 8th

We all motored to the King's to see *Ruddigore*. It opened slowly, but after Leonard Osborne came on the scene in the character of Richard Dauntless everything went with a swing.

November 9th

Listened-in to the first of a series of Reith lectures by Professor A.C.B. Lovell: an interesting summary of the stage which astronomy has reached, all completely fantastic, with stars and nebulae rushing away from one another at some incredible speed, with apparently no risk of colliding with any other object in the vast emptiness of space.

November 11th

Called for Robert Irvine, with the object of going round some of the old Calton Ward members and trying to persuade them to resume their connection with the Party. Our first couple thought all parties were the same, out for what they could get, and the husband got involved in a long argument with Irvine about misdeeds of shop stewards, an office which Irvine himself happens to hold in the foundry where he works. But even this couple invited us into their kitchen, cosy with a blazing coal fire, and received us hospitably. Mrs O'Hara, at the far end of Brunswick Road, also took us into a kitchen where there was a fine blazing fire, and Mr O'Hara shaving at the sink. It turned out that she worked for the Lord Advocate, giving daily help in the house, and she recounted with gusto how Mrs Milligan had said to her that they would rely on her, Mrs O'Hara, at election time, and how she had replied that she was sorry but they were staunch Labour supporters and always would be. This reply had evidently been much appreciated in the Milligan household—of which Mrs O'Hara spoke highly, while preserving untarnished her political philosophy. I found them a delightful couple. Finally we visited Mr McFettes, poring over NUPE papers spread over his kitchen table: an old hand, who is a member of his Union's National Executive, and seemed to have things to attend to more important than going to listen to Cecil Gordon. He struck me as a shrewd old fellow.

November 14th
Procedure Roll before Strachan. The pursuer, a part-time fireman in Hawick fire brigade, was called to a fire at the Theatre cinema. The escape ladder of a vehicle called a Merryweather escape suddenly slewed over and fell on him. He blames the sub-officer responsible for positioning the vehicle. The defenders say that the accident was caused by an unknown member of the public 'who is believed to have been desirous of assisting the firemen' and who slewed the escape round by taking hold of one of the wheels. In reply to this the pursuer avers that if that were so the accident was still caused by the fault of the leading fireman, who should have warned the public to stand clear and sought police assistance if necessary. It seemed to me that this was a somewhat unforeseeable intervention, but luckily the alternative case was supported by an odd averment of the defenders', that 'as is usual in such circumstances various members of the public were anxious to help in the fire-fighting operations'. Ross for the defenders.

I was unable to stay to listen to him, having to go along to the First Division for an advising: *Nicoll v. North British Steel Foundry*. Clyde held that it was impossible to interfere with the Sheriff's finding that the shot blast and the swing frame grinders contributed to the pursuers' incapacity—so the pursuers won. Macvicar told me later that after we had come out of court Clyde spoke to him about the case, and said he hoped Macvicar would not think they had been too cowardly—they felt there was nothing else they could do. Meanwhile in Strachan's court a proof had been allowed: in a case of this kind it did not matter much whether it was tried by a judge or by a jury.

November 15th
Glasgow. To the Grand Hotel for a meeting of Labour candidates, addressed by Harold Wilson. He dealt with economic policy, and gave an excellent address. He has the facts at his finger-ends, and really got down to the problems: in this kind of thing, he is in a class by himself.

Finished reading *Voss*, by Patrick White, a novel which seems to have been deliberately written in a laborious, stylised manner, with conversations reminiscent of Ivy Compton-Burnett. Here however the style is applied not to a domestic situation but to a disaster which overtakes an expedition exploring into the interior of Australia. Nothing much happens, though what does happen is extremely unpleasant. The novel is not so much about the expedition as such as about the interaction between their sufferings and what takes place, apparently by a kind of telepathy, in the mind of a young woman who as a result of a couple of casual meetings has fallen in love with the expedition leader. I was thankful to get to the end of it.

November 18th
A jury trial before Wheatley: *Brown v. Hemphill*. The pursuer was the father of a man of 27 who had been employed by the defenders as a long-distance lorry driver. The defenders operate a fleet of road tankers, used for the carriage of oil and other liquids. When the tankers were in the garage, before being taken out to collect the next load, it was usual to clean them out, by steam or high-pressure water hose. Men were employed for this purpose, but the ultimate responsibility for ensuring that his tanker was clean rested on the driver. Brown's tanker, which was standing in the garage after having been cleaned, was driven out into the street by a mechanic. Shortly afterwards it was found that Brown was missing, and after a search he was discovered unconscious inside the tank. He had evidently climbed in, either to mop out the interior or to make sure that it was clean, and had been overcome by the fumes: and, while he was lying unconscious

inside, the vehicle had been driven out. The result has been serious brain damage. Brown is now an inmate of Bellsdyke mental hospital. He cannot give any coherent account of himself. He has no knowledge of time and place: he cannot identify money, or name an apple or an orange. When asked if he ever looked at television, he replied 'Jimmy Shand and his band' and kept repeating this in a vacant way. The action was on the basis that the defenders had failed to provide a proper system in not taking care that another man was always standing by whenever anyone had to go inside a tank. It was obvious that if we won the pursuer would get a very big award, but all the evidence indicated that the defenders had instructed drivers never to go inside a tank unless there was a man standing by, and that all the employees were fully aware of this rule. Accordingly it seemed very doubtful whether the case would succeed, and at a meeting with the pursuer on Saturday I made a strong effort to persuade him to accept £2,500 which had been offered. But he was determined not to accept, and the case went on. The witnesses were worse even than I had expected. All except Brown's brother stressed that there was a generally observed rule that no one was to go inside a tanker without someone standing by: and even the brother agreed that there was such a rule, as every driver knew, while maintaining that it was not regularly enforced. But in the afternoon the defenders, instead of being content to leave the case where it was, led one witness, one of the company's directors, and he gave me the material I wanted to present the case to the jury. I was able to put to him a printed document of 'Standing Instructions to Drivers of Tanker Waggons' which for some unaccountable reason had been lodged by the defenders and which, though dealing fully with cleaning out tanks and various safety precautions which had to be observed, had no word about not going into a tank without a man standing by. The cross-examination of this witness enabled me also to read a letter that the company had written to the hospital, in which it stated that the method of discharging used fuel oil, which this vehicle had been carrying, was to feed the exhaust gases from the petrol engine of the vehicle into the tank, thereby raising the internal pressure sufficiently to syphon off the load—and incidentally of course leaving the interior of the tank full of exhaust gases. The tank had then been steam-cleaned. As nobody could say who had cleaned this tank, or whether Brown had been aware of this situation, I was able to introduce into the case an additional element of considerable danger which had not been mentioned on Record. The cross-examination was quite effective, and I was satisfied that everything possible had been done. Wheatley gave a full and fair summing-up—fair in the sense that it was impossible to tell which side he favoured, and in that respect probably more favourable to the pursuer than the evidence warranted—and the jury found for the pursuer by 10 to 3 and assessed damages at £17,500. They found Brown 40 per cent to blame, so the pursuer gets £10,500. I believe that the assessment of £17,500 is the biggest ever made by a Scots jury.

November 25th

The pursuers' reclaiming motion in *Borough of Ramsgate v. McGhee*, in the Second Division. Migdale had allowed a proof. I had thought of another possible point, and this, though it did not meet with much favour from the Court, enabled us to fill up the day with an entertaining discussion. I think they will probably adhere to Migdale's allowance of a proof and we shall accordingly succeed in putting off some time—which seems to be the only real object the defenders have.

November 26th

Television included a Guildhall banquet at which the Prime Minister proposed the toast of Anglo-American friendship and Nixon, the Vice-President of USA, replied. Nixon made an excellent speech, eloquent and full of good sense. He struck me as a man who knew what he was about.

November 28th

A television 'press conference' at which Mr Nixon gave further evidence of his ability and adroitness.

December 6th

Bennett made a remark to me about a midget woman we had seen in the lobby during a jury trial: 'That's what we call a short witness'. This reminded me of something O'Brien had said about a witness described as a 'catch boy'. The case had concerned means of access, and all the witnesses before this one had agreed that the only means of access was by climbing up a high bulkhead. The catch boy however said he never used that way, but always went by the ladder. All the other witnesses had said there was no ladder, but as it was obvious that this boy could not have got up the bulkhead it seemed that he was telling the truth: and the pursuer's case accordingly collapsed. O'Brien said he had never known before what a catch boy was, but now appreciated that it was a witness who said in the witness-box the opposite of what he had said on precognition.

Motored to Arniston for a Scottish Junior Cup tie. I was supporting the local team and was disappointed when in the last three minutes of the game the red-jersey team, whom I took to be Arniston, scored a second goal to win the tie. I have since found out however that in supporting the blue-jersey team I had been under a misapprehension, since they in fact were Newtongrange, so the local team had won.

December 8th
Consultations fixed for 2.30, 3 and 3.30, then at 4.15 a consultation which took considerably longer: a lady who is seeking to divorce her weathy husband and who had strong views about how her case should be presented. She had already quarrelled with the Dean of Faculty, who previously represented her, and after a long argument I got her to agree that I should conduct the case in my way, not hers. She has been concerned in recovering some letters which she thinks have been wrongly withheld by a London solicitor, and after her capitulation remarked that that meant that no further efforts were to be made to recover the letters. I replied that I did not say that: all I meant was that I should decide whether such an effort was to be made, and if so how and when it was to be made. She is obviously an extraordinarily difficult client, whom it was necessary to tame from the outset so far as possible. Caplan, the young junior at the consultation, remarked after she left that it had been most instructive.

December 9th
Judgment in *Borough of Ramsgate v. McGhee*. They have confirmed Migdale's allowance of a proof, so we may get some more fun out of the case yet before our clients have to meet their obligations.

December 12th
Some talk at lunch time about Migdale: Emslie recalled an occasion when he had solemnly told a jury that they were 'masters and mistresses of the facts'.

December 19th
Shaw told at lunch about one of the few occasions when David

Maxwell appeared in court. He had been against Shaw in a defended divorce, and his client and the client's father proceeded to give different accounts of what had happened. Stevenson, who was trying the case, was doubtful of their credibility, and had pointed out to Maxwell that their evidence differed in a striking and peculiar manner. 'How do you account for it, Mr Maxwell?' 'Heredity, my lord', said Maxwell, 'heredity'.

1959

1959: the long-awaited General Election, with the consequence of four more years of Conservative government, and the incidental result that I was not going to be Solicitor-General for Scotland. My practice had reached the dimensions at which acceptance of office would mean financial loss, and I was by no means altogether sorry that I should be continuing in practice in the accustomed way. There was hardly a court day on which I did not have at least two proofs or trials entered in my diary: and though the vast majority of cases settle before the date of the enquiry is reached enough remained to keep me fully occupied. Politics were dominated by the election: and the electorate, enjoying their new-found prosperity, regarded the Tories as the working-man's best friend. Those who had come up in the world—a description applicable to the majority of the electors—were not interested in social reform: and a party that promised new hope to the downtrodden and defrauded workers had nothing to offer to workers who were no longer downtrodden and had no realisation of being defrauded. Mr Gaitskell was a pleasant surprise. Night after night, he argued the Labour case reasonably and convincingly: but he was not a likeable person. The electorate preferred Mr Macmillan—if it were not for his politics, I should have done the same. In my own election I had as my only opponent the Lord Advocate, Mr Milligan. He did not exert himself unduly in the election, nor did I. The meetings were well attended, and question time was interesting, particularly on the topic of nuclear disarmament, on which a number of young people pursued me throughout the campaign. I had a good deal of sympathy with their views, but my position was clear: that throwing nuclear weapons overboard and going back to a position in which war with 'conventional weapons' might once more be a reality was by no means a desirable policy, apart from being a chimera—since if war began in these circumstances nothing could prevent nuclear weapons from being developed all over again in the course of it. In home affairs I was content to stress the crudity of the 'never-had-it-so-good' campaign, and to show how little we were doing for those in need, in comparison with the vast potential resources of the modern world. The result left me rather disillusioned about the workings of political democracy:

189

but I enjoyed the election while it lasted. Our pleasant cul-de-sac at the foot of Mountcastle Drive had been gradually losing its character, and the fields which had been a glorious picture of golden barley waving in the wind had been covered with bungaloid growth. When a giant bull-dozer appeared, to drive in piles for the bridge across the park and the Figgate Burn, we knew it was time to go—to Midmar Gardens, a quiet street with a view over to Blackford Hill.

January 1st

As the weather was bad, I settled down with the children before the fire and played cards: vingt-et-un, rummy, German whist, beggar-my-neighbour, snap, pelmanism, Jacob, Old Maid, donkey, cribbage, sevens, Newmarket and comette.

January 3rd

Finished reading *Causes of Crime*, by Lord Pakenham, a book which must constitute the most long-winded way possible of saying that there are many causes of crime and nobody knows precisely what they are.

January 6th

Pike is clearing out the house at Liberton: it appears that his father kept everything—papers, tins, bottles, anything that came into the house.

January 7th

Looked in at Pike's. Jim assured me that the house was clear compared to what it had been like when he started work, but every room was still filled with an extraordinary miscellany of stuff. Every drawer and shelf had its quota, carefully arranged and labelled, but all completely useless: 'Gas Mantles', 'Curtain Remnants', 'Brown Paper', and so on. The books included an old edition not only of the *Encyclopedia Britannica* but of *Harmsworths'* and *Chambers' Encyclopedias*, with books referring to every conceivable trade and profession, including a *Grocers' Manual*. Logs were stacked all up the back staircase, and the garden was filled with planks, stacks of timber and the like. There were foodstuffs of all kinds, dating back ten or twelve years.

January 12th

To Glasgow, to take the evidence of a witness in the Elder Cottage

Hospital in Govan. He is suffering from cancer of the throat, but gave his evidence clearly and lucidly. He told me afterwards that he was very well looked after. 'If you could get better anywhere, you would get better here', he said, rather sadly.

As the next train which had a buffet car was at 12.30, I declined the offer of a taxi, and said I should prefer to walk. We set off on foot, and after walking some way reached a crossroads with a notice pointing to 'Govan Ferry'. I said we had better go across, and we boarded the ferryboat, in a little passage on the deck railed off from the vehicles which occupied most of the space. It is a free ferry: neither we nor the vehicles had to make any payment. The point from which the ferry started is in the middle of Harland & Wolff's premises, and we had a good view of the shipyard, with a big ship on the stocks nearly completed.

In the evening motored to the City Labour Party's rooms in Picardy Place for a meeting of parliamentary candidates and election agents. Marshall gave a useful summary of the kind of work which should be put in hand now: but with the usual Labour Party fondness for discomfort the meeting was held in a poky little room, heated only by one small electric radiator. I had my papers for tomorrow's jury trial, and worked on them spasmodically while the discussion was going on: and before it ended had the preparation of the case completed.

January 13th
The pursuer, a waitress at the Royal Hotel, Rothesay, was asked to remove an apron from a drying pulley. The rope broke and one end of the pulley fell. The pursuer says it struck her on the forehead, and she has since suffered from a neurotic condition which has made her feel unfit for any kind of work. She is very stout, and has put on three stones in weight since the accident. Duffes cross-examined her old mother about this, and was told by her that she had been instructed by the doctor to give her body-building foods. She was now fourteen stone. 'You rather overdid it', Duffes suggested. We had advised her beforehand that she should accept any settlement she could get—there is a tender of £250, which she would not consider, saying she expected £2,000 at least.

January 14th
I was instructed today for cases in five different courts: Scotland said

he did not remember such a thing before. Three were debates, and two of them I had to leave to my juniors. A High Court continued hearing I left John McCluskey to look after. I thought I made a fairly good speech to the jury, but the verdict was unanimously for the defender.

Finished reading *The Rainbow Comes and Goes*, by Diana Cooper, rather a fascinating volume of autobiography. She gives an interesting and not unattractive picture of the life of the younger members of a ducal family and their friends, in the days before the first war. But the highlight of the book is a series of love letters passing in 1918 between the author, then working as a nurse in a London hospital, and 2nd Lieutenant Duff Cooper, serving in the front line in France. At times he writes in a light, almost teasing vein, but it is impossible not to appreciate the emotion which underlies this strange correspondence, its poignancy heightened by the terror which all the time overlays it as the writers' contemporaries and friends are mown down one by one. The reader knows that in fact this couple will survive, but that hardly affects the intensity of feeling which, along with their candour and honesty, is the main impression left by the letters.

January 15th
A jury trial before Wheatley: an unusually interesting and enjoyable little case. My pleasure in it was completed when John Shaw phoned in the evening to say there had been a unanimous verdict for the pursuer. Cuthbert Thomson was a member of the jury, and when I phoned him told me he had enjoyed the experience very much, though he had not thought the jury's deliberations were of a very judicial character. Oddly enough, he had preferred the pursuer to his mate, whom he thought 'rather aggressive'—a strange description of this mild-mannered, sensible man.

January 16th
Television press conference with Harold Wilson. He was first-rate, with all the facts at his finger ends—answering his questioners with good humour, conviction, and complete confidence in the soundness of his case: an encouraging performance. It is a pity that Wilson is not the party leader instead of Gaitskell.

January 18th
Cramond church: a recital of piano pieces by Betty Brown, and two

sonatas for violin and piano. In spite of a bad cold, Betty played beautifully. I began to get a little tired of it by the middle of the programme, but later on, refreshed by a Beethoven sonata, I got into a more receptive mood, and felt when Betty finished her three final pieces that I could have stayed there very comfortably listening to her for quite a while longer.

January 22th
Some awful American trash on television, called the Burns and Allen show, which the children like to have and are allowed instead of children's television, which is usually at least as bad.

January 23rd
North Edinburgh Labour Party social at the Gordons' house. Nancy had made sandwiches with ham from one of Mr Pike's seven-year-old tins, which when opened seemed perfectly good. I was surprised to see how many of the ladies could sit down at the piano and play or sing as required: it seems that the art of making our own entertainment is by no means dead, despite wireless and television. One young lady, Miss Sutherland, not only could play anything required, but recited the whole of *Tam o' Shanter*, with sufficient expression to make it intelligible but in no way overdoing it.

February 6th
Heard from Migdale that Blades was dead: a great misfortune, since it means that Strachan moves automatically into the Second Division, and the chance of having Strachan and Guthrie together in the First Division is gone. It follows that there is no hope for the First Division in the foreseeable future, as the judge next in seniority after Guthrie is Migdale.

February 11th
A debate before Migdale: *Thomson v. Glasgow Corporation*. The pursuer had gone with her washing to a washhouse in Govan, and was standing beside a spin dryer waiting for it to stop. Somehow or other, in a manner by no means clear, her rubber apron caught in the dryer. Her arm was pulled round the spindle and injured, so that she had to have it amputated. The ground of action against the Corporation is that they failed to have a guard on the spindle, or their servant in charge of the washhouse removed the guard before the motion had

ceased. I had another debate to attend to, on a plea that the defenders' averments were irrelevant. Ewan Stewart embarked on an involved argument about the effect of a supervening act of negligence, and this argument failed to convince Guthrie. It was not long before Ewan sat down, remarking to me *sotto voce* that as Guthrie was clearly against us it was useless to flog the argument further. But after Peterson had made a short reply I put the argument on the more commonsense ground that had occurred to me, and it was not long before it seemed that Guthrie was beginning to appreciate the point. Peterson had really no answer and Guthrie gave judgement sustaining our plea. This was satisfactory, and showed how before a reasonable judge no case need be regarded as lost until the argument is over. I happened to meet Guthrie in the lobby and had a word with him about the debate and how I had been unable to get my junior to see the point, though I had been sure I was right about it. 'He was perhaps a bit too metaphysical for you and me', was Guthrie's comment.

February 24th
A divorce before Guthrie: *Murray v. Murray*. The pursuer had ordered his wife out of the house after 27 years of married life, but immediately after the separation embarked on an extensive one-sided correspondence with her. The letters, although containing a good many offensive observations, included also requests to her to come back. On the view that the approaches were not genuine, she ignored these letters. The letters became more objectionable, with scurrilous accusations against the defender and the family. He sent the eldest son the model of a gallows, and his wife a copy of Dante's *Inferno*, which she in the witness-box described as a book about hell and said she had burned in the garden. In a curious incident averred to have taken place last year, the pursuer appeared out of the blue at the defender's house and hit her on the head with a hammer, so that she had to go to hospital. McKechnie in his examination of his client the pursuer made no reference to this, and I started my cross-examination by questioning him about it. He admitted frankly that he had hit the defender with a hammer, and did not seem to think there was anything odd about it. He had taken the hammer, he said, with the object of breaking up some furniture, and when the defender for some reason unknown to him cried, 'Murder, murder' there was nothing to be done but to hit her, which he did. McKechnie had refrained also from putting to him all the letters damaging to his case,

so he was left rather at my mercy trying to explain them under cross-examination. When I had been badgering him for some time he remarked that it seemed to him a lot of suggestions were being made that he was never given an opportunity to answer, whereupon Guthrie turned on him and said, 'Murray, that is contempt of court, and if it were not that I am not sure that you are completely responsible for what you are saying I should deal with you very severely'. The poor old fellow was much taken aback, it being obvious that he had been accustomed to domineer all his life and never had his pronouncements questioned. I thought myself that he was a pretty crazy fellow.

February 25th
Guthrie assoilzied the defender, smiting the pursuer hip and thigh in the course of his extempore judgment.

March 7th
Ayrshire Yeomanry point-to-point at Torcross Farm, Tarbolton. I had thought of leaving the car in the village, but could not find a convenient place and carried on a mile up the hill to Torcross—though grudging that one always has to pay to park a car at a point-to-point. I had to stop in the gate while parking money was being taken from cars in front, and on starting off again was waved past along a row of men who were taking the money, so as to make room for the cars behind: and before I knew it I was past all the men and in the field. I had had no intention of going past without paying, but having done so found no inclination to draw attention to the fact and be mulcted of the exorbitant charge. My first choice was a winner—a horse called Solemn John—and brought me fifteen shillings, so though I had no more winners my afternoon's racing cost me only a shilling.

March 8th
Finished reading *Along the Road to Frome*, by Christopher Hollis. It is autobiographical, but the author is more concerned to reflect on the people and things he has encountered than to give a formal account of his life—and very honest and thought-provoking reflections they are. He is a convert to Catholicism, and the book is pervaded with genuine religious feeling and what one might call enlightened commonsense. He is highly critical of Catholic institutions, as he is of Eton and Parliament, of both which he has had personal experience. Catholics, he thinks, are at their best when living as a small minority,

under obligation to preach the Gospel to all nations but not surprised or disappointed if the preaching has apparently little effect. He always sees the other point of view. The sceptic had, he says, a formidable case. If we were faced with the astonishing claim that two thousand years ago, millions of years after the universe was created, there lived an obscure Syrian peasant who was its Creator, it would be a wild understatement to say that at first sight such a tale was more likely to be untrue than true. His answer to this is not altogether convincing, but he does not imagine that it is, and it is manifestly sincere and worth thinking about. His comments on politics are equally acute, and include a delightful character-sketch of Attlee, whose prose style 'was, and remains, my unending delight. There is a flatness about it that is not of this world'. He has good, constructive things to say about any number of subjects: Ireland, America, elections, war propaganda, Suez. This book left me with greatly enhanced respect for its honest, thoughtful, fair-minded author.

On television tonight: Rachmaninov's *Concerto No 2*. We were much impressed by Moiseivitch's playing, and his complete concentration on the music, without the least trace of show or affectation.

March 9th
The Cameo: *Wild Strawberries*, a film well worth seeing, not always easy to understand in all its implications, but full of vitality and truth, absorbingly interesting. A remarkable use of silence, particularly in some realistic dream sequences. What makes it so moving and impressive is the reality of the people in the story, the development in their character during the old Professor's car drive to Lund to receive an honorary degree after fifty years in the medical profession, and the haunting, nostalgic beauty with which the story is told.

March 13th
Tonight on television included an interview with John Stonehouse, a Labour MP who has just been expelled from the Central African Federation because he made a speech to Africans which did not please Sir Roy Welensky's Government. He dealt fairly but courteously with the questions put by the interviewer, and made an excellent impression.

March 15th
To Morningside with the object of calling on George Herbert Brown.

In the last week or two I have had an unprecedented number of taxation Memorials, which have meant a lot of work on unaccustomed ground: but in the last one I could not understand even what the Inspector of Taxes had been purporting to do, and thought I had better have some expert advice. But no one was in.

March 16th
A useful talk with Brown.

March 20th
With Nancy to the Playhouse: *Operation Amsterdam*, a dull, ineffective film. It contained every cliché of the suspense film, but whoever made it had not realised that no amount of chasing and shooting could make a film exciting unless there was some point in it.

March 21st
Haddington: a junior football match—an unusually friendly occasion, particularly as regards the spectators, who were few in number, and seemed to be mostly local worthies and to know the members of their team by name. At one point when play was proceeding on the far side of the field the Haddington wing forward came up to the touch line and asked some of the spectators what had won the Grand National. At another time one of the players was tying his bootlace for quite a lengthy period while the game was going on round him.

March 22nd
A service from St Cuthbert's on television, with Leonard Small, now a Doctor of Divinity, preaching on Matthew 21,10. We then motored to Portobello Church: a service in celebration of the 150th aniversary. Again Dr Small preached, on Psalms 87,6: another excellent sermon. He preaches with a wealth of stories and illustrations, all carefully worked in and completely to the point, and with a mounting air of drama and excitement which carries everything before it to a magnificent climax—all without a single note. He never smiles, even when he brings a laugh from the congregation—as he did more than once even with the Portobello members—but preaches with a quiet concentration which seems to have tremendous force behind it.

Finished for the second time *The Facts of Love*, by Stanley Wade Baron, which again I thought rather delightful, with some shrewd ideas. 'People can always get along, I am certain of that, if they are two normal and rational people, but where there is love—well, it is a strange thing but love makes everything a little more difficult'. I had forgotten there was a happy ending, and was relieved to find that all came well at the last.

March 24th

With McGarvie, Irvine and a young fellow named Buchan, who is in an insurance office, to Bothwell Street, where we split into two pairs. McGarvie came with me, and we tackled an enormous tall tenement of five floors and a basement. Visiting each house in this building took us the best part of a hour. I found it interesting, and we got quite a lot of red marks on our Register cards, as well as selling fourteen copies of a pamphlet. Buchan recalled a previous occasion when he had been canvassing and an old woman who came to the door had told him she was not going to vote for anyone until we got a better Government.

March 25th

A debate before Walker. The case was very simple, but I was in doubt up to the last moment whether he would allow a proof or a jury trial. The general view was that he did not know himself until he was in process of giving his opinion, when it looked as if he had been going to order a proof and then could not think of any reason for refusing a jury trial. Anyhow, a jury trial was what he decided on, with expenses to the pursuer.

We had last night a Conservative television show, with Mr Butler interviewed by three journalists and showing himself an adept at saying nothing in as charming a way as possible. He never put a foot wrong: and the producers of this broadcast had at least done their viewers the compliment of expecting them to take serious questions seriously.

March 26th

Finished reading *A Time to be Happy*, by Nayantara Sahgal, a candid but sympathetic picture of Indian life before and after independence. It is all set in a low key, but it is an even-tempered book, suffused with kindliness and quiet wisdom. 'One can't go through life rejecting every situation and opportunity because of its limitations. If we did, very soon there would be no choice left for us'. I liked the story of the fancy-dress competition for children at the hotel's annual party, where an Indian girl was awarded first prize and then after a protest by a group of women was superseded by a little English girl in a crinoline and had to surrender her teddy bear and take a box of chocolates as second prize. The hotel manageress had gone up afterwards to the room occupied by the Indian girl's mother, a well-to-do and valued client, in order to console her, but found her in no need of consolation but merely about to have a cup of tea and anxious that the manageress should join her. A listener to whom the story was told, who thought the Indian mother might have shown a little more pride, was asked 'What are five thousand years of culture if they haven't taught one to be polite?' and on asking whether politeness was the only thing that mattered got the reply, 'That men may live together in civilized accord—it is very nearly the only thing'.

March 27th
Finished reading *The House in the Heart*, by Elizabeth Coxhead. A review I read of this novel suggested that it would be a good thing if the author devoted her talents to something more worthy of them. I can see what the critic meant: but this little tale is so movingly and attractively told that I should not myself wish the author to do anything else than what she always does so well.

March 30th
Finished reading *Too Much of Water*, by Bruce Hamilton, an excellent murder story set on board a ship carrying a small number of passengers to Barbados. In a short space of time the author manages to make the reader well acquainted with all the passengers, their characters and foibles, in a most entertaining manner. The murder is a secondary consideration, but that part too is ingeniously done, with a neat ending after the murderer is known.

April 2nd
Train to London. The children behaved well, being much taken up with a scoring game for things seen from the train: a point for a signal-box or a herd of Friesian cows or a pond, two points for a diesel train in motion or a herd of Herefords, and so on.

April 4th
Underground to Westminster, and finding a launch setting off for Tower Pier paid our two shillings for adults, one shilling for children.

The pier is just at the entrance to the Tower, and we thought we had better visit it. On Saturdays admission is free, and this had the disadvantage of making the place rather crowded. A curious fashion among teenage girls of carrying a large wicker basket instead of a handbag—dozens of them.

April 5th
To church: St Paul's at Knightsbridge. The congregation was dowdy in the extreme, their only peculiarity being that they all genuflected before taking their seats and bowed now and again when the name of God was mentioned. But there was some fine music. The Bishop of Basutoland preached. He simply appealed for money and 'priests' for his diocese, and gave an extraordinarily naive, unconvincing account of the work there. He seemed to have no sense of reality or any understanding of the problems that one supposes must arise in an African diocese. It was simply a matter of converting the heathen, in the manner of some nineteenth-century missionary. What the Basutos can make of him passes one's comprehension. But he was short, and so peculiar that one could not say he was dull.

April 6th
The Crazy Gang's revue: excellent, with everything required to make up a first-rate family show—speed, humour, a friendly atmosphere, spectacle, a bit of comedy juggling, a chorus of 24 high-kicking good-lookers, and a pair of brilliant specialty dancers. Elizabeth thought it the best thing she had ever been at, and I have no doubt she was right.

April 7th
Madame Tussaud's waxworks: the wax models having only a remote likeness to the people they were intended to represent. The distorting mirrors in the amusement hall were more of a success.

April 8th
Came down at 10 to the television room to hear Harold Wilson's criticism of the Budget. He was very good, but attracted only a small audience from the hotel inmates. One of the old ladies, leaving as Mr Wilson started, said if she stayed to listen to that man on the television she would want to smash it.

April 9th

My bill for the week, *en pension* for the four of us, £43.17.9. At Holborn the children had their last escalator. To celebrate the end of the holiday they went up the ascending escalator again to the Central Line level, and had a second run on the downward one. Then after getting off the train they stood on the platform waving goodbye to it until it disappeared into the tunnel.

April 10th

Finished reading *Let Him Have Judgment*, by Bruce Hamilton, a novel which it would be misleading to describe as a murder story. There is a murder in it, or something that looks like a murder, but in fact it is an exciting, absorbing tale, with convincing character development and a denouement which brings out with horrifying force the disastrous possibilities of a mistake in capital cases.

April 16th

To St Mary's Roman Catholic cathedral, to attend Alex McClusky's funeral service. The small frontage gives no idea of what an imposing building it is inside, and it was well filled by a big congregation. When the service had been in progress for some time, the woman sitting next me asked, 'Do you know who this requirem is for?' My answer apparently conveyed nothing to her. It was a very odd service. There was no music, and the whole proceedings were deliberately conducted in a manner completely inaudible to the congregation. The latter took no part in the service, except to stand up occasionally from a kneeling position. The officiating priest, McClusky's brother-in-law, rattled through the Latin at a great rate, while we were supposed to follow in a little booklet. A man behind me obligingly leant forward now and again and said 'Page 11', or 'Page 16', or whatever it might be. But the robes and candles were quite imposing, and it was interesting to see, for once in a way. The archbishop sat at one side in his purple robe, but did not participate. Towards the end, the priests came down to the coffin, and there was a strong smell of incense as censers were swung round. During the early part of the service there was a good deal of coming and going by members of the congregation, and towards the end a lot of them went up to the front for communion, to receive which they stood in a kind of queue. The communicants included quite a number of children, who were dotted about the congregation, and walked back to their seats with clasped hands, like the adults. The proceedings did not suggest the remotest connection with anyone's funeral, and there was nothing in any way moving or uplifting—merely a kind of archaic interest. At the cemetery the brother-in-law rattled through the service at the grave just as quickly as in the cathedral, but the mourners were allowed to take part in the responses, giving the officiating priest Latin for Latin in what sounded like the *De Profundis*.

April 17th
Lyceum: *Change of Tune*, a new comedy by Alan Melville, extremely entertaining, and beautifully staged and acted. I enjoyed it immensely, and was enchanted by both leading ladies: Geraldine McEwan as the wife, and Dilys Kaye as the courtesan. The latter was ravishing in her lovely nineteenth-century get-up. The play's wit and invention never flagged, and if it does not have a long run in London it will be through no fault of its own or those taking part in it.

From Mr William Muir:
Register Number 198/57   H.M.Prison, Inverness   24.4.1959
Dear Gordon Stott I humbly acknowledge your letter it is very kind of you to think of me & you have known me for a long time If I am spared to be released I will write a book. I will not forget to wallop the Jewellers & so Diamond merchant such as Mrs Henry & her son Louis. The whole Judicial system is wrong. I did wrong to defend my self and was deaf I never heard much of course it was all cut & dried before I went near the Court. The Police to come out to my house without a warrant I lost my Diamonds and £175 who stole the money has never been known the police never tried to find out I was the victim not the Jeweller I lost every thing & 5 years for what George Dawson got 6 years for hundreds of thousands is there any fairness in our system The same with the no hanging law. A man can get Drunk and kill and get away fight or kill a Cat or a Dog it is not even reported I am in favour of Hanging especially those that kill to steal or Sex Cases take the Manuel a perfect scandal to Scotland I wrote a Petition from here stating I was in a position to reveal valuable information about the Lanarkshire murders Ann Klenland & the Watt case. no attention was paid I received a reply stating the Police were quite capable of investigating the case and declined my information Little did the know I was in a position to hand

over a small case left in my charge by a Friend of Manuels I got acquainted with a man in Saughton Prisin who was serving a short sentence from Glasgow transfererd with a draft He was discharged october I was a trusted Prisoner he knew where I lived at Barton. I was visited unexpected by him an a Girl. I was asked to keep the case. He never returned I opened the case & found valuable evidence concerning these Lanarkshire murders I read in the Press later that a Girl was missing from Coatbridge Lanarkshire. I see by the press Mrs Mann member for Coatbridge raising Hell in the House of Commons about the slackness of the Lanarkshire Police for failing to trace these missing Persons unfortunately she digs at the Lanarkshire for having to call in Glasgow Police I think they are no better than Lanarkshire. Glasgow has many unsolved crimes and my opinion now is that many of these crimes has been taken for granted Manuel done them all the contents of this case proves without doubt he murdered Ann Kelnland the Crown to prove it it also proves he was associated with another Person in the Watt case I see a book and many articles has been written in different Papers about the Manuel Trial all built up on imagination not facts I was sorrow they refused my help I am certain Manuel and his friend would both have been arrested & hanged before he had a chance to murder Isabella Cook and the Smart Family I could do nothing I am in Jail true Manuel hanged himself by talking much what he said was true. Mrs Mann asked the question is their still a murderer in our midst. I quite agree their is this Friend of Manuels I mention I believe is a murderer Now I have mentioned about this case to many people all they are interested in where is this case containing many articles letters Photos Diary clothing etc I would have handed over this case if I had requested to do so no person was interested a man in Jail must safeguard himself What I done for you I got nearly murdered for it at Peterhead I will never again help the Police I plead guilty to that charge and you got me 2 years it was fear that made me plead guilty Glasgow Police promised to help me I was not being charge by them after it was found out I was giving evidence against Dickson & Duffy 2 men went out to Tarbrax and threatened my wife I complained and was interviewed by a Det in Saughton nothing was done she got so ill had to be removed to Hartwood Mental Hospital where she died it was cruel piece of work nothing was done for me or her only I

got a mauling from a Friend of Dickson & Duffy the so called John Ramnesky he escaped & got away from any punishment for assaulting me. Now I am sent up to Peterhead for this offence and placed almost next door to Ramensky threatened again I was removed here for safe keeping I took very ill and had to be removed to a Hospital and operated on, all from worry and fear. I am glad to say I have recovered and I am well and happy here this is a Hydropathic. The governor and his staff are very considerate and allow me a good deal of rope I get all the papers printed I am out in the garden Now when I come out I intend to put this case I mention to the Fire I realaise some papers would make head lines of these articles I am not interested now I dont want murdered in Prison for that is the reward when one gives information to the Police I will call on you when I get released
Yours truly

May 8th

A lot of discussion in the Hall and corridors about the next Dean of Faculty. Since Shearer is the establishment candidate, the position has unfortunate possibilities. I had approached Ian Fraser as a candidate who might expect fairly general support, but he apparently had never considered standing: and having heard that Leslie wanted to stand I made a virtue of necessity and phoned him. With his usual air of possibly unconscious humbug, he insisted that he had never had any desire to stand, but if the upsurge of feeling from the floor was such as to make it seem his duty to go forward he would not feel entitled to refuse. I gathered that he intended to be a candidate. Meanwhile Kissen had been following up an approach I had made to Jack Hunter as a possibly formidable opponent to Shearer, and was to speak to Ian Fraser about whether he would propose him. I got E.F.G. Stewart to agree to sound Hunter. Since by the Faculty method of voting no one can be elected on a minority vote, it seemed desirable that both opponents go forward in the hope that one or other would get sufficient support.

May 9th

Brand this morning said he had persuaded Fraser to stand after all, on condition that I would propose him. This was awkward, in view of my conversation with Leslie, and I had to tell Brand that I did not think I could, though I should very much like to see Fraser as a candidate.

May 10th

Accounts for last week included £100 which the pursuer in *Miller v. South of Scotland Electricity Board* has chosen to make me out of the damages received in settlement of the action: a generous gesture, as total damages were, I think, only £600. It is of course intended to recompense me for my trip to London, which in an *in forma pauperis* appeal would otherwise go unpaid for.

May 13th

Four candidates were nominated today for the office of Dean: Shearer, Hunter, Leslie and Fraser. I had phoned Fraser on Monday, and he came up to Parliament House to see me. In view of my defection, he had come to think he should not go forward: but he changed his mind when I suggested Bobby Johnston as his proposer. I later got Bobby on the phone: he said he would be delighted to propose Fraser, and so it was arranged.

May 14th

Jury trial before Lord Kilbrandon—Shearer for the defenders.

May 15th

Shearer's speech was very fair: his nomination as a candidate for Dean seems to have mellowed him, and he conducted this whole case with courtesy and moderation. The jury found unanimously for the pursuer. His wife gave birth to a son this morning, so he had an eventful day. An amusing feature of this case is that before I came into it it was submitted to the Legal Aid Committee, and on legal aid being refused came before me in the Appeals Committee, where we all agreed in turning it down on the ground that there was no case. The solicitors—not a firm for whom I had ever acted—then approached me and asked if I would take it on a speculative basis, which of course I agreed to do: and I have succeeded in proving that myself and my colleagues on the Legal Aid committees were wrong.

May 20th

The Faculty met to elect a Dean. T.P. McDonald presided, and explained that there would be a general vote, then a vote between the two lowest, and finally a vote between the winner on the second vote and the one who had topped that poll on the general vote. On the first vote the result was: Fraser 35, Leslie 39, Shearer 39. Thus there was no decision as to who were the two lowest, and after consultation with the Clerk and Treasurer T.P. decided to give a casting vote—which on grounds of seniority he cast in favour of Leslie. This meant that Fraser and Shearer were the two lowest, and the vote between them was even closer: Fraser 52, Shearer 50. Finally Fraser beat Leslie by 59 to 49. I voted for Fraser throughout, with some misgivings in view of what I had said to Leslie but in the firm belief that Fraser was the best candidate.

From Mr William Muir:
Register Number 198/57   H.M.Prison, Inverness   28.5.1959
Dear Mr Stott I received your letter. Oh yes I would be glad to write a book & I Pray I will be spared to write one you shall have a book. Lawyer's of your standing are good judges of Character especially if you are for the Prosecution I am in the best of Health at least I think that but I am gettng old & easly upset my nerves get the better of me some of the young blood in Prison are perfectly villain and get far to lenent a sentence they come in here with the air of a Peacock & they are as arrogant as a Pig Gov & his staff have their hands full and what thanks do the get from the Public who ought to be getting medals and regonintion from the Crown perhaps when your Party gets power you will see to these Prison administrators. (I dont no when your party will get in again) you never know you might be a judge I pity Willie Muir if he comes up against you for *Diamonds*. This is a wonderful wee Prison about 40 or 50 the highest I have seen it very few real *Criminals*. Cheeky wasters would do nothing to help the administrator I argue & tell them off it is no use you might as well talk to the wind I am a great believer in doing what I am told for instance the Authorities here dont like to see the Pigeons fed why they come about these places I am certain they are the spirits of ex Governors & Officers long since gone to the Happy Land I feel sorrow for them. The Gov says they are vermin I must not fed them so I have stopped. God will not punish me for neglecting them. I expect to come back to earth as a Cat I will be some old womans Pet. The general Assembly is in session a funny lot these Auld Kirk ministers they have rejected having anything to do with Anglingene church. John Knox is still uppermost in their minds I wonder what your Father opinion would have been if he was still at Crammond Kirk I dont think he would have approved

of it. They are kicking up the devil about the Colered quartrs in *Blantyre Africa* I would like to see all whites clear out of that Dark Continent we have done our part let then administrat their own affairs some day there will be a clash between Black & White. Now about Home affairs McMillan & Co are doing fine I am sorrow we lost Mr Dulles at the time we needed him some of your party will not agree with that he fought for a principle I am a bit guilty of that my self I believe in Principal stick to your views whether it pleases the other fellow or not I criticise a lot of things in Prison today it is completely revolutionised gone to far to reform these teenagers they take liberties. Segration and more Buildings to house these Pests as far as I am concerned they would not need more than 2 Officers here. I am sure they could find hundreds like me in these places dont require a Officer as long as they have Hard cases Homo Sexual Fly men all together the jails will be full and they should appoint ex Governor & Prison Officer who has proved they are good judges of Character to sit on Committee. You dont mean to tell me a Man who has put in 25 or 30 years among the criminal element he could not be a good judge of who should be seperated from the mob & given a chance to work out their own destiny in a seperate Prison. I dont mean a Governor that has been appointed from another Dep such as the Army or Navy only men who have risen from the ranks they understand and know every trick of the criminal A great fuss was created by the Hanging of Manwool their is a flaw in the law I agree all should be hanged I notice a decision in the High Court yesterday Ramansky appeal a just verdict it would be a farce if a man do P.D should get away with committing crimes such as he did & expect to get away with it I am not sorrow for Gently Johnny as they call him a typical Criminal a common thief seeking Publicity now dont bother to answer this epistel I will watch the Scotsman and when I see you in action winning the case I will no you are very much alive

I will have a lot to tell you some day I am happy up here they pull my leg a lot I take it all with good humor.

I hope you are well

I remain Sincerly

June 2nd

A jury trial in which Alastair Johnston appeared for the pursuer: he was not as slow as I had expected. In a jury trial against Duffes last week, which Duffes won, I am told he asked one witness the same question seven times.

Finished reading *The Bell* by Iris Murdoch, a peculiar story but a gripping one. It poses some interesting problems of character and conduct, and the author's sympathetic treatment of the people in her novel won a ready response from me. The dying fall on which the book ends, though perhaps not wholly satisfying, is attractive.

June 4th

On television, Miss Leontyne Price: a negro soprano of primitive power and dignity whose static composure was in attractive contrast to the restless wriggling which characterises many singers on television.

June 6th

A production that has been lodged in one of my cases—an application for an appointment: 'Date you last attended Doctor: 26/2/1919. Reason: birth'.

June 8th

Kirkcaldy: an arbitration under the Agricultural Holdings Acts. The arbiter was a farmer from Strathmiglo, a simple-minded old fellow who was obviously very unwilling to be involved in a legal wrangle. He made a number of prejudicial remarks which indicated that he was not favourably disposed towards my client, but agreed that he would have to decide in accordance with what the law laid down. He was anxious that Charles and I should have an opportunity to tell our 'story', though equally anxious that we should not go beyond one o'clock. The debate was over in not much more than an hour, but what the arbiter will do remains a mystery.

Finished reading *A Room in Moscow*, by Sally Belfrage. No doubt it was praiseworthy of her to want to stay for a while in Moscow in order to find out that people there were much like people anywhere else, but though she has the right instincts she is a silly girl and has produced a tedious book.

June 9th

A motion to take the evidence of an Indian witness on interrogatories, in cross actions of divorce, *Warden v. Warden*. The parties went through a form of marriage in 1948 and lived together in Bombay, where the husband is a wealthy merchant. They subsequently found that a divorce which his former wife had obtained in Nevada was invalid in India or Scotland. He accordingly divorced her in the Scots courts in 1951, and the parties then married again—although they both insist that they did not get on together at all. The wife makes some extraordinary allegations about the husband's unsavoury conduct, which as the conduct took place in private are not susceptible of corroboration. She further says that he did not support her in disputes with servants, and left doors open so that they could see her undressing. The husband says his wife displayed complete lack of affection towards him, except for wanting him to stroke her back when she was in bed. She ridiculed him in public, and demanded large sums of money for various objects, which she then invested. She twice switched on the current while he was repairing electric lamps, with intent to injure or murder him. In May 1957 he went out one day, ostensibly to play golf, and never came back. She had a message that he had left for England. She later followed, and though the parties have not again cohabited they have had a number of meetings and scenes, including one in a clinic where the husband had gone for a face-lift. I do not know what the husband is like: but the wife, who is my client, is an impossible woman who insists that everyone is out to trick her and is apparently prepared to go to any lengths to achieve what she is after—incidentally, of course, failing in her object. She burgled her husband's hotel room in Brighton and removed all his private papers: she ransacked the desk of his brother's office: she is at present engaged in litigation with her former London solicitor whom she accuses of keeping some documents from her. Her husband says that in February 1958 she came to a flat where he was staying in London and turned on the gas, with the result that a budgerigar in the adjoining room was seriously affected. Both parties say that the other's conduct has gravely affected the health of the complaining party: and I should not be at all surprised. Mrs Warden's objection to today's motion was that the witness whose evidence it was sought to take knew nothing about the case and must have been got at. She arrived in Parliament House armed with some affidavit, which, in accordance with the methods I have found it necessary to employ with her, I did not ask to see.

June 10th

A Handel concert on television from the Royal Festival Hall, conducted by Sir Arthur Bliss, a delightful old gentleman who presided at the rostrum with much dignity and aplomb. This was followed by *Scottish Press Conference* with the Lyon. The full force of his peculiar personality did not get across on television, but it was possible to appreciate that he was certainly something very much out of the ordinary. I was unable to do any work tonight, having left my brief-case at Parliament House—at least I hoped I had since it was not in the car when I got home.

June 11th

Found my brief-case in the robing-room where I had left it. I had a proof before Lord Kilbrandon, a case under the Building Regulations. I had been assured by everyone that the hearing could not take place today, as the defenders had had the evidence of their foreman—now in the West Indies—taken on interrogatories, which had not yet come back. I was accordingly rather taken by surprise when Grieve, after leading only the evidence of a doctor, closed his case without saying anything about the evidence on commission. I had made no preparation for a speech, but it was not a case in which much preparation was required, and fortunately I had on arrival at Parliament House this morning looked up and noted the authorities on the point. So I had no difficulty in putting the case, once I realised I had to speak, and actually got under way.

June 12th

A Faculty meeting to consider an interim report from a committee appointed to consider possible reforms in Court of Session procedure. Ian Fraser's handling of the meeting left a good deal to be desired, and his grasp of procedural matters seemed limited: but he at least conducted the proceedings with courtesy and good humour.

June 13th

Offered to take James Leechman home. At Hope Street two policemen were directing all the traffic down Glenfinlas Street, explaining that the road was up. This led into a complete jam in Randolph Crescent. An enquiry into a scheme to remove the trees there and replace the wooded mound with a traffic roundabout has been proceeding in the City Chambers for the past fortnight, and I could not help wondering if today's exercise was somehow directed to proving the Corporation's point that the existing lay-out led to congestion.

We were held up for about a quarter of an hour, something that had never happened before in my experience in that area: and our suspicions were increased when, a policeman having at last appeared and directed traffic, we observed the kilted figure of Harald Leslie, leading counsel for the Corporation, standing idly at the corner of the Crescent where it emerged into Queensferry Street—apparently doing nothing but observe what was going on. We wondered whether he had been told about what was being done at Hope Street.

June 15th
Phoned Kemp Davidson to tell him as counsel for the Cockburn Society in the Randolph Crescent enquiry about my experience on Saturday. As the commissioner was to be visiting the locus this afternoon, I went round by the West End to make sure that nothing untoward was happening. Everything was normal: and I learned from Davidson that Mackenzie Stuart, one of the other counsel concerned, had known about Saturday's happenings and said something about them this morning.

June 23rd
Innes, the assistant in Connell & Connell who is attending to the sale of the house in Midmar Gardens came up to see me. The figure indicated is something in the region of £5,500, and Innes suggested that if I now put in an offer topping that figure there seemed a good chance that it would be accepted.

Finished reading the memoirs of Viscount Montgomery, which left me with my admiration for its author considerably enhanced. He is highly intelligent, and quick to grasp the essentials of a problem. He is willing to see the other man's point of view while at the same time rigid in his adherence to the doctrine that decisions have to be made and adhereed to: and it is difficult not to feel that in the disputes that arose on strategy his decisions were absolutely sound. He is a complete master of the art of war, and perhaps his only weakness is his failure to see that it is an art that can never again be practised on any extensive scale.

July 3rd
Ross McLean, who had lodged at 32 Dundas Street with Mrs Loutit, recalled that he had asked Norah—at the time only a little girl—whether she preferred having him there to Hector McKechnie, his

predecessor. It appeared that she preferred him, because he spoke to her. All that Mr McKechnie had said to her was, 'Bring the corkscrew, Norah'.

July 6th
To Sun Insurance office to arrange fire cover for the new house, which I was surprised to find from Green's *Encyclopedia* was apparently at my risk between the date of acceptance of the seller's offer and the date of entry. Posted a letter to Connell & Connell confirming the bargain.

July 7th
The Warden divorce action. Jack Hunter, who appeared for Mr Warden, moved that the case be heard *in camera*, but Cameron refused, evidently thinking that if the parties were determined to wash their dirty linen in public they must do so. Mrs Warden for the most part gave her evidence with restraint, and I handled her as tactfully as I could: but though she may well have been speaking the truth she did not emerge as anything but a very tiresome character. I think her chances of getting a divorce on the ground of her husband's cruelty are infinitesimal: the husband's prospects in his action may not be much better. One of her complaints against him is that he never lost his temper, which she found most exasperating.

July 8th
Hunter cross-examined Mrs Warden. She was no match for him, and her triumph in the English courts, where she recovered correspondence to which she had attached such exaggerated importance, proved her undoing—she was quite unable to explain the damaging passages in her own letters. At one point in the late afternoon when she paused before answering and Hunter asked her 'What's the difficulty?' she replied rather pathetically: 'There's no difficulty, except that I can't get anyone to believe me'. It must have been an exhausting experience, for I myself was quite exhausted simply sitting in the court, which got hotter and stuffier as the day wore on.

July 9th
Ian Fraser told a story of an anti-aircraft site he had been on in the war, when the gun crews took advantage of the peaceful days in the

early months of the war to grow some seeds between the guns. Unfortunately when the seeds came to fruition the growers were moved to another station, and their successors took the benefit of the crop—to the indignation of the former commander, who sent a message, 'Messis sementem sequitur'. The commander of the new crew was James Muirhead, a Glasgow lawyer, who was equal to the occasion and telegraphed back a reply, 'Inter arma silent leges'.

July 10th
Mr Warden continued his evidence, and I started cross-examining him. I got on reasonably well, and my client cheered up a little.

July 14th
The Warden case: I did not think I got on so well today—Mr Warden did not fall into my traps as nicely as I had hoped.

July 15th
The evidence was concluded, and I addressed Cameron on the wife's behalf. She has seemed more cheerful since I started cross-examining her husband and at long last showed her there was someone batting on her side.

July 24th
A custody petition in the Second Division, *Gibson v. Hagen*: a young married couple suing the wife's parents for delivery of her child. The child was born in August 1955, when the mother was unmarried, and to avoid a scandal it was arranged that the grandmother should pretend that she was pregnant and pass the child off as hers after it was born. This was quite a success, everyone being under the impression that the child was the grandmother's. But now the mother has married the man she says is the father of the child, and wants the child back: and the grandparents will not give it up. They deny that the first petitioner is the father, and say that at the time the mother was associating with another man, Dalgleish, who she at one time said was the child's father. She had said she did not like the child because 'John Dalgleish was staring out of her face'. Gibson also, they say, exhibited an antipathy towards the child, and on one occasion said she put him in mind of what had gone before. The Court allowed a proof before answer.

From Mr William Muir:
Register Number 198/57   H.M.Prison, Inverness   30.7.1959
Dear Gordon Stott

This is a epistle on Politics I know your opinion of the Tories. Yes they are going to win the next Gen Election much you will regret it, if you had been in the swim for Labour I would have voted for you. I wrote you in answer to your last letter but it was rejected I dont know where it landed. all are Labour Supporters here. Well Sir my sentence is slipping away whether I deserved it or not, God no's he is my judge & if I have spent many years behind Prison Bars I cannot be all bad I must have been very very good all those years. true when I got out The Crooked Jewellers tempted me with Hot stuff I feel they were trying to Con me I done them and of course the Police had to stick their nose in I suppose they had some benefit from all willies transactions when it comes to Diamonds. I am a tory and I hope Milligan losses his seat...I think Inverness is the best run Prison in Scotland just one big Family you never hear off any thing happening here they know how to run a Prison but unfortunately they are not recognised by the Powers that be and get any medals at the Queens Birthday it is a few Governors & Chief Officers should be rewarded and I must include my old aquantince Mr Hancock & Mrs Hancock they have both taken a great interest in Prisoners especially at their annual Sports the Public never get to know about these things I am very happy here the air is good...God has spared me not to handle any more Diamonds...now for a bit of Poetry.

How clearly memory brings to mind the days of long ago.
Twas when my hair was black as coal: tho now it is white as snow.
It brings to mind fond memories of many a childhood scene—
Of the dear old home and grassy yard down by the deep ravine...
Thus passed my happy childhood days as quiet peaceful dream
Secure from all alarms down by the old mill stream
Untill one day, in early spring—it all comes back to me
Altho 'tis many a long sad year I still the picture see.
I was nigh sixteen, and thought twas time for me,
To be a man and have my way, and be as men should be
Father was getting old—his step was very weak
And ofttimes in the morning you scarce could hear him speak
Twas on this day near to its close: my father said to me

Willie wont you go and find the cows for I can scarcely see
I knew his step was weak, and getting very slow.
But anger rose within my heart, I said I will not go
Father turned away and this is what he said,
'Well' never mind, I will try to although I should be in bed
And down the road he slowly walked toward the pasture green
The sun had set behind the hill, and already it was late
My anger died away as I saw him go from sight:
But somehow pride forbade me from doing what was right
I heard him call the cows, but the came not at his call,
For they had wandered up the hill where the hemlock grew so tall
Twas getting dark and in the west, a heavy black cloud lay:
I heard the leaders clanging bell, but knew it was far away
I thought that father must be tired, and knew he scarce would see
And once, I thought I heard his voice so gently calling me.
I started for the pasture, and as I walked along—
I said I will tell my father I know that I am wrong
I will tell him I am sorrow and ask him to forgive
and will promise not to speak that way again as long as I shall
live.
Before I reached the gate the lightning sharply flashed
And every now & then, a peal of thunder crashed
I called aloud to father, but no answer could I hear,
Save the cruel echo's mocking which made me start & fear
When I reached the pasture gate, the rain was falling fast
I called again to father, but was answered by the blast,
Just then the lightning flashed and my father I could see
Leaning on the pasture gate, but he did not answer me.
Father I quietly said, but no answer came from him.
No more would those palled lips ever speak my name.
Oh father, still I cried, Oh father please forgive me
Ill never speak that way again as long as I shall live
But all was still, save the fierce winds dreary moan.
How often have I tried for that night to atone.
And oftimes I wonder, if when we meet in heaven
Before the Judgment Bar of God I will hear that I am forgiven.
Mr Stott that has been just like me I deeply regret if I have hurt
any living soul & pray I will be forgiven if every little Boy would
think seriously of these words & think of Father & Mother I hope
you are well & winning lots of Law Suits I will call on you when

I am free again
Twilight shadows have found me dreaming
in a sad & dismal cell.
Haunted by a life of scheming
Schemes that paved my road to Hell.
Yours sincly Willie

August 1st
Nethy Bridge. Elizabeth has been keeping up her diary:

We went to see the ospreys after breakfast, they are very big birds
they are the only birds of there kind in Scotland there terribly
rare. We took the Bongo but when we got the notice board directing to the ospreys it said no dogs allowed. Mummy stayed behind
to look after the dog. To see the ospreys you looked through a
pair of binocilars. They were really a wonderful sight there was a
whole lot of old ladies there so we could only see for a little. We
had a lovely bathe at Loch Garten.

August 2nd
Nethy Bridge church: the parish minister, Rev. Ian Macalister,
preached on I Peter 5,7—a sensible, interesting sermon from a fair-
minded, thoughtful preacher, careful not to say anything he did not
feel able to justify.

August 3rd
When Nancy and I went out for a walk before going to bed, the
mountains to the east were a brilliant red, like hot copper, in the
relection of the sunset. The red faded, and within a few minutes the
hills had returned to their normal dark blue.

August 6th
Elizabeth arrived in our room about 4 am, complaining of a bumble
bee in her bed. I did not take this seriously, but Nancy went through
and reported that there was indeed a bee in Elizabeth's bed, though
a dead one.

August 7th
To Boat of Garten, where a film about Highland birds was being
shown. We found the hall packed: and a man appeared, apologised

for not being able to get us in, and promised that the film would be shown again next week. A middle-aged couple in the vestibule had come from Nethy Bridge, where they are staying in the hotel, and we gave them a lift back. They had earlier had the opportunity of an excursion to the ospreys' nest, but had thought it was the name of some public house, and had only since learned that there was a real osprey. So on the way back to Nethy Bridge we came round by Loch Garten and walked up with our passengers to the hide. We had an excellent view of the mother bird and two of her young, who had returned to the nest and were consuming a fish brought in by the male bird. The couple from the hotel had hardly an idea of what they had seen in the three or four days in which they have been 'doing' Scotland—Inverness one day, Fort William another, and so on. It appeared that the man was postmaster at Norwich.

August 11th

At breakfast time two lads arrived from the moor, wanting to use the telephone. They were at the RAF training camp beyond Boat of Garten, and had been out four days and nights in the forest on an exercise, the idea being to evade capture by the Army and reach some rendezvous of which they did not seem to have any clear idea. Though one was the son of a headmaster in Buckinghamshire, they did not seem to be able to work a telephone, and I had to get the number for them: the Boat of Garten police. Nancy meanwhile having found that they had had to live during their days and nights in the open on iron rations and such tinned foods as they were able to carry proceeded to fry bacon and egg for them—which they consumed with great relish, along with quantities of toast and marmalade. They then went off again into the moors.

August 12th

A game of canasta lasted till 10.15, so that it was dark when Nancy and I went out for our walk with Bongo. It is odd how completely still this countryside is after dark: no night life among animals and birds, and when we stopped not a sound to be heard.

August 13th

Finished *Women and Thomas Harrow*, by J.P. Marquand. The story moves backwards and forwards in time in a manner which threatens to be confusing: but the author is a master of his craft, and what he does is always well done: readable, convincing and interesting throughout.

The children went off into the wood, and later I was unable to find them, though I went right through the wood from corner to corner. No doubt they were hiding from me: and it turned out that they were having an Army exercise, having fitted themselves out with overcoats and mufflers, and their 'rations' in a tin picnic box. It was two hours before they appeared, having had a fine time.

August 16th
Nethy Bridge church: Mr Macalister preached to a large congregation, on John 14, 22-3. An interesting sermon, which threw a lot of light on the text so far as I was concerned.

August 18th
Finished reading *The Light of Common Day*, by Diana Cooper. I had hardly thought it possible that she could improve on her first volume, but I think she has. The highlight of this book is a correspondence with one Conrad Russell, a relative of the Duke of Bedford's. In one of his letters Russell speaks about her ability to bring those she is writing about to life.

> 'You scribble forty words—punctuation, spelling, syntax, grammar and construction all faulty, I strongly suspect—but the result is: Colonel Beck in his habit as he lived is before me. I might read his life in three volumes but it would only be stuffing and padding and would not tell me anything more essential about him'.

This is absolutely true, and the result is remarkable. Her other merit is her candour about herself: she never hesitates to expose her own silliness even though well aware of it. All in all, she is rather a darling. Russell's own letters are very entertaining: learned, allusive, affectionate, kind.

> 'I live here with Father Felix, a Benedictine monk and a sad serious man. He has not smiled since he came, and God knows I've been funny enough to make a cat laugh its ribs out. When I go to bed he sits up and says his Office. When I light the bedroom candles he says: "Oh, I haven't said my Office". Then I say: "Not said your Office, Father? That's bad. You must say it now". When I am snug in bed I like to think as I go off to sleep "There's a monk downstairs saying his Office".'

August 19th
Old Mortality, by Sir Walter Scott. The character who gives his title to the book has nothing to do with the story, and after a kind of prologue is completely forgotten about. The story itself is not bad at all. Some of the plot is rather phoney, as when the hero, adopting an assumed voice, is not recognised by his own servant in a lengthy conversation but shortly afterwards is instantly recognised by an opposing soldier who gets a glimpse of him in passing. But the author paints a lively picture of the Covenanters and their battles, and one is quite keen to know what happens next.

August 21st
We motored along to Causer for an extra pint of milk—the dairyman had left only 8 pints instead of our usual 9—and then to Loch Garten. Richard had gone off by himself for golf. The charge of one shilling for a child entitles him to as much golf as he likes for the day.

August 23rd
Loch Garten. Two or three eels at the water's edge came up to the surface for pieces of cake that Richard threw to them.

From Mr William Muir:
Register Number 198/57   H.M. Prison, Inverness.   24.8.1959
Dear Sir:—This is a continuation off my last letter To distinguish between what I believe and what I would like to think I believe in is the prelude of distinguishing between the thoughtful and the thoughtless, and between them can be no compromise. I believe in the word of Shakespeare that 'There is nothing either good or bad but thinking makes it so, and we are not the creatures of circumstance but circumstances are the creatures of ourselves, our thoughts. A person told me recently I imagined things I believe there is truth in that. I see that these thoughts and beliefs are my origin and the source of all things gained or lost. The mould my character, affect my health and determine my success or failure Everything I do comes from this generating force of thought. I no this is a power if I ignore it I am easily persuaded by what I see or hear If I believe in the power of my own positive thought, and act on it I overcome all the hostile influences like fear, anger selfishness and weakness. For those are not present if not manifested in my thoughts. Paracelsus said that men who are

devoid of spiritual perception what I call thought—are unable to recognise anything that cannot be seen externally I come into this condition of awareness when I find my self. I believe I have not seen your name recently defending or prosecuting I suppose you will be interested in the Election. Oh yes the Labour has a chance. And frankly I would wecome a change of Government. I would like to see you back at the Lord Advocate Office or even a judge I predict you will get there some day. I think it quite wrong to invite the Russian Leader to America, I am afraid some fanatic will kill him & then the balloon will burst What a lovely summer we have had here I am allowed out in the Garden when raining I can come inside I have been well treated here I will be very sorrow to leave it I have got attached to a old cat 13 year old he has adopted me I like the old fellow I give him a Tit bit now and again His owner is ill and he misses him We had a very severe storm here Friday I got a real frieght it hit a part of the Prison and it was a miracle no one was killed. Now for another wee bit of Poetry (In the hour of Death)

In the hour of Death, after this life whim—
When the heart beats low, and the eyes grow dim,
And pain has exhausted every limb
The lover of the Lord shall trust in him.
When the last sigh is heaved and the last tear shed
And the coffin is waiting beside the bed
And the widow & child forsake the dead—
The angel of the Lord shall lift this head.
For even the purest delight may pall
And the power must fail and the pride must fall
and the love of the dearest friends grow small
But the glory of the Lord is all in all.

I hope you are well and have had a pleasant holiday I am well & look living for 23 more years when I will be a hundred and the queen will be sending me a telegram. I hope the address will not be Willie Muir P.D. Peterhead.

Yours sincerely

September 5th
Cameron issued his judgment in the Warden cases. He disbelieves Mrs Warden entirely, and has granted decree to Mr Warden assoilzieing him in Mrs Warden's case.

September 17th

In Parliament Square I encountered Milligan and told him I was looking for a copy of his 1955 Election Address. He said he would send me one, unless on looking at it he found it would give me too many arguments.

From Mr W.R. Milligan:
38 India Street, Edinburgh.   17/9/59.
Dear Stott,
I simply hate to think of you tiring yourself out looking for a copy of my 1955 Election Address. I have only 2 copies, but gladly send you one. Could I have it back, please, in due course.
Yrs sincerely

September 19th

A Conservative political broadcast. Mr Macmillan sat facing four of his Ministers and asked them questions, for all the world like a well-meaning but rather gruff schoolmaster with his prize pupils. I thought it rather comic.

From Mr Compton Mackenzie:
31, Drummond Place, Edinburgh 3.   21st, September
Dear Mr Stott,
I would willingly have taken the chair for you if I had not promised Douglas-Home I would attend his rally in South Edinburgh on October 7th. I hope you will be successful in North Edinburgh.
Yours sincerely,

September 23rd

Got my first batch of Addresses from the printers. I found the printers had done a very nice job, but was suddenly horrified to observe that in 'Labour's policy of expansion' I had included '£3.10s. for the old age pensioner'. I had been working on notes for a speech about old age pensions among other things, and had it now well in mind that the Labour proposals, to add ten shillings to the existing pension, would mean £3 for the pensioner. It was obvious that to allow the Address to go out in its present form would be disastrous, since it would mean either that I was trying to bribe the pensioners by offering more than the Labour Party had promised or else—the true explanation—that I knew so little about the position that I had not realised what the amount of the pension was. After some cogitation, and a discussion with Nancy, I phoned Warwicks but found Drew Warwick had gone. I got him on the phone at his house and explained the situation. He was going back to the works, and I motored down and met him there. He had already stopped the machines and made the alteration, so that the copies now being printed had '£3', but all but a thousand or so of the Addresses had been printed. All that could be done, he said, was to run them through a machine which would block out the 10s. and leave a blank. Even this would involve a lot of extra work and time, but would avoid the very great expense and delay involved in reprinting. I accepted his proposal thankfully as the best we could do. It is a pity that we have to spoil the appearance of a very attractive little leaflet, but very much preferable to the hopeless position I should have put myself in by issuing the Address in its present form. I have the Earl of Dalkeith to thank for saving me from disaster, for I had not meant to speak about pensions this week, and it was an absurd remark he made in opening his candidature against Willis in East Edinburgh that set me working on the pensions question and put the proper figure into my mind. I had taken in a copy of the faulty Address to show McGravie my blunder, but although I pointed out the offending paragraph to him he could not see what was wrong. Buchan, when he came in, agreed with me that it would have been fatal, particularly as the three pounds ten shilling pension is the Communist Party's proposal.

September 29th
Usher Hall: a demonstration addressed by Gaitskell. He made what I thought were some minor errors of taste which a party leader's speech would have been better without, but he has improved a lot, and viewed from the back looked much better than when one has to face him. Tonight's meeting in Canonmills School was packed: an excellent meeting, with a lot of questions. Hecklers included Wendy Wood, who let me down gently when I refused to vote against my party on Scots Home Rule. Freda White thought I had handled the meeting well, and even Buchan, who took a poor view of my performance at Leith Walk School, seemed to think I had done a bit better.

September 30th
Broughton School: another packed meeting, but my speech a complete flop.

October 1st

To R. & R. Clark's printing works for a dinner-hour meeting: everything went well. I was cheered not only by this but by finding in today's *News* a first-rate report of last night's meeting: curious that the worst meeting of my campaign has produced far and away the best report.

October 2nd

To Sanders Street for a meeting of Stockbridge Old Age Pensioners that Mrs Laidlaw had told me about. No one knew I was coming, and a somewhat hostile old gentleman sitting near the door recognised me and said he did not think they would want to hear me, as they had a lot to get through. I sat down on a bench beside the others, and joined in singing the 23rd Psalm. Minutes were read, and after some formal business another old fellow got up, drew attention to my presence, and suggested that I might be asked to address them. 'Not on politics, of course', said the acting president, in a perturbed tone of voice: but she invited me forward, and I gave a little address, complimenting the members on their Association and urging them to go and vote either for Milligan or for me. It was well received, and I spoke to the accompaniment of murmurs of agreement. It looked as if people there were my supporters after all. To the committee rooms until 5, helping with the Addresses. Phoned the post office, and was relieved to be told that men would not be back until ten tomorrow morning—when with a bit of luck we thought we should have everything complete. We had decided that Elizabeth might go to tonight's meeting—which delighted her. The chairman allowed question time to run on too long and the meeting degenerated into a wrangle about nuclear weapons, with the audience speedily diminishing. Elizabeth however thoroughly enjoyed it, and at the end of my speech applauded enthusiastically, smiling all over her face and remarking that it was super.

October 3rd

We have run into more trouble with the Election Addresses, when it was found that there was still a box of unfilled envelopes and no Addresses to fill them. I phoned Warwicks and learned that we had got the full supply ordered. We were working on an absurdly narrow margin, but as only a little more than 24,000 have been sent off and 26,000 were ordered it seems that nearly 2,000 have gone astray, enough to fill the empty envelopes. Mrs Charlton had addressed about 200 to postal voters, and until the postmen arrived I occupied myself in taking the Addresses out of some of these envelopes and transferring them to envelopes addressed to ordinary voters—on the theory that postal voters would probably have completed their vote before the Addresses reached them. When the postmen arrived and were taking the bags downstairs, a tremendous uproar arose, which turned out to be the caretaker screaming at the postmen for dragging the bags down the stair and spoiling her paintwork. A stand-up fight developed, but luckily we had the same sensible supervisor who came yesterday, and he pacified his subordinates while I tried to restrain Mrs Malcolm. A somewhat uneasy peace was attained, and the last of the Addresses were safely removed. I took the afternoon off and motored to Yetholm for the Border Shepherd Show.

October 4th

Synod Hall: a demonstration addressed by Frank Cousins, general secretary of the Transport and General Workers Union. He made what Willie Marshall rightly called 'a good hustings speech'. He lambasted the Conservatives and the 'employing class' in a bitter, incisive style, and made plenty of telling points: but I felt that he had not thought very profoundly on some of the things he was talking about. His speech would help to rally the faithful rather than per-suade the unconverted. He was certainly interesting: and, as he himself remarked towards the end of his hour-long speech, the time seemed to have passed very quickly.

October 5th

To Chancelot Mills at two for a factory meeting. A good audience crowded into a little bothy, and heckled me in a friendly way for well over half an hour. The manager presided, and urged everyone present to vote for the Labour candidate. I proceeded to Easter Road for a meeting of Abbeyhill Old Age Pensioners Association. Tom Oswald's car was standing outside, and I could hear him bellowing away as I approached the hall. He gave an out-and-out political speech, telling quite a good audience of pensioners that the Labour Party meant to look after them and they had to vote Labour for their own benefit. I contented myself with a few sentences about the place of old age pensioners in politics. Questions were invited, and a woman immedi-ately asked where the money was to come from: a question which brought quite a lot of applause. At Abbeyhill School the hecklers included a Tory youth with a prepared list of questions, who played into my hand every time he intervened. The people who had volunteered to attend the counting of votes had all been summoned tonight to take the oath of secrecy, which John Rhind as Justice of the Peace administered with great solemnity, making everyone stand up and raise the right hand. Unfortunately he proceeded to read everything on the form except the oath of secrecy.

October 6th
Norton Park School: Anne Simpson, now a town councillor, presided, and caused a big laugh at the end when in thanking my supporting speaker, Sam Pollock, she got the name wrong and said how grateful we were to Mr Milligan for coming and giving us such a helpful speech.

October 7th
Canvassing lower-middle-class tenants in Brunton Place: highly respectable middle-aged ladies who when they told us they would have to see how they would vote obviously were telling us in a polite way that they would vote for Milligan. We visited about twenty houses before we found a supporter: a young lady who when I asked if we should have her support replied enthusiastically, 'You certainly shall'. I had to ask her to say it again before I could be sure I had heard her aright.

To the committee room at seven. Ian Taylor was there with Forsyth's jeep. Nancy got in the back, while I sat in the front with Taylor, and he drove along to Easter Road haranguing through the loudspeaker at a crowd making for a football match. No one paid the slightest attention, and after a few minutes he agreed to go to Stockbridge. We stopped at various points, when he and I took it in turn to make a brief exhortation to the electors: he effectively, I much less so. Actually most of the time was occupied in trying to get the microphone to work. Back to Nelson Library for the eve-of-the-poll rally. I had one effective moment when I was troubled with the electric lights flashing at a point in my speech when I was dealing with Conservative estimates of the costs of the Labour programme. I remarked that I was not surprised that the lights were behaving strangely when I was quoting these figures, but they should wait and see what they would do when I came to the next figure: what the

Conservatives had spent during their term of office. I gave the figure, and immediately the lights went out completely, amid loud laughter and applause.

October 8th

I gave the local electors a shout through the loud-hailer exhorting them to vote for Willis, before we set off for Holy Cross Academy, and repeated the same process at a few points as we made our way through Willis's constituency. At Restalrig this attracted the attention of some women who wanted a car to take them to vote in Craigentinny School: and as the East Edinburgh result seemed to be much more in the balance than North Edinburgh I thought it a good piece of work to take them there. We had two trips to make—finding another lot of voters wanting to go down when we got back with the first lot. For the fun of the thing, I took the car through the well-to-do parts of the constituency, and gave them a shout through the loud-hailer in Drummond Place, Great King Street and Dundas Street. I was kept occupied for two hours taxi-ing voters to Bellevue School. With an hour to go, I took the opportunity to come home. Nancy was still working somewhere in Broughton Ward, and when I phoned the committee room at 9.15 she had just come in. I boiled three eggs for supper before leaving for the corn exchange at Gorgie, where the Edinburgh votes were being counted. Harry Hawthorn, a Labour official from one of the Edinburgh constituencies, had a little portable wireless in one of the booths, and as I had no real interest in our own count I settled down with him there. The first few results showed a considerable swing to the Conservatives, and it was apparent that the Government was going back with an increased majority.

October 9th

Our count: Milligan 19,991, Stott 11,235—a 74 per cent poll. East Edinburgh was hanging in the balance. Mrs Willis was in a highly nervous state, but the Countess of Dalkeith as radiant and smiling as ever: she is an extraordinarily attractive girl. Someone introduced me to Lord John Hope, the member for Pentlands, who whatever his intellectual weaknesses also seemed to me to have quite a bit of easygoing charm. When the East Edinburgh figures were totted up, it appeared that Willis had won, by some 240 votes. Found from the morning paper that John Mackie had been returned for Enfield: I cannot imagine what he will do as an Opposition member. Poor

Douglas Johnston was condemned to another term as MP for Paisley, where he had a good majority. Labour had done well in the west of Scotland, winning two Glasgow seats, but this of course makes little impression on the massive Tory victory in the south. I think the majority of electors, who have no idea of the potential wealth of this country, and cannot conceive how much of it is snaffled by financial and business interests, have succumbed to the scare about the cost of the Labour programme. It is obvious that a detailed programme of expensive social reform, so far from acting as a political bribe, is Labour's greatest liability.

At Parliament House I changed into wig and gown, and got down to some work. But as the day went on I felt increasingly weary, and soon after three decided to come home. I have not felt tired at all during the contest: as I told John Mackintosh, who remarked to me how tired he was when I saw him at Gaitskell's meeting, it was a good deal easier for me who had no organisation to bother me. I managed my whole programme myself, and simply went where I felt it necessary to go. A lot of work has been by T.D. Smith, the school-teacher whom I had never seen before and who has been constantly out and about, canvassing or doing other work in a sensible, business-like way but so unassuming that one hardly noticed him. In contrast, Bill Smith, our talkative party member, never turned up, and luckily Cecil Gordon hardly turned up either. But the three who really ran the election were Mrs Charlton who looked after the committee rooms all day long with unvarying efficiency and geniality, Joe Luke, an old pensioner living in a lodging-house who took round messages and showed unrivalled knowledge of every street in the area, and—above all—Buchan, who gave up a week's holiday, went everywhere and did everything. I do not know what I should have done without him. We had a good meeting every night. I put a lot of work into my speeches this time, speaking on a different topic each evening, and after I got into the swing I quite enjoyed it. Having no real doubt about the result in North Edinburgh, I did not worry much about how I was getting on. McGravy arrived about 4.30 with Nancy's car, when Mason was just coming off work in the field opposite, and the three of us had a chat about the debacle—reaching no conclusion except that it was difficult to see how, if after what they have done in the past five years the Conservatives can get an increased majority, it will ever be possible to get rid of them. It looks as if we shall have to have Home Rule for Scotland after all.

October 13th

To St Andrews House to give evidence on behalf of the Faculty before the departmental committee on artificial insemination. Most of the questioning was done by the chairman, Lord Faversham: the questions were pretty obviously from a brief prepared by his civil servants, and I did not think he had much grasp of the subject. From time to time the questioning was held up while the committee argued among themselves, Mr Justice Melford Stevenson taking a prominent part. He seemed somewhat opinionative, but got the point of the answers more quickly than the chairman. It must have been obvious that we did not know much about the subject, but we kept our end up, and I found it entertaining.

October 19th

Legal Aid Central Committee: and home thereafter. Nancy arrived from the new house, to which we got entry today. She seemed in despair about the condition of walls and floors now that the carpets and furniture are away. The Browns have been completely uncooperative and had not even informed us about word that had come regarding delivery of furniture from Lebus, with the result that the furniture had come and been taken away again. Nancy had found a communication from the Post Office stating that the phone number was to be changed in the spring although Mrs Brown, in trying to sell her some headed notepaper, had assured her there was no prospect of a change. The date of the communication from the Post Office was actually before her conversation with Mrs Brown. Luckily she had declined to buy the notepaper.

October 20th

Nancy had been to Midmar Gardens and had meetings there with an electrician and a plumber. The electrical wiring is all in a dangerously defective condition, with no proper plugs and everything as unsafe as it can be, so that the floor-boards will all have to come up for rewiring of the power installation. Lighting can apparently be left over for a year or two until we are going to redecorate the bedrooms: but Nancy has instructed Dunsmores to go ahead with work on the power right away. It does not look as if the house will be very habitable on 31st October. The tradesmen had however agreed that it was fundamentally a good house, and that we should be able to make a success of it.

From Mr William Muir:
198/57 H.M.Prison, Inverness   20/10/59
Dear Gordon Stott

Now the Election is over & of course I regret your defeat If I had a been a free lance I would have heckled Milligan he is not a true blue Tory...I hope to have an opportunity to voice my opinion I well no it would (not) be believed because I have a criminal record...The Cat will not stop crime forbid smokes that is the answer to keep Criminals out of Prison and hang all murderers segregate all vicious Criminals & reorganise the Labour Party This is a very well conducted Prison this is a exception Barlinnie Peterhead & many others want a shake up appoint Governors from the ranks who no's all the answers how to keep Criminls in their place their are many capable men in the Prison service. I wish I had been in Politics instead of being in Jail...

October 21st

Mrs Warden was appearing in person to ask for interim aliment and expenses to pursue a reclaiming motion against Lord Cameron's judgment. She has thrown over her agents and counsel, and is to conduct her own case. I spoke to her before she went into court, and said I thought she was wise, as it would enable her to say what she pleased about the conduct of the case in the Outer House. She seemed rather subdued, but I was told she livened up in the Motion Roll. Her motion was refused.

October 23rd

Nancy in deeper despair than ever about the house, complaining tearfully that the Browns had actually cut off the rambler roses and dug up the roots, leaving the dead branches sticking to the wall. I phoned Farquharson to have this added to my list of complaints.

October 24th

Motored with Nancy to the house. We found a big hole above the fireplace in one of the bedrooms, and there is a horrid mess near the foot of the garden, where they had had a bonfire on which they had put a mass of old tins and broken glass, as well as several old disintegrating bags of cement. I tidied away the glass and pieces of old iron, into the dustbin, but it is difficult to know what to do about the cement. We thought the house had possibilities if only we could get it into reasonable order.

October 25th

The electrician had been up in the roof space, and found the electricity junction box had been smashed to admit some additional wire, with the consequence that water had got in and rusted it. It seemed that all the lighting, at any rate in the upper floor, would have to be rewired.

October 27th

Nancy told me it had now been discovered that there were no junction boxes for the electric lighting, and material had to be got to remedy this. The electricians said there was a month's work to be done in the house. A Labour Party questionnaire in which they asked for candidate's comments on party policy at the election. I have replied that the policy was good but there was far too much of it.

October 30th

At midday I motored to Midmar Gardens to see how the house was getting on. Found it full of tradesmen—electricians, plumbers, tilers, painters—picnicing in various rooms. I made no comments, and did not stay long. To the crematorium for Mr McVittie's funeral. I got wedged in a mass of Freemasons or some such body of organised mourners which are the curse of cremations and make the whole affair artificial and meaningless.

November 2nd

The removal van arrived, and soon after 11 we set off for Midmar Gardens. Here there was a certain amount of chaos: painters working in the kitchen, and a great hole in the floorboards of the hall, though which a man's face could be seen below looking up from where he was lying flat on his back beneath the floor. This had to be stepped over whenever any furniture had to be taken upstairs. Another electrician was working on a meter board behind the front door, so that everything had to be brought in by the french window leading into the study. The electrician under the floor was still there when I left for a Legal Aid meeting at 1.50. Our bedroom was in order, and we were able to settle down for the night in comfort and the complete quiet which seems to be a feature of Midmar Gardens.

November 5th

A jury trial. The pursuer was a Pole, and his evidence was taken through an interpreter. He gave it in a graphic way, with long, vigorous discussions with the interpreter illustrated by a copious use of gesture and demonstrations. His mate was a Highlander, living on the island of Scalpay, and made an even odder witness than the pursuer. He pondered for quite a while before assenting to my first question: that his name was Morrison. From the certificate of election expenses, it looks as if our campaign in North Edinburgh has been one of the cheapest on record: the constituency party has evidently made a small profit.

November 8th

North Edinburgh party meeting. Mason pointed out that it had been a very happy election, and Ian Clark said that had been the outstanding feature. Everyone seemed surprised that it had been possible to conduct an election without acrimony and ill-will among the candidate's supporters.

November 16th

A consultation in *Black v. Glasgow Corporation*. Frank McClusky and Isabel Sinclair duly arrived and sat down at the table, but, after we all were seated, solemnly announced that they had come to tell me that the case was at an end, since Mrs Black was dead—a piece of information they could just as well have given me over the telephone.

November 21st

I was interested to find that the number of proofs and jury trials fixed for me up to the end of May was no less than 62.

December 1st

A proof before Kilbrandon. An odd quirk of pronunciation by the first defenders' foreman, who when asked if bricks were being loaded by a travelling crane replied, 'Yes, a traivelling cran'.

December 4th

Working on a complicated action between a German company and a firm of joiners in Orkney—work on the case not assisted by the fact that much of the correspondence is in German, while even the letters in English were not easily comprehensible.

Dear Mr Tait, Thursdynight last week I yet arrived in Holland after a bad weather flight...Sowing-machines are on way to you. You can use them for the huts. When you will buy them afterwards is this possible. Other offers for sowing-mchines, when we haven spoken about, are coming. With the faith in your working, we remain with kindest regards.

Fortunately there is a delightful gentleman named Mole, a public works contractor in Stourport-on-Severn, who keeps writing helpful letters to both parties, saying to each in turn that he is completely fed up with him and has been let down by him over and over again, and utterly refuses to have anything to do with the matter—and then immediately after is writing to the opposite party using every conceivable argument in favour of the other man and doing his best to get his claim accepted.

December 23rd
A letter from Farquharson: Connell & Connell declined to make any concession in my dispute with Mr Arnold Brown.

1960

*In 1960 we all settled happily into our new home in Midmar Gardens.
Politics were not such as to arouse enthusiasm. Despite growing protests
from nuclear disarmament enthusiasts, particularly against the new Pola-
ris atomic submarine base in the Holy Loch, and unrest and continued
fighting in Algeria, Cuba and the Congo, the atomic bomb enforced an
uneasy truce on American and Russian leaders. They continued to slang
one another, but realised they could go no farther without destroying
civilisation. At home the Government's prosperity propaganda gave place
to warnings of an economic crisis, a recurrent feature while our financial
welfare was dependent on persuading foreign investors to leave their money
in London: but I doubted if many people would notice the difference
between a period of prosperity and a period of crisis. In Parliament,
everyone was aware that much of what was said had no relation to
reality. We became regular attenders at church, having joined South
Morningside congregation. We had got the children into the way of coming to church every Sunday as a matter of course: and to make a little
variety I took them every other Sunday or so to hear some other preacher
in one of the numerous Morningside churches. Early in the year our old
orange cat ended its days. Though it never got the length of having a
name, it was a kindly, gentle cat, and a remarkable mouser. It tried to
live up to its new surroundings and kept its white front scrupulously
clean—something it had never done at Portobello—but in contrast to its
habits at Portobello it seldom went out. We had an unfortunate experience
when attempting to replace it, losing two attractive kittens in turn through
an infection: but a third kitten thrived: a black-and-white half-Persian,
a real beauty, friendly with everyone and afraid of nothing.*

January 4th
Motored with the children to Crichton. Nicholas and Sally came too
and brought a friend, seven-year-old Sheena Birkett. The castle was
a great success: the children swarmed over the walls, and explored
the quarry from which the stones for the castle must have come. I

had left the car at a field gate, and starting off carelessly found the backwheels failing to grip, so that the car spun round into a hollow, at right angles to the road. With no one to push, it was impossible to get it out. I explained to the party that we should be last for lunch, and we all set off in excellent humour to walk up the hill to Crichton village to seek help. We knocked at a cottage door, and the woman who answered it suggested that we go on to the farm and ask for the grieve. There was a big house before the farm, and Sheena and I went into the drive. We at once encountered a shooting brake, driven by a youth, an older couple with him. They could not have been friendlier or more helpful, and agreed without the slightest demur to come and give us a hand—'provided', said one of them, 'you don't mind being driven by a learner'. So Sheena and I climbed into the van, where we knelt on the floor. As we were starting they remarked with surprise that there was a little corgi on the drive—I had forgotten about Bongo, who then had to be hoisted in beside us. Even with two men shoving, it took an effort to get the car out, but it came up by degrees. I introduced the children to our rescuers, and thanked them warmly. We all gave our helpers a friendly wave as the van disappeared round the corner, and we set off for home—again forgetting Bongo until one of the children drew attention to the fact that he had been left standing on the road. We were home by one—everyone in the party delighted at our adventure.

January 10th
South Morningside church: Mr Reid preached on John 5,11. He is not a spectacular preacher. He misses all the subtler points, and one feels that he is not troubled by any difficulties simply because he does not see them. But what he says is sensible, and his general outlook on life seems fair enough.

January 12th
Jury trial before Guthrie. A young woman employed by the defenders claimed that she had contracted dermatitis through the fault of the defenders by providing her with rubber gloves which were not thick enough or long enough to protect her skin from being penetrated by spicules of fibre-glass. I appeared for the defenders. We had the pursuer examined by three doctors in the hope that one would suggest some other cause, but all agreed that fibre-glass was responsible, with the result that we were not in a position to lead any

medical evidence. However, we got a favourable charge, and the jury were out for only five minutes before coming back with a unanimous verdict for the defenders. The jury, contrary to the ususal result of the ballot, was almost entirely working-class: another indication that the working-class is as ready to favour the management side as to support one of themselves.

January 15th
An interesting consultation with two business men from Aberdeen over whom W.R. Fraser, the drapery tycoon, had tried to pull a fast one. Luckily we seem to be going to be able to find a way of getting the better of his scheme.

January 17th
Braid church: Rev. Roderick Smith, the minister, preached on Luke 2,51, a vigorous attack on modern social evils, such as excessive resort to the divorce court. As he put it in an original way, and was willing to see the other point of view without weakening in his own convictions, he preached a very effective sermon, though he was not above distorting scriptural history at times in order to make his point. He spoke rapidly in a curious Highland accent: an occasional word wrong added to the picturesqueness of what he was saying.

January 19th
On television a wonderful Leni Riefenstahl film of the Olympic marathon, brilliantly photographed and working up to an almost unbearably exciting climax. I had never seen anything like it. Absence of commentary is one of the most striking effects.

January 21st
Scullion v. Aitchison Blair. The pursuer had been sent to Rothesay Dock to help in installing machinery in premises there. He was working on the top floor when two of his mates on a scaffolding above asked him to look up and check the position of a sling. He stepped back to do so, and his left leg went down an uncovered hole just behind him. As a result, he strained his back. In the case under the Building Regulations there is the difficulty that a duty to guard openings in floors arises only to holes through which anyone is liable to fall more than 6.5 feet: and though there was certainly a drop of more than 6.5 feet to the next floor it was doubtful whether this hole was

big enough for anyone to fall through. The pursuer in his evidence did not seem to think it was. It did not look as if Cameron was regarding the pursuer as a very credible witness, but the evidence came out well when we got to defenders' witnesses: a foreman who stressed that all holes had to be guarded, and assured us that extreme care was taken to cover every hole on the premises, followed at once by an engineer who said that holes there were as often as not left uncovered.

Nancy's starter was out of action: and I started the car with the handle and drove it to the garage in Braid Road. It turned out to be a simple defect which the garage people were not long in putting right, for a charge of one shilling and sixpence.

January 26th

I have been unfortunate this week, having had to return four jury trials. Next week I have nothing but a couple of absurd speculative actions which I should have been delighted to return but shall have to take since there is nothing else left in my book for either Tuesday or Thursday.

Finished reading *Inside Europe Today*, by John Gunther, a sensible book and no doubt useful reading for Americans who think every Russian is a murderous hooligan. But it was rather dull. The author is at his best dealing with personalities, and this is not a book about personalities at all.

January 27th

Free for tomorrow after all. Mr Shaw had not been able to find a suitable senior counsel, and arranged that I should get the papers back.

January 28th

Jury trial: the pursuer an assistant machineman in Stoneywood paper mill, pushing a bogey down a passage, with a long, heavy reel which was to be fitted into a machine. The pursuer says that a wheel of the bogey caught in a depression in the concrete floor, with the result that the bogey and reel swung round and his hand was caught. The case was a light-hearted affair, particularly when Dr Muir gave evidence on the pursuer's behalf that he had taken a bogey and run it through the hole some months later in an attempt to reproduce the conditions of the accident. 'What happened?' he was asked: and replied

'Nothing'. He had a reasonable explanation: a change in the depression in the intervening months.

February 4th

Finished reading *Lolita*, by Vladimir Nabakov. I think that for good or ill it might well tend to corrupt established ideas of morality, but, as one of the critics puts it, it is very moving, very funny and very true. A macabre sense of humour runs through the book, but it has a lyrical quality as well. It is about love, and one is left with the conviction that it is true enduring love: that despite all her weaknesses, and his, the narrator's love of his Lolita is indeed 'love at first, and last sight, at ever and ever sight'.

February 9th

A proof before Kilbrandon: *Gardiner v. Motherwell Machinery & Scrap Co.* In consequence of counsel's advice that the pursuer had no case, the Legal Aid committee had wanted to withdraw the certificate, but instead had decided that the solicitor remit it to some other counsel for his opinion. It was remitted to me, and though I thought it difficult it seemed impossible to say that it could not succeed. I advised that it should be allowed to go on, and as a result apparently came to be regarded as counsel who should conduct it. The action is in respect of dermatitis which the pursuer says he contracted while employed in the demolition of boilers at Blochairn Works. He says he was exposed to oil, grease, soot and dirt, without any washing facilities except a bucket of hot water. The difficulty is that there is no practice in the demolition trade of supplying washing facilities.

February 10th

The defenders led three skin specialists—all as usual disagreeing wildly with one another, but more or less agreed that this could not be an industrial dermatitis. One of them insisted that the whole trouble was due to washing with soap and water: he had been told by the pursuer that he had taken soap to work, and thought that very significant. Nobody else supported this ingenious theory.

February 11th

McDonald v. Provan, an action by a trade union official who had bought a second-hand Ford shooting brake from the defenders. Three months later he had a visit from the police, who told him the vehicle was stolen property and removed it. It appears that the front half of the vehicle, including engine and gears, had been part of a Ford car stolen by a man named Faldon, who had it welded to the back of an old shooting brake which had been involved in an accident, and the vehicle sold to the pursuer was this composite vehicle. He is suing for return of the price he paid, but Forsyth, who appeared for the defenders, argued that the pursuer's case was irrelevant because under the doctrine of specification what had been created out of two different entities mixed together was a new piece of property to which the defenders, who had bought it from Faldon in good faith, had a good title. His argument was that the pursuer's only claim was against Faldon, who had used stolen property to make up part of the new entity. Clyde was much amused by the case.

February 12th
Cameron in the Scullion proof assoilized the defenders, holding that the hole was not an opening through which anybody was liable to fall.

February 13th
Midmar Gardens an excellent sledge run, with plenty of deep snow.

February 25th
Proof in *Thomson v. Glasgow Corporation*, before Wheatley. It was a pity that Migdale had disallowed a jury trial, for the pursuer turned out to be a very sensible, honest woman who gave a frank account of the spin drier and the accident in which she lost her arm. The demonstration of how she operated her artificial hand would in itself have been sufficient to win votes in most juries. As it is, we have quite a good judge for this kind of case, and as this was an old, badly guarded machine I think there is a fair chance of success. But the defenders may win on a technical point which would hardly arise before a jury: that our attack in the pleadings is directed against the spindle of the machine, while our expert thought that the danger arose in the revolving cylinder. Kissen was against me, and pursued every possible point with his usual diligence, but even he could not suggest that the pursuer was untruthful.

February 26th
A jury trial I had to return yesterday had the curious name of *Collumbine v. Concrete*.

March 1st

Finished reading *Collected Poems 1925-1948*, by Louis MacNeice. Mostly he makes difficult reading, but read carefully is a poet who has very much something to say. In his long poems every word has its meaning and force.

March 2nd

A cheque for 30 guineas in payment of Portland Cement opinion: the biggest cheque I have ever had for an opinion.

March 3rd

A jury trial before Strachan. The pursuer was employed in the defender's quarry close to a big pile of stones, on the other side of which a mechanical digger was operating. He claims that the driver of the digger brought his bucket into contact with a 0.5 ton stone on top of the pile and knocked the stone down on top of him. As a result he had a serious injury to his leg. Part of the main artery was destroyed, and a piece of dead artery had to be inserted, to restore the circulation. This seems to be a comparatively new discovery, and a very competent-seeming surgeon from Aberdeen, who described the case to us from the witness-box, said it was uncertain how long such an artery would remain open. Because of lack of elasticity, it was supposed that it might block up after five years or so. The case on the merits was nothing like as good as on damages—none of the witnesses supported the pursuer's case that the excavator driver's carelessness had caused the accident. We had a subsidiary case against the foreman for putting the pursuer to work in a dangerous place, but as even the pursuer said he was not sent to work in any particular place this did not seem promising either. I thought the best course, as we had no favourable witness, was to put in the unfavourable ones. None of them gave me much encouragement, but I did get a sentence in re-examination of the eye-witness and the foreman to the effect that from what they saw of the stone it looked as if something like a bump might have been required to bring it down. Alex Thomson, who appeared for the defenders, remarked that the new technique seemed to be for a pursuer to put in all his witnesses and take some innocuous evidence, ask for the cross-examination to be disregarded, and take a critical sentence in re-examination when he could not do anything about it. Though a difficult case, it proved unexpectedly pleasant and easygoing: I took all the witnesses quietly and informally, and was not at all tired.

March 4th

Strachan's charge was scrupulously fair, as always, but he pointed out that the pursuer's case depended on proof that the digger had hit the pile, and the only corroboration of this was in re-examination— which, he said, often consisted of statements by counsel to which a witness was asked to assent. The jury by a majority of 9 to 4 found for the pursuer, assessed damages at £3,500, and found the pursuer 15 per cent at fault.

This evening to the Lyceum: *A Lodging for the Night*, an excellent play about press exploitation of the innocent young wife of a house-breaker who has murdered a policeman. The main theme is put over with great effect, and though a serious play it is full of wit and sarcastic humour which add to the effectiveness.

March 8th

A debate before Mackintosh. The pursuer, a member of the crew of the trawler *Mount Keen*, was standing on the deck of the trawler when it was fishing off the Faroes. Vibration caused by shooting the trawl caused a lens glass to fall from a lantern on the mainmast, striking the pursuer on the head. In reply to a call upon the defenders asking them to state how the glass could have fallen without their negligence, they suggest that the glass had been broken in rough weather or by a bird. Although it was a flat calm when the glass fell, they say the trawler had encountered rough weather since leaving Aberdeen nine days before. Alastair Johnston opened the case for the defenders in what his junior, Croan, later described as an 'exhaustive' speech. He spoke all morning.

March 9th

A debate before Strachan: *Swain v. Benzie's Trustees*, a Will case which had been debated in March, when Douglas Johnston had appeared for the pursuer and asked for an adjournment so that he could amend. When the papers came into my hands this week, it seemed to me that there had been no need for amendment. I had McIlwraith with me. I had no difficulty, in a short talk with him, in persuading him what was the proper line, and he put the points in his usual succinct, effective way. T.P. McDonald had no clue as to what it was all about. His remarks in reply to McIlwraith were beside the point, so that in the final speech I required only to set out the argument in commonsense order, considering the possible methods of division and showing why ours was right. An interesting debate: an illustration of how a case can go off the rails if counsel have failed to understand their real point. Douglas had written an opinion recently advising a compromise on the basis that the pursuer would get a small fraction of the estate—which the pursuer, fortunately perhaps for her, had rejected.

March 10th
Jury trial before Wheatley. I never feel happy in road-accident cases.

March 11th
Wheatley giving judgment in *Thomson v. Glasgow Corporation*. I was disappointed, but hardly surprised, that he had found for the defenders.

March 12th
Five Thistle Street Golf Club outing to Musselburgh, where the Town Council had granted us the use of the links free of charge—described as the Club's home course, though I doubt if any members had ever played on them. We were each restricted to three clubs, and I had brought a putter, a niblick, and a No 3 iron. The greens were a mass of weeds and bare patches, but otherwise the course was in wonderfully good condition, and most of the nine holes were a good length. In the evening to the Roxburgh Hotel for the dinner. Sir Hugh Watson I have always thought of as a stodgy, humourless personality, but he spoke in a pleasant, easy style. Old Jackson the cashier replied: reminiscences of the firm when he joined it sixty years ago, when the partners wore top hats and tail coats, as did the Parliament House clerk, and the cashier when he was attending a taxation.

March 13th
Spent the evening working, with a short interval to hear Miss Nancy Thomas sing 'Homing' on the wireless, with great power and dramatic effect.

March 18th
In the lobby I encountered Mrs Warden, who had been appearing on her own behalf in an application to lodge some documents. She told me she would have to go for a new trial. I replied that that would be

at all events a novel form of procedure, and we had quite a friendly conversation.

March 19th
Citizen Kane on television. I never believed sufficiently in Mr Kane to be emotionally stirred by what happened to him, but brilliant direction makes it exciting, and it held my interest throughout the two hours.

March 20th
University Chaplaincy Centre: a 'memorial meeting' for Cecil Gordon, who died on Thursday. A comprehensive gathering representing Gordon's varied interests: University, politics, medicine, the arts. A tribute was paid by the Dean of the Faculty of Medicine, Professor Brotherston. He was excellent: factual, unemotional, free from humbug. The poem 'Fear no more the heat of the sun' was read—also very well—by a young member of the University staff, and finally W.H. Marwick said a few words about Gordon's connection with the Quakers, whose meetings he attended in his latter days. His remarks were followed by a period of silence, ended by an organ voluntary excellently played by a girl. I was greatly impressed by the whole proceedings. Despite their matter-of-factness, and the absence of any reference to God or religion, they were dignified and moving, and, in contrast to many normal services, seemed throughout to be concerned with Cecil Gordon, not some abstraction or idealisation. They led me to think well of him, about whom I had often thought less well.

March 22nd
An Opinion for Robert McIntyre, who claimed to have been slandered by the BBC through their political commentator's having referred to him as a former MP who had refused to take the oath of allegiance. He pointed out that he had at no time refused to take the oath, but had not been allowed to take it unless he came forward with two sponsors.

March 23rd
Forsyth spoke to me about the impending by-election in North Edinburgh, it being accepted that Milligan will go on the bench at Russell's retiral, and asked if I intended to stand again. I gave a negative answer.

April 8th
A word with King Murray, whom North Edinburgh Labour Party have expeditiously adopted as their candidate.

April 12th
Forsyth is taking silk, along with McIlwraith—sad to lose my two best juniors. It has been a pleasure to see a Forsyth record among the papers: it seldom needs much revision, in comparison with the rubbish that many juniors produce.

Finished reading *Voyage to the Amorous Islands*. There is clearly much to be said for the Tahiti way of life before its discovery, free from the evils of civilisation and its artificial code of morality. The book leaves one feeling envious of Captain Wallis' sailors and their five blissful weeks among the unspoiled beauties.

April 13th
Ashton's ballet *Cinderella* on television, followed by a short session of Cliff Richards, the bongo-like youth whose singing and posturing into the microphone is sending teenage girls into hysterical frenzies of screaming and fainting. He and his accompanists certainly worked hard, and the result had a kind of wild impressiveness that one could not ignore. I really found it more interesing than *Cinderella*, despite Margot Fonteyn and Michael Soames.

April 23rd
I have at last, I think, found the answer to an Estate Duty problem which someone has set me. Memorials on subjects like this, about which I know nothing, mean a lot of work, but in a way they are interesting recreation provided one has plenty of time to wrestle with them.

April 25th
To the Central Hall for a meeting under the auspices of the Scottish Council for African Questions: Dr Hastings Banda, who has just been released after a year's imprisonment in Rhodesia. He knows all the tricks of the trade, and gave an excellent account of himself—reasonable, persuasive, witty, good-humoured.

May 1st
With Elizabeth to Waverley Bridge, where we joined the May Day

procession. We marched in the second row, behind Willis, Willie Marshall and Judith Hart—the pipe band behind us—along Princes Street and into Castle Terrace. Elizabeth thought it was super.

May 5th

Finished reading *Bend Sinister*, by Vladimir Nabokov. An amusing passage where the pseudo-scholar gives a new interpretation of Hamlet —a passage which like several others has nothing to do with the case. The gruesome ending is effective in an ugly, sadistic kind of way, but by and large this book is rubbish.

May 6th

Princess Margaret's wedding. Television re-showing of the ceremony was well done, with the Archbishop of Canterbury carrying out his weird part with admirable dignity and aplomb, and the bride radiant and attractive—in contrast to the Queen, who stood at one side solemn, melancholy and plain. We were struck by the delightful way in which the Duke of Edinburgh conducted his sister-in-law down the aisle: a perfect blend of humanity, humour and poise.

May 8th

This seems to be a good year for fruit blossom: looking down the line of back gardens over our wall we have a wonderful view of the mass of blossom on the cherry trees.

May 9th

Bar Foursomes at Muirfield: the expense much less than usual, since enough members of Muirfield were playing to enable the rest of us to be regarded as guests, so that we got our day's golf for six shillings instead of a pound.

May 10th

Taking the chair for King Murray at a North Edinburgh by-election meeting in St Mary's School. He spoke at a tremendous rate, denouncing the Government with vigour and violence, and answered questions for the best part of an hour: voluble, lengthy replies on a great variety of subjects. I did not find him very convincing, but he put plenty of energy into it. His party-political fury would make a change from the last candidate. I motored home with a feeling of relief that I was not going through all the rigmarole of an election again.

May 11th
Some work to do on the case for tomorrow, but afterwards a lazy evening reading the Sunday papers: it concluded with two charming little concertos by Telemann on the Third Programme.

May 12th
Finished reading *Llewellyn Powys*, a selection from his writings by Kenneth Hopkins, full of good things, and of Powys' wise, discriminating writing. There is no humbug about Powys: everything is simple, down to earth, and true.

May 15th
Augustus John on television 'face to face' with John Freeman. Freeman had a strenuous job getting anything out of him: though a quaint old fellow he had nothing interesting to say.

May 18th
A recording of Dr Banda on the wireless was cancelled to make way for a press conference held by Mr Kruschev in Paris today after the breakdown of the much publicised 'summit' conference which collapsed before it began after much rancorous talk which could all have been avoided if the statesmen concerned had stayed at home.

Finished reading *Anatomy of Prison*, by Hugh J. Klare, the secretary of the Howard League for Penal Reform. Though some of his ideas seem odd, there is hardly a sentence which does not set one thinking about the problems and how to deal with them. The emphasis of the book—quite properly, when one thinks about it—is much more on the position and status of the prison officer than that of the prisoner. Another good point he makes is the excessive and wasteful emphasis on security for every prisoner, when it is required for only a minority. It seems true that it would be much better and cheaper to have a few prisoners escape and have to be recaptured than to expend a disproportionate amount of time and effort in keeping everyone under constant surveillance.

May 20th
The result in North Edinburgh: Lord Dalkeith 12,109: King Murray 6,775: McPake 3,458.

May 22nd

We all motored to church, where Rev. David MacDougall, minister emeritus of Dalry Church, preached on Isaiah 55,1. Though obviously a nice, kindly old fellow, he was about the worst preacher I have heard. He could not read his own writing, and frequently read out the wrong word. All his illustrations went wrong. Quite often he began a sentence and forgot what he was going to say before he got to the end of it. Sometimes he stuck altogether, when he would say 'I'm sorry' and start again. He was however brief, and his sermon as he preached it could not be described as dull.

May 24th

A jury trial before Wheatley. The pursuer, a passenger in a Bedford van run into by a Standard car, sustained fractures of a shoulder and hand. It is a case which wins itself since one or other of the defenders must have been at fault, if not both, and as regards the accident I was content to put in all the possible witnesses, including the two drivers, and let Robert Reid and McIlwraith argue over them. The witnesses turned out to be about the woolliest I had ever encountered. Although a violent collision had taken place either within a few yards of where they were, or involving a vehicle in which they were travelling, every single one declared that he had not seen the collision, and it appeared that neither of the drivers had seen the other vehicle. After the accident a Wolseley car had come into the back of the van, but the driver of this car maintained that he too had seen nothing of the accident. As a final absurdity, a policemen who had been called to give evidence about damage to the vehicles spoke about damage on the offside of the van, and had to admit when I re-examined him that he had mistaken the nearside for the offside because the van had been turned round and was facing the wrong way. I thought it lucky for the pursuer that fault on someone's part was conceded, and that I did not have to try to establish it on such evidence.

May 25th

The jury awarded the pursuer £1,156, finding the defenders equally liable.

We lost *Swayne's Trustees*, Strachan having dismissed our action: extremely disappointing, as I was not only convinced that we were right but was sure I had convinced Strachan. It just shows how mistaken one can be.

Consultation at 4.30, and home thereafter. I had a lot of work to do, but did it lying on the drawing-room sofa. I lit the fire and had everything cosy and comfortable, and got to bed much less tired than I had felt last night.

May 26th

Wason v. British Transport Commission: the pursuer the widow of an engine-driver who had been killed at Dailly goods shed driving his engine out of the shed. The engine had shunted two trucks through the shed, tender first, and stopped with the funnel still outside. The engine was a biggish one, Mogul type, for which an old shed was not really adapted: at one side there was only five inches clearance at the entrance. Wason had not noticed this, or had forgotten: he put his head out to look back when starting to move out and sustained fatal injuries. The case against the defenders was that they should have prohibited engines of the Mogul type from entering the shed, or put up a warning in the form of a 'Limited Clearance' board. There was some evidence that such a board was to be found at Bellahouston and at Mauchline, but seemingly nowhere else in Scotland.

In the course of the morning Scotland came in and handed me papers on which an opinion was required by tomorrow morning. As I was to be in court all day, he thought I would hardly be able to take it on: and having read the Memorial and found it was a matter of company law I agreed and handed the papers back to him. I had work in hand this evening anyhow in preparation for a debate in Glasgow Sheriff Court tomorrow. But after Scotland had left the court it occurred to me that I might as well do the Opinion too and make a night of it. So I went out after him and recovered the papers. Actually, on reading the Memorial more carefully at lunch time, it occurred to me that the questions did not seem very difficult. I thought I could find an answer to all of them.

A consultation at 4.15, at which I had to bludgeon a pursuer who got a nervous shock when jolted in a bus into accepting a tender of £400. Only the combined efforts of her husband and all her legal advisers at last prevailed with her.

June 8th

In Wason's case the Second Division decided to order a new trial on the ground that the damages were excessive: a decision I had expected, but a weak, silly decision.

June 10th

Kilbrandon giving judgment in *Gardiner v. Motherwell Scrap & Machinery Co*: in favour of the pursuer. He awarded £3,000.

June 12th

Finished reading *W.B. Yeats and T. Sturge Moore: Their Correspondence 1901-1937*. In the middle of the book there is a lengthy interchange of letters on the meaning of reality, arising out of Yeats' contention that a cat which had existed only in Ruskin's imagination nevertheless existed just as much as any other cat. This Moore sets out to controvert with great patience and pertinacity. But when he seems to have proved that Ruskin's cat is distinguished from other cats by being thought by most people not to exist Yeats scuppers him by some 'evidence' of a thought process which has appeared on a photographic plate, or such a query as 'How do you account for the fact that when the Tomb of St Theresa was opened her body exuded miraculous oil?'

June 23rd

McInnes v. British Transport Commission. The pursuer, a relief stationmaster at Elvanfoot, was returning at night in an empty carriage train to Carstairs, sitting in the left-hand front seat of the brake van immediately behind the engine, with a forward facing window. As the train came round a slight curve on to Lamington viaduct over the Clyde, something smashed through the window and shattered the glass, seriously injuring the pursuer who has lost the sight of one eye. On arrival of the train at Carstairs a piece of coal was found lying on the floor of the van among the broken glass, and it is assumed that this is what broke the window. The pursuer maintains that it came from the tender, and blames the driver for not seeing that the coal in the tender was properly trimmed or for driving too fast, thus causing the tender to oscillate and coal to be thrown back.

June 24th

The jury found for the pursuer and awarded him £2,850. I was told that what may really have happened is that the fireman threw the coal off the footplate for the benefit of a fisherman kindling his fire in the twilight on the bank of the Clyde.

July 1st

A word with Mrs Warden, who had been up to hear the First Division give judgment on her reclaiming motion—she argued it before them herself for four days last week. As expected, they refused her appeal in both cases, but she is determined to take them to the Lords—'even if I have to scrub floors to do it', she said. She did not seem surprised at the result, nor particularly despondent: simply as vindictive and impenitent as ever. She was quite amiable to me, and I seem to have got off comparatively lightly in the general offensive she conducted against all concerned when she was arguing her case.

July 2nd

This was the last day of the *Bulletin*, which we have always had every morning in addition to the *Scotsman*. It has been far and away the best daily picture paper—the only picture newspaper in the proper sense of the word—and one often got news in it which was not readily available elsewhere, besides some quite sensible, fair-minded comment in the editorial column. Unfortunately George Outram & Co., which publishes the *Bulletin*, has got mixed up with Fraser the multiple draper, who seems to put a blight on everything he touches from a quality point of view, and no doubt the *Bulletin* was not making sufficient profit to please him and his colleagues. But it is sad to see the end of Sandy Seal and Mr Potter and the other *Bulletin* features.

July 7th

A debate before Wheatley: *Pickard v. Pickard*. The pursuer is a wealthy, eccentric old gentleman from Glasgow who made his money in the cinema trade and invested it in heritable properties in and around Glasgow. He took the title to a number of the properties in the name of some one or other of his five children, but himself administered the properties, collected rents and included them in his own funds, and when he found it desirable sold properties or parts of them, getting the nominal owner to sign the disposition. In 1953 his wife died, and he married a lady with whom he had lived for forty years but who was not *persona grata* with the younger generation. In consequence of their refusal to have any dealings with her, there was a family dispute, and the children having taken legal advice intimated that henceforward they intended to control their own property. The pursuer's response was to raise these actions, for declarator that he was the true owner. He says the defenders hold the subjects in trust for him. The defenders, for whom I act, maintain that the properties are theirs. In addition to two leading Glasgow solicitors, I had Angus Pickard behind me along with his brother Peter, an English barrister. They seemed to enjoy the debate.

From Biddy Derham-Reid:
Two Firs, Jacob's Well, Guildford, Surrey,   July 7th 1960.
Dear Gordon
I did write to you a fortnight ago—and then I decided I had written a dreary & uninspired epistle and so I tore it up—and even tonight, I have no faith that I shall find inspiration...

I was glad to get all your news in your last letter—which I am ashamed to say I never answered, though I did take it all the way to Spain before Easter. I imagined I might find leisure to sit in the sun & write—I hoped, amusingly on life in Barcelona—We didn't do anything wildly exciting but we did see Franco's triumphal procession—& all of his army turned out—needless to say he kept us (on the pavement) and the army (lined up for 3 miles or so in the road) waiting a long time—the army waited from 8.a.m. till 11.30 a.m. and so by the time we arrived, the army was drinking coca-cola & smoking like chimneys. Franco had two Rolls Royces, one to ride in (bullet proof) & one just behind that, as a spare. He is—as you know, not popular in Barcelona, & the tension during his 2 weeks visit was terriffic. We much admired his bullet proof saluting base, it looked like a Victorian Bedstead, and the brass rails were all polished. They built this erection (which had come from Madrid) into the road—& planted a garden round about, even to real turf & climbing plants up the back—and then the whole thing was cleared away over night. The Tramcars & lamp standards were dressed over all, but as the two weeks grew to a close, the flags fell down or off, & the bunting cascaded across the main procession route at the peak of the Rush hour, which necessitated a policeman standing holding it up—he was there over an hour to our knowledge. Everyone in Barcelona was heartily bored, & there was a great outcrop of anti-Franco stories—& very off jokes...

I shall be in Scotland in September—we might meet—Ayrshire is my destination.
Yours with love.   Biddy
I learn with sorrow of the death of 'The Bulletin'.

July 9th

Finished reading *Trustee from the Toolroom*, by Nevil Shute, the author's last book in every sense of the word, for he died some months ago. It is an excellent book, displaying all its author's qualities, including his gift of narrative, with a description of a storm never surpassed in my experience—tense, matter-of-fact, exciting and moving —and his gift of portraying kind, friendly, interesting people. The philosophy of the book not a bad philosophy.

July 10th

Ampherlaw. We stopped after turning off the Lang Whang and took Bongo for a walk up a rough track across the moor. A van was parked some way along, with a man and a woman in it: and on our way back they stopped us and asked if we had a match—they had only one left, and were afraid to use it. Nancy had a book of matches in the car, and she and Richard started off back to the van with it. I backed the car along the track and picked them up, after which we resumed our journey. Half a mile farther on, Richard asked where Bongo was, and we realised we had left him on the moor. When we got back, he was starting at full pelt along the track towards the van, having been rushing round on the grass since we left—so far as we could judge from his out-of-breath condition.

July 12th

An interesting debate before Mackintosh: *Cunninghame v. Cunninghame's MC Trustees*. Mr Cunninghame directed his trustees to hold the residue for his wife in liferent and on her death to convey it to such persons from his own blood relations or their issue as might be named by his wife. His widow left a Will under which she purported to exercise her power of appointment in favour of a great-grandson of Mr Cunninghame's uncle. The main question is whether when the testator refers to 'blood relations or their issue' he must be restricting the meaning to something like 'next of kin'—which would cut out the appointee and allow our client to succeed as heir male. The solicitor from London who had been sitting behind me was impressed by the friendly, informal atmosphere of Mackintosh's court, which he said was very different from that of the Chancery court.

July 16th

On television we had John Freeman's *Face to Face* interview with Dr

Jung: a fascinating three-quarters of an hour not so much for anything the old psychiatrist had to say as for the skilful, restrained way
in which Freeman's questioning brought out all the interest and
drama of his ideas.

July 21st

Mackintosh giving judgment in Cunninghame's case: I was not surprised to hear he had been against the pursuer on all points.

Powderhall: the greyhound races an attractive picture, with three
dogs running round the arena in a bright light while all the surroundings were in shadow.

July 25th

Haddington: the Enquiry in applications by Associated Portland Cement Manufacturers to work limestone and shale at Oxwallmains and
erect a cement factory. The mineral workings are expected, at the
rate of 6 acres per year, to last about 52 years. The factory is to cost
£4,000,000. Taylor, who appeared in person for APCM, made an
announcement of which we had prior knowledge: that a deal had just
been concluded with the Duke of Roxburghe, whereby he sold all his
land in the area to the company and withdrew his objections. Thus,
as a cost of some £250,000, the company had got rid of its principal
opponent.

July 26th

Evidence from Sir James Hope: that the project should go on, provided they paid him sufficient—and of course, he added, it was roast
beef he lived on, not sweeties. He had produced the brand of potato
'What's Wanted', the best in the country. The Commissioner announced his intention of viewing the site—where Hope insisted that
Johnston accompany him through a field of potatoes to see some
restoration that had been carried out in the old days when some
limestone working had been carried on with spades and barrows by a
man known to his grandfather.

July 30th

Finished reading *The Affair*, by C.P. Snow: beautifully done, with
every motive analysed and accounted for, and quite absorbing to
read. But in the end one is left wondering what it all amounts to.

August 3rd
Finished *I Know the Face But...* by Peter Bull: a lot of funny passages, but its outstanding feature is its forthrightness and spontaneity. When the author feels that a success in which he had been concerned is piffle—*Waiting for Godot*, for example—he makes no secret of his feelings. He makes no secret either of the strain and worry of an actor's life, however frivolous he may be in telling of it. He is interesting too about people he has encountered: his favourites, like Pamela Brown and Stewart Grainger, and those he does not like, about whom he writes with good-humoured frankness and commonsense.

August 4th
Grantown. We had engaged a pony for the children for an hour: a very docile pony, proceeding throughout at a walking pace. The charge was only two shillings and sixpence.

August 5th
Nancy thought Bongo's foot was swollen, and at her instigation I phoned the vet and we motored with Bongo to Grantown. The vet sold us some eye ointment, in a tiny tube that looked like a free sample, for seven shillings and sixpence, saying it was very good stuff for taking down inflammation. As Bongo had been all round the golf course with us, rushing round each player at every stroke, I was not inclined to take his bad foot very seriously, and possibly the vet felt the same.

August 6th
I have pretty well given up getting papers at the Nethy Bridge shop: when I go down, the *Scotsman* is always finished, and the *Press and Journal* has not come in.

August 11th
Motored to the village and called at the baker's to get some cakes, but was told they would not be in until about one. As this was early closing day, it required careful timing to get the cakes.

August 12th
An error in judging at Grantown Show, the supreme championship having been awarded not to any of the sectional champions but to a calf that had been left in the judging ring by mistake.

August 13th

Finished reading *The Faber Book of Modern Verse*—Michael Roberts, the editor, has a mind of his own, and has produced an interesting selection, starting with Gerard Manley Hopkins' wild, exciting 'Wreck of the Deutschland', which is about everything except a shipwreck. The editor contributes an illuminating introduction, full of useful ideas.

August 14th

We all set off for Dulnain Bridge—my father's first mission when he was a Divinity student. The minister, Rev. H.G. Jackson, was a weird bird with big horn-rimmed spectacles and what looked like a black wig with ringlets. His sermon was in accord with his Dickensian appearance, but it was short and to the point, and though it was not much of a point he made it confidently and clearly.

In the afternoon we motored to Loch Morlich and on up the valley to see where the newly completed motor road to the skiing ground at Coire Cas had been washed away ten days ago in a cloudburst, leaving several cars stranded on the Cairngorms on the wrong side of the flood. £20,000 damage is said to have been done to the new road.

Just before we went to bed Nancy came through from the kitchen in a state of slight alarm to say there was something flying about there. I went through, and found a bat flying round the ceiling. I thought I had managed to catch it when it settled on a cornice, but lost my footing coming down from the chair I had got up on, and in the melee the bat escaped. I put the light off and left the window open.

August 18th

Sheepdog trials were being held today in a field on the Boat of Garten road, and when we were in bed, before 8 o'clock we heard the sound of someone passing, calling 'Moss' to a dog. 'There's a sheepdog going to be tried', Nancy remarked.

August 19th

Motored to Inverness and took the train to Lairg: day return, fifteen shillings. Lairg Crofters Show and sports. From Inverness I had a clear run home in gathering darkness, reaching Nethy Bridge within the hour. Found Nancy listening to a radio programme in which

John Freeman was answering qustions put by Barbara Wooton, Malcolm Muggeridge and another man. As I had expected, I found Freeman's views and ideas congenial. To many questions, on religion, politics and attitude to other people, he gave just the answers I should have liked to be able to give. He could not envisage himself actually hating anyone, and when asked what part of his life he enjoyed most he replied 'The present', adding that if asked the same question at any other time he would probably have given the same answer.

August 21st

Boat of Garten church. The local minister, Rev. Peter Lovie, preached on Acts 17,32-34. He was the best preacher we have heard in these parts this season, and preached an eloquent sermon.

August 24th

Elizabeth, sent out for a bag of potatoes and a cabbage, came home instead with a lettuce.

September 3rd

Finished reading *Hons and Rebels*, by Jessica Mitford. It has amusing passages about the home life of Lord Redesdale and the Mitford family, but despite its silly title is by no means a frivolous book. On the contrary, it is remarkably courageous: whether one agrees with the author or not it is impossible not to admire and like her. Her story of her short but abundantly happy marriage is beautifully done.

September 7th

Finished reading *And Mr Fortescue*, a selection from the nineteenth-century diary of Chichester Fortescue. Though Under-Secretary for the Colonies, Mr Fortescue appears to have been of a modest, retiring disposition—his friends are always urging him to 'bring himself forward'. His diary consists simply of jottings, but they convey a remarkably good picture of the political and social personalities of the day: a most interesting, likeable book.

September 8th

With the children to the Cameo: *Jazz on a Summer's Day*, a film of the jazz festival at Newport, Rhode Island, which has been hailed by the critics as a masterpiece of cinematic art. I saw nothing artistic about it: a monotonous succession of people working at jazz instruments or bawling into a microphone, generally in the dark with an arc-light glaring right into the camera, while the awful noise goes on and on. Came home feeling distinctly unwell as a result of the afternoon's entertainment.

September 11th
Church: Mr Malloch preached on the stories of the Good Samaritan, and Eve and the apple, pointing out that both were very true and applied to all of us. The question was, where was each of us in the story? A lively, pointed sermon, not only cogent but entertaining—it caused Richard to give a loud guffaw at one point. The address to the children, by contrast, consisted of a lengthy, lurid attack on Roman Catholics, to whom Mr Malloch is not well disposed.

September 14th
Finished reading *The Fall of Singapore*, by Frank Owen. Though in rather strident terms, this book gives a concise, readily intelligible account of the short campaign in which the Japanese over-ran Malaya: too one-sided an affair to make anything but dismal reading. The author is critical of mistakes made by the defenders, but with the odds so heavily against them it is difficult to think that anything they could have done would have had any greater effect than to delay the inevitable. Churchill was determined that Singapore should never be surrendered, but luckily the military people had more sense.

September 15th
Got up before seven, and after breakfast set off in the car for Stirling, en route for Oban and the Argyllshire Gathering. The connecting train from Waverley to Larbert was taken off a year ago, and to go by train all the way would now mean leaving Edinburgh at 6.50. I reached Stirling in good time to catch the train there at 8.48, and was pleased to find that this way of going had another advantage: a day-return ticket available from Stirling at only seventeen shillings. I got into an empty compartment, but hearing American voices along the corridor moved along and joined a couple from Iowa—a retired farmer and his wife making a tour of Europe as their 'first vacation'. They were going to Iona, and produced a copy of their local church paper with an article about George MacLeod. They had been to Rome for the Olympic Games, Oberammergau for the Passion Play, and Haarlem for the Flower Show, and were interested in everything they saw:

historical, agricultural, scenic. The lady had a notebook in which she jotted down any information I could give her about the places we passed, and they always had an interesting comment—whether about Wallace, or cows, or bog myrtle. On the way back at 5.15, I was sorry to find the dining-car replaced by a buffet observation-car at the back of the train—the company in the car being harangued by a prosy employee of the railway, who was telling them they had a view of Oban Bay and then that they had a view of someone's factory. I hastily got a cup of tea and an egg sandwich and retired to the next carriage. It happened to be a guard's van, and I sat down in a little seat with a view out of the backward-facing window.

September 17th
The conclusion of the Proms on television, with Constance Shacklock singing 'Rule Britannia' with her customary appearance of dogged determination.

September 21st
Motored to Semple Street and exchanged my National Insurance card at the Ministry office—impressed by the speed and facility with which this was carried out.

September 22nd
Finished reading *To Be Young*, by Mary Lutyens. This account of the author's 'childhood, girlhood and first love' is fascinating, mainly because of its absolute candour and honesty. It contains delightful examples of a child's way of thinking.

September 24th
Lammermuir Pastoral Show. At the auction I joined in the bidding for a great number of lots, and finished up with half a dozen eggs, a gingerbread, a bag of queen cakes, and two pots of raspberry jam.

September 27th
With Nancy to the Dominion picture house: *Tiger Bay*, a fine picture, all the more harrowing because it was so good. It had its lighter moments, little touches that showed the powers of observation of those who had made the film, but the bitterness of the ending was almost intolerable. It was bad enough to have a happy ending snatched away once not far from the finish, but then when it seemed to have

been given back to us to have it snatched away again was almost more than one could bear. Hayley Mills gives a magnificent portrayal of the tough, lying, unsentimental child of the Cardiff dockside who befriends the fugitive murderer and then unwittingly destroys him through her devotion. One shudders to think what the Americans would have made of this child—in this film she is absolutely convincing. The photography is excellent, right up to the final shot of the police launch heading for the shore in a choppy sea, with the steamer in which the fugitive might have escaped gradually fading into the distance.

September 28th

Finished reading *Strawberry Fair*, by Osbert Wyndham Hewett, the earlier book about Chichester Fortescue and the Countess Waldegrave. Her letters are revealing and put her in a very attractive light. She seems to have been an outstanding personality: wise, tolerant, vivacious, considerate, without a trace of humbug or affectation. Her death at the end came as a personal loss: I felt genuinely sorry to think I should not meet with her again.

September 29th

Ross McLean is to be Sheriff of the Lothians in place of Gilchrist: a good appointment. I remarked to Spears that it would incidentally give pleasure to members of the Senior Bar. 'It doesn't matter to you', he said. 'You've got plenty already'. But Scotland demurred a little, apparently thinking I could do with a little more work.

Another account from the *Readers Digest*, described as very much overdue. I shall put it in the envelope they have sent me and post it back to them unstamped, as I did with the last one.

October 1st

Gave a lift into town to an old lady who lives opposite and who was speaking about the floods in Berwickshire in the year when the railway bridges were carried away. The water tank at Cumledge Mill was carried off, so that the mill could not work. The miller was thinking he would have to instal a diesel engine when he overheard two farmers talking in Berwick market, one saying to the other, 'We've nae shortage o' water now. I've got a fine tank'. The police on investigation discovered that he had found the tank washed up on the beach at Berwick.

October 2nd
To church. Mr Reid, newly returned from holiday, preached a ridiculous sermon on Psalms 65,5.

October 14th
Croan told me we had succeeded in getting a jury trial from Kilbrandon in *Roberts v. Sir William Arrol & Co*. Having ascertained from him what the case was about, I asked if he had taken the debate himself, to which he replied, 'No, you took it'—reminding me that this was the debate in which he had given way to me at the last moment, to make the reply. I had completely forgotten I had taken part in any debate in that case.

October 15th
Finished reading *All in a Lifetime*, by Walter Allen, an agreeable story of an old man recalling his youth and early history coinciding with the rise of the Labour Party: nothing much in it, but it rings true.

October 18th
A damages case. Just before I came to address the jury, I broke one leg of my spectacles, and had to stand holding them up to my eyes with one hand while I held my notebook in the other, all the time I was speaking.

To Alexanders, where my new Consul was awaiting me. I traded in the old one for £450.

October 22nd
The two American presidential candidates debating on television. Though they debated skilfully, neither impressed me as the kind of man we should like as President.

October 23rd
To church. Mr Reid preached on Revelation 12,10. His sermons are dry and far from convincing, but he does not play down to his hearers, so that though one does not feel greatly edified there is at any rate nothing objectionable about his preaching.

October 24th
Finished reading *Sir Charles Dilke*, by Roy Jenkins. His expensive,

eminent legal advisers seem to have made every conceivable mistake, so that he was saddled with the commission of an offence which it now seems reasonably certain he did not commit: a remarkable example of how a man's life can be ruined by something for which he has no responsibility. Apart from this dramatic affair, the book is of interest as showing the remarkably progressive views which Dilke held, far ahead of his contemporaries, on social and economic questions.

From Mr John Taylor:
Wanborough House, Cranleigh, Surrey.   24th October, 1960.
Dear Gordon Stott,
I am sorry be be so long in acknowledging your letter of 1st October...

You will, I am sure, be interested to know that Hope, out of the blue, visited me in London on his own on 3rd October with a view to trying to settle the purchase price for his lands. He suggested that we might revert back to the figures we talked about when we made the offer to him in March last and indicated that he would accept an offer on those terms and forget the other high figures he had in mind. Obviously he had suddenly wakened up to his position and was on the run and rightly or wrongly I felt he had to be taught a sharp lesson in view of all the trouble he has caused. In the result I settled on a price of £10,000 less than we had offered to him earlier this year and that offer has now been accepted. I look on the £10,000 as being no more than a partial recompense for the time I wasted in negotiations with Hope.

I am glad, therefore, irrespective of the terms of the Permission, that in dealing with Scottish landowners I have brought both Roxburghe and Hope to heel. If Brooke won't fight the blackmail which is going on in land values I feel we have made some little contribution which might encourage others not to be held to ransom. We have indeed paid fair prices with quite a good profit to both the owners but we have not given way to exorbitant terms nor am I prepared to do so with any landed proprietor in the United Kingdom.

Yours

October 27th
A play on television: *A Moon for the Misbegotten*, by Eugene O'Neill,

a corny affair which I endured for an hour before it became too much for me and I turned it off.

Finished reading *Mostly Murder*, the autobiography of Sir Sydney Smith, which gives an attractive picture of his candid, straightforward personality and his commonsense, unpartisan view of life—all completely free from humbug or affectation, and enlivened with a macabre sense of humour. This persists to the last paragraph of the book, when the author is reflecting that murderers are quite ordinary people: 'So ordinary, indeed, that sometimes when I have watched them going to execution I have been inclined to echo the famous words uttered on a similar occasion by the sixteenth-century divine, John Bradford, and say, "But for the grace of God there goes Sydney Smith". I have always refrained, however, lest I tempt Providence, knowing the fate of John Bradford. The grace of God apparently deserted him in the end, for he was convicted of heresy and burnt alive'.

October 28th
Sinclair Shaw is much incensed that Shearer has been appointed Sheriff of Renfrew and Bute in succession to Ross McLean and in preference to me, and has apparently been corresponding with Labour MPs on this subject.

October 29th
Finished reading *Senator Joe McCarthy*, by Richard H. Rovere. Though he has written a fair-minded and fairly impartial book, the most shocking thing in it seemed to me that he, a professedly liberal journalist, thought it necessary to denounce an ex-Communist working in administrative service in case damage should be done if McCarthy got to hear about him. The man was dismissed, and Rovere's only reaction appears to have been relief at getting him safely out of the picture before McCarthy got round to his presence in it.

October 30th
Elizabeth retired to bed with a cold.

November 1st
Elizabeth still in bed: and as I had taken four seats for *Iolanthe* tonight I went across the road to Mrs Bruce's to see if Pamela, the prettiest of our local teenagers, would come. Pamela, like the peers in

Iolanthe, would not I think pretend to any intellectual eminence, but she seemed a very nice girl.

November 2nd

A consultation in *Cunninghame v. Pearson*. Some other parties interested in the reversion had taken Shearer's opinion, in which Shearer poured scorn on the arguments so far put up for the pursuer and suggested a new line of his own. I found on looking into this that it was unsupportable on the authorities. It had been decided to have a joint consultation to thrash the matter out. Being senior to Shearer, I presided, and was pleased to find that on a subject of which I have little experience I was able to keep complete command of the consultation—really, I think, because I had done some work on the case.

Finished reading *The Darkness Outside*, by George Johnston, an effective story about a small party of archaeologists working in Mesopotamia, cut off from the outside world, who come across an old man wandering in the desert with rumours of some catastrophe that has happened to European civilisation. They have no means of knowing what truth there is in this, and the book concerns the reactions of the various members of the party, male and female. It tends to degenerate into melodrama before the end.

November 4th

For the fourth successive day I had a debate before Migdale—most unfortunately, as today's debate was important, on the construction of an agreement. I was virtually certain I was right, but, as I had feared, it proved impossible to get Migdale to see it. It was an action by Bryce Morrison, former managing director of the *Glasgow Herald*, against George Outram & Co. In November 1958, when he was 77, he got a letter from Sir John Spencer Muirhead, the chairman of the Board, saying he was authorised to say that the board would grant Morrison a pension of £2,500 per annum, which would be paid as from December 1, 1958, on condition that Morrison retired from the Boards of four subsidiary companies, of which he had been chairman. The pension was paid in monthly instalments for a year, and the defenders then stopped payment, intimating that the pension was being paid during their pleasure and they intended to make no more payments. Thinking this an impossible interpretation of the agreement which Morrison had accepted, I had had no hesitation in advising an action. The defenders had replied with lengthy averments obviously designed to throw mud at the pursuer—they had no bearing on the issue in this case, and any other judge would, I think, have been distinctly annoyed about them. Migdale merely remarked airily that they had been put on to explain why the pension had been stopped, and as the agreement had not provided in terms for a life pension he did not see why the defenders should not stop it. This seems fantastic—it must involve that as soon as the pursuer had resigned his directorships the defenders could have terminated the pension without making a single payment, so that the agreement was really to do anything or nothing. It seemed to me that there was no doubt about what the parties intended, but though I thought I put the case clearly it did not seem to be clear enough for Migdale. He took the case to avizandum, but with observations that were ominously favourable to the defenders' pleadings. The Aberdeen solicitor, who was in court, told me that Munro, the publisher who has taken my advice on a number of points, has got to the state of mind when he will do nothing without my approval—which is very flattering, but makes it all the more annoying that the Morrison case came out before Migdale instead of a judge who would deal sensibly with it.

November 6th
With the children to Greenbank church. Rev. Dr R.T. Cameron, formerly of the West Church of St Andrew, Aberdeen, preached on the outlook of the author of Ecclesiastes: a good sermon, sensible, honest and well organised.

November 11th
This Week on television: an interview with Mr Chester Bowles, suggested as Secretary of State when the new President, John Kennedy, takes office. If this is right, it looks as if a new wind of friendly commonsense and tolerance will be blowing over the American outlook in world affairs. I was much impressed with him, and the way in which he did not take himself or his nation too seriously.

November 12th
To North Bookshop in Dundas Street to ask about a copy of the *Children's Britannica* which I happened to see advertised in last night's *News*: a new production in twelve volumes that has just been published at the price of £45. The bookshop were offering a copy at £16. It was second-hand, but gave the appearance of being new and unused

—the seller, I was told, had decided to go to Canada just after he acquired it. I was impressed by the book: British, factual, thorough, well illustrated, just what the household required. I bought it forthwith. A real piece of luck, for one thing I never read in the *News* is the advertisement column. It just happened last night that I was feeling lazy, and when sitting by the fire started looking at the advertisements for lack of anything better within reach.

The Festival of Remembrance on television tonight from the Albert Hall: some noteworthy spectacle, particularly the upstanding, bearded prelate who conducted the religious part of the proceedings, looking and sounding exceptionally magnificent in his mitre and robes. I believe he was the Bishop of Birmingham, Dr Wilson.

November 13th
To church: Cubs and Brownies in the Remembrance Day parade. Mr Reid preached on Psalms 20,7. Though he vigorously disclaimed any imputation of pacifism, and did not seem fully to appreciate the implications of what he was saying, it was in effect a pacifist sermon. At any rate it showed manifest signs of much internal wrestling with himself. Apart from having no children's address, he made no concessions to the young people present in church in unusually large numbers, and indeed ignored their presence completely.

Finished reading *Jonathan Swift*, by John Middleton Murry. It suffers from repetition, and from the author's assumption of a degree of knowledge on the part of his readers that a good many would be unlikely to have. If I had not recently read other books about the period, I should have been completely at sea. Apart from that it is interesting and readable, and gives a convincing account of Swift's life and works.

November 14th
Another copy of my 'overdue account' from the *Readers Digest*: I have stuck it into the envelope provided, and posted it back to them unstamped, as I did with the last one.

November 15th
Proof in *Brown v. Brown*. The pursuer is seeking divorce on the ground of her husband's cruelty. Two months after the marriage he became morose and taciturn, sitting in the house staring at his wife, and on one occasion pulling a silk stocking tight round her neck.

After some persuasion, he was induced to enter Gartnavel mental hospital, and he has been there as a voluntary patient ever since. His schizophrenia has now reached a stage of complete apathy, with occasional violent interludes. Two specialists agreed that the defender was almost certainly of unsound mind, and could have been certified if necessary. The question of law remains: whether this is a valid defence to an action on the ground of cruelty. In the course of the afternoon I had to come out to speak to Lloyd, and asked my junior, Davidson, to cross-examine the pursuer's mother, who was then in the witness box. This was the kind of request I disliked very much when I was a junior—having to cross-examine out of the blue without being prepared to do so—but Davidson as usual acquitted himself well.

November 17th
Continued my speech in the Brown case. Cameron is most interested in it, and kept me on my feet most of the morning, discussing every conceivable aspect of the law of cruelty and insanity.

Finished reading *Act of Mercy*, by Francis Clifford. This story about a young English couple employed on a plantation in South America, who get involved in succouring an ex-President on the run, is told with the maximum of tension and suspense, continuing right up to a neatly ironical ending.

November 29th
The cement-works proposal to proceed—we had got substantially what Taylor wanted.

December 7th
Second Division: *Thomson v. Glasgow Corporation*. The point at present is whether we are entitled at this late stage to amend so as to make a case that the washing machine was dangerous as a whole with its lid open, instead of limiting ourselves, as we had, to a dangerous spindle. Strachan seemed sympathetic, but the others were dubious. Thomson kept insisting that they were not there to do abstract justice but merely to see that the game was played according to the rules. They seemed to be adopting a curiously cynical attitude. Their main difficulty seemed to be that the defenders having been led into cross-examining on the line that the machine was obviously dangerous, other than the spindle, would now be prejudiced in maintaining the opposite. Strachan alone seemed to wonder whether this was a

form of prejudice which should be recognised by the court: all the others apparently took it for granted.

December 8th
Cunninghame v. Cunninghame's Trustees in the First Division. Wylie opened the case on our side in a half-hearted way: the court seemed to be against him, and Ross had an easy passage in his reply. I did not want to embark on any important argument at a late hour in the afternoon, and was content to play out time by referring to some authorities: with the assistance of Clyde and Sorn, I had no difficulty in doing this. We skated amiably round the point at issue, without coming to grips on any important matter.

December 9th
I did not handle Clyde so well today, having the feeling afterwards that I had returned rudeness for rudeness—never a good policy. So, though I do not think I missed any point, I was not pleased with my speech. Anyhow, Clyde had the final say, when at three o'clock he produced several sheets of manuscript from under his desk and proceeded to read the 'extempore' judgment that he had prepared last night. The English solicitors who had come up for the hearing were as courteous and gentlemanly as they always are, showing no sign of resentment or pique but thanking me for what I had done and apologising for asking me to argue a case that had met with such scant respect from the bench. But what really pleased me today, and served to offset this disaster, was news that Migdale, contrary to all my expectations, had decided *Morrison v. Outrams* in favour of the pursuer, finding that he was entitled to his pension for life.

December 16th
Gardiner v. Motherwell Scrap & Machinery Co. The point was very simple. Two specialists on the pursuer's side said he was suffering from industrial dermatitis, but as each of them had seen the pursuer on only one occasion, a long time after the initial outbreak, it was arguable that, as the defenders said, Kilbrandon should have preferred the evidence of their three doctors, who had been actually concerned with his treatment. Kilbrandon however held that their evidence that this was not industrial dermatitis was vitiated by being based on a mistaken hypothesis. What happened was that the pursuer arrived at hospital with a line from his doctor, who said he had been

suffering from cheiropomphylix, and with his skin covered with red paint—*pigmentum castellani*—which he had applied himself somewhat in excess of his doctor's instructions. Dr Dewar, the first hospital doctor, had been unable to see any dermatitis at all because of the paint, but knowing that cheiropomphylix was a common sequel to ringworm of the feet, and that *pigmentum castellani* is a common treatment for that condition, assumed that the pursuer had been suffering from ringworm of the feet—*tinea pedis*—and entered that in the hospital record. His two colleagues accepted this record, assuming that Dr Dewar had examined the man and made this diagnosis: and since *tinea pedis* was never industrial in origin they naturally concluded that this was not industrial dermatitis—cheiropomphylix, according to their use of the word, consisted of big blisters on the palms of the hands, the part of the hand least likely to be attacked by industrial dermatitis: this, Dr Dewar said, was much more likely to begin on the back of the hand. In fact, on the unchallenged evidence of the pursuer and his doctor, his dermatitis had started on the back of his hand, and it was never suggested to him that it had started on the feet or on the palms of the hands. None of the defenders' doctors would say that from his own observation he could say that the dermatitis was non-industrial. Each said he was going on the 'history'—in other words, on Dr Dewar's mistake. I tried to make the point clear, ignoring Clyde for the most part and concentrating on Guthrie, but I doubt very much whether it got through. Clyde made no attempt to understand it.

December 18th

To church with Elizabeth. It was supposed to be the children's Christmas gift service, but Mr Reid's only concession to the presence of children was to leave out the children's address.

December 20th

The First Division unanimously reversed Kilbrandon in *Gardiner v. Motherwell Scrap Co*. It will be an excellent case to take to the Lords as the first Legal Aid appeal if my colleagues on the Appeals Committee can be persuaded to grant legal aid. I have no doubt that an appeal would succeed.

OPINION of LORD CARMONT

The question to be decided in this Reclaiming Motion is whether the pursuer contracted 'industrial dermatitis' when engaged on his work...It is necessary, therefore, to have a clear view of what industrial dermatitis is, as distinguished from the other diseases and forms of disease referred to in the evidence and which I personally find somewhat confusing. I mention for example: oil acne, dermatitis herpetiformis or a dermatitis venenata, Cheiropompholyx, tinea pedis, a dermographism, folliculitis, monilia, and the English equivalents mentioned by the various witnesses at the proof such as 'athlete's foot, papular, vesicular, pimpled and blistered dermatitis, an eczematoid ringworm of the feet, a sensitization eruption on the hands, skin writing, fungus infection, a blistered eruption and oil plugging'. References were also made to impetigo and eczema, erythematous and follicular eruptions and primula dermatitis which all help to make the evidence more difficult to understand...

December 28th
Glasgow: a commission to recover documents in *Pickard v. Pickard*. We proceeded to old Pickard's office, a ramshackle place with 'Dr. A.E. Pickard, L.S.D.' in big letters above the door. The 'Dr', I was told, stood for 'Debtor'. As expected, the pursuer proved a difficult witness, and Maguire as Commissioner spent a good deal of the time shouting at him to keep quiet and answer the questions. At first he refused to produce anything, saying the properties were all his and we had no business with his books: but eventually he said that his clerkess had all the books and he did not object to our having them. We wanted his rent books, which to my surprise show allocation of rents among various members of the family to whom we say the properties belong. Otherwise I was content to take from him that he had no other books—though it was obvious from a big pile of books that had been deposited on the floor that this was inaccurate. Pickard had recovered his good humour, and showed us a deposit receipt for £20,000 he was carrying loose in his pocket, made out to 'A.E. Pickard, field of Bannockburn'—apparently one of the properties of which he is owner. He said he had heard that the Scots had defeated the English at Bannockburn and taken the field from them, so he had come and bought it back for the English.

December 31st
To Kate's for Bridge: and home by 11.30. We took the dog up the

road, and were back in time to hear Big Ben strike midnight at the end of the year.

Index

Where appropriate, entries give the position of a person at the time of writing of the diary. In some cases what the person later became is given in parentheses

Index

Index